ECONOMICS:
AMERICAN VOTER'S GUIDE TO BASIC ECONOMICS - DISCUSSION GUIDE 1

Yes, YOU can bring America's prosperity to all Americans

Author:
Charles Francus, CPA

Provided by:
Rethink America LLC
Empowering America's Voters

Copyright Charles W. Francus, November 2, 2015
Registration Number TXu 1-983-853
United States Register of Copyrights and Director

UPDATE TO COPYRIGHT REQUESTED AUGUST 2017
FILE **1-5735661271**
Date/Time :8/18/2017 11:03:50 AM
[THREAD ID: 1-2MUYPOZ]
United States Copyright Office

Licensed to Rethink America LLC

Provided by Rethink America LLC
Empowering America's Voters
www.rethinkamericausa.com
rethinkamericausa@gmail.com
Admin@rethinkamericausa.com

➤ Information on the book and the author are available at www.rethinkamericausa.com. Additionally, a sample section of the book; a practice set for Appendix B of the book "Penny Money Flow;" and tips on starting a discussion group are provided via the website. Further, a few pages of the book refer to 2017 tax laws. Once the tax laws are revised and the IRS has completed its interpretations – such pages may be revised. If so, revisions will be available via the website.

➤ Videos on subjects depicted in the book as well as other subjects will be available at www.YouTube.com. A list of current and upcoming videos is on the Rethink America website.

➢

Special thanks to:

Peter Hamner

Kimberly Morey

Sharon Swedlow

And, many others

Dear Reader,

It is both possible and probable that citizens who read this book will learn more about that which is important about America than they will learn from fifty other books on the subject.

The power of the book is that knowledge comes not only from what is written but from good exploratory discussion with others.

Additionally, the book presents a complex subject in terms that the majority of Americans can follow with relative ease.

This is learning power; plus it is a great way to expand one's circle of friends.

Having said this – it is a very interesting read to be undertaken by the individual reader.

I belong to two discussion groups. One meets twice a month at a Parks and Recreations building and the other meets once a month at a restaurant. The second group meets, also, once a month for a social get together.

I worked in England for a while and there I saw a pub/restaurant which held a discussion meetup on the first and third Tuesdays of each month; apparently to attract business on a slow night. Also, I saw another pub/restaurant which alternated between Trivia Night and Discussion Night and, additionally, a book club which met on a commuter train.

You can start up a group to discuss this book at your religious organization, civic club, community action group, political group, volunteer fire department, etc., or as a group independent of another organization (e.g. at your local public library).

You can use the announcement board at the local laundromat or library, your church, meetup.com, or any other means for calling together folks who will be interested. (See tips for starting a discussion group on the Rethink America website.)

Whatever approach you take, you will both enjoy yourself and learn about your country.

Yes, **you** can bring America's prosperity to all Americans,

Charles (Chuck) Francus

All things in nature come from God. Most things in politics (the country's commitment to quality education, healthcare, defense, Social Security, etc.) come from the structure of the country's economic system; the balance comes from God.

PREFACE

Many have recited, in some form or another, James Carville's catch phrase used by the Clinton campaign – (it's) *the economy, stupid*.

Yet, even though many have echoed the phrase, very few Americans know much about how the American economic system operates. Probably no more than one in 500 Americans possesses the basic level of understanding needed to vote knowledgeably and responsibly on issues of economics. Examples of political issues that fall under the umbrella of economics include funding for education, healthcare, defense, law enforcement, Social Security, and the structure of the tax system.

The group of individuals who do not understand how the American economy works, unfortunately, includes almost all of our politicians; both those at the federal and state levels of government (this includes members of US Congress, past and present, and Presidents, past and possibly present).

Too often many voters and politicians **confuse myth with substantive knowledge**. If Americans want an economic system that works well for all citizens – then voters must elect politicians that understand the difference between myth and knowledge. (NOTE: prior to writing this book – I shared many of the same thoughts that many politicians and others subscribe to.)

Does every "responsible" voter have an obligation to learn BEFORE voting? If you think this is the case – then you need to read this book.

The *American Voter's Guide to Basic Economics* provides the citizen with the understanding needed to vote with his/her head held high and shoulders square.

The book has been written as an exploratory review:

- It starts with an introduction to the discussion guide

- The next four chapters review the structure of the American economic system

- Having examined the fundamental structure within which solutions to current economic issues must fit, the guide, in eight chapters, reviews current issues.

We learn better and enhance our learning experience when we discuss a subject rather than simply picking up a book and reading it. Therefore, this book is written as a group discussion guide.

While written to facilitate group review – the independent reader will enjoy contemplating the content him/herself.

Important to understanding how the US economy works is the development of an understanding of how money moves through the economy (i.e. transactions). "Appendix B – Penny Money Flow Exercise" provides an exercise which every reader should attempt; either with a group or individually.

A review of the transactions for Monday and Tuesday (already completed in the appendix) may be adequate; however, readers are encouraged to attempt to complete the exercise, on their own, for Wednesday and Thursday. An example is provided for Wednesday and Thursday on the Rethink America website – but, you should use your own transaction values (see www.Rethinkamericausa.com for an example).

The exercise demonstrates how government spending relates to the private sector income and how private sector spending relates to the government's revenue (i.e., tax collections).

It is assumed in the exercise, for simplicity, that one government exists (not federal, state and local). This government both spends money and collects taxes.

Prior to reviewing Appendix B, the reader may find it helpful to first review Appendix A - Percentages.

SUMMARY OF CONTENTS

STRUCTURAL ECONOMIC ISSUES:

CHAPTER 1: Introduction to Discussion Guide provides the reader with a general overview of the book and **why learning about the US economic system is important to every voter**.

The US economic system affects a large part of every citizen's life. Yet, very few citizens, **this includes our Presidents and members of Congress**, know much about how it works and fewer know how it affects their families.

Everything, in the form of defense, social (e.g. Social Security, Medicare, law enforcement), economic (e.g. oil and agricultural subsidies, R&D credit), etc. programs, relies on the structure of the underlying economic system.

CHAPTER 2 – Developing a Sound Foundation addresses the mindset of most US voters; then, provides some questions (with answers) designed to help the voter determine his/her level of understanding of the US economic system.

Included in the questions is a question related to the relocation to China of a US Company's manufacturing operations. The chapter examines the question **"Will US companies continue relocating operations to China if the USA corporate income tax rate is reduced to zero?"**

Next, the chapter covers select economic fundamentals including **the Federal Reserve System's dual mandate to control inflation and employment levels**, basic definitions, and the key classes of Economic Units.

This is followed by an **eye-opener exercise** which "follows the money" from the point of a Federal Government expenditure through the private sector economy.

*CHAPTER 3 - Basic Economic Relationship*s explores the relationships that exist within an economic system. Subjects addressed include:

- Where does an economy come from?
- Development of an economic perspective
- **What is money?**
- The relationship amongst supply, demand, and cultural views.

CHAPTER 4 – Applied Wealth reviews the "hows" of the accumulation of personal wealth and the determination of earnings distribution.

CHAPTER 5 – Types of Economic Systems examines the key aspects that differentiate one economic system from another and the major types of systems.

CURRENT ECONOMIC ISSUES:

CHAPTER 6: CURRENT ISSUES -Welfare Payments assesses the effect of welfare payments on the US economy.

CHAPTER 7: CURRENT ISSUES - Investment Shortfall, Idle Money, Repatriation and Job Creation discusses a hot current topic, **US Corporate Tax rates** and the whether or not changes to the tax rates will result in an **increase in investment in America**. This chapter complements the discussion in Section A, of Chapter 2 where an analysis of a project to relocate a US manufacturing operation to China was reviewed.

CHAPTER 8: CURRENT ISSUES - Education and Welfare to Work covers the economic effects of raising the education level of the workforce and of moving citizens off of welfare and into jobs.

CHAPTER 9: CURRENT ISSUES - Minimum Wage assesses another hot current topic. The voter is asked to create in his or her mind a "standard" of fair pay. Subsequently, a review of the impact of raising the minimum wage is completed and various pros and cons of raising the minimum wage are examined.

CHAPTER 10: CURRENT ISSUES - This Project Needs Your Support, using the Keystone Pipeline project as an example, examines how the voter should consider proposed projects that require citizens' approval or input. The approach used to review the Keystone Pipeline project is applicable to projects such as the construction of a new high school or convention center, approval of zoning for a new big-box retail store or race track, etc.

CHAPTER 11: CURRENT ISSUES - National Debt explores various aspects of this very hot topic. The national debt cannot be reduced through a reduction in government spending – the math does not work. Why?

CHAPTER 12: CURRENT ISSUES - **"Fix Social Security"** starts with a brief summary of the support retirees currently receive and then explores several options for truly "fixing Social Security." The impact of various options on the average family, worker, and grandma and grandad is reviewed. Options covered range from a "pay-as-we-go" system to a significant raise in the qualifying retirement age.

CHAPTER 13: OPINION – Why are there Different Economic Theories? discloses the author's opinion as to why various economists subscribe to differing economic philosophies.

Table of Contents

AS MENTIONED IN THE PREFACE, IT IS RECOMMENDED THAT YOUR GROUP COMPLETE THE "PENNY MONEY FLOW" EXERCISE IN APPENDIX B

Completing the exercise is not necessary – but, you will find it helpful

CHAPTER 1: Introduction to Discussion Guide

Chapter 1 covers:

- What this book will do for you
- About economics
- Arithmetic and relative position
- Qualifier
- Explanation of citations

The discussion guide does not present any political positions. It is written as material for use by religious organizations, civic clubs/associations, community action groups, etc., as well as, informal groups (its purpose is for all). Therefore, it is politically neutral so as to protect the tax status of non-profit organizations utilizing the guide in their groups.

NOTE: The US tax laws are in a state of transition at the time this book is being published. The book, therefore, is written in a transitional character. After the IRS interprets and finalizes changes made – the book may be updated (it is possible an update will not be necessary). However, this version may have more educational value than an updated version; as the reader can better see the effect of the tax changes. NOTE, also, only a limited portion of the book's content relates to tax laws.

****

WHAT THIS BOOK WILL DO FOR YOU

This is not a book for economists or big investors. This is a book for you – the American voter.

The USA economic system affects a large part of every citizen's life. Yet, very few citizens know much about how it works and fewer know how it affects them. This leaves the typical citizen open to being misled, as some politicians and others try to manipulate us to vote against our own best interest and that of our family. The information provided will give you a fighting chance.

How important is an understanding of economics?

Everything, in the form of defense, social (e.g. Social Security, Medicare, law enforcement) economic (e.g. oil and agricultural subsidies, R&D credit), etc. programs, relies on the structure of the underlying economic system. Yet, none of the 2016 US presidential candidates demonstrated an adequate understanding of the system. For that matter, neither have any members of Congress. A sound understanding is necessary for developing substantive solutions that will both work and stand the test of time. The voters must, themselves, have a solid understanding so they can meaningfully (versus emotionally) decide which political candidates are the best fit for the job.

When first written, *American Voter's Guide to Basic Economics* was designed to be used by discussion groups at places of religious teaching (churches, temples, mosques, and other religious houses), civic clubs, community action groups, etc. However, I found that friends wanted to read it and simply discuss the material with themselves - in their own mind. The book is overall an excellent tool for learning the basics of economics either as part of a group or as an individual reader.

There are many areas of economic study; research Wikipedia for a very extensive list. I have grouped these into the following areas of study:

- Structural economics
- Statistical economics
- Behavioral economics, and
- Ethics in economics.

This guide is focused, primarily, on structural economics.

The basic structure of the economic system and several current economic issues are explored in a manner designed to demonstrate the type of thinking voters should apply when assessing the political positions of a candidate. The book does not tell the voter what positions to take.

ABOUT ECONOMICS

Economics is the study of what people do regarding the creation and exchange of goods and services of assumed value; including the systems employed by society to facilitate and govern such creation and exchange (condensed definition).

Everything within the framework of economics is <u>relative</u>. There are times of boom and times of bust, but what the citizens of one country call a bust would for citizens of some other country be a time of boom – if such citizens could only have things so good. There is **money which is active** (circulating to support the trading of goods and services) and **money which is idle** (stored in savings accounts, traded bonds [traded in the secondary market; also called aftermarket], traded stocks, etc.) <u>but active money is not completely active nor is idle money completely idle.</u> **Active money and idle money differ from one another in matter of degree (relative level) of activity**. There are businesses that do better; better than what – better than others. There are businesses that do worse; worse than what – worse than others. There are economic systems that are good for a few (relative to others) and economic systems that are good for all (relative to being good for a few). **Everything in economics is relative**.

Rarely is there an exact statement that can be made regarding something of an economic nature. This is because many other factors impact on any given economic factor. For instance, you might place money into a savings account. This money will be idle for a while. However, the bank that is holding your money might use your money to make a loan to another customer to buy a car: <u>your idle money is now active money</u>.

<u>Active money contributes to a strong economy, and idle money slows down an economy</u>. While the concept is clear, explaining it in definite terms is not entirely possible. This statement is true for almost all aspects of the study of economics. Economists must speak within a framework that is both conceptual and typical. In simple terms, they must say "this is the way something happens for the most part."

This guide addresses the subject of economics within the frameworks of:

- This is the way something happens for the most part, and
- Only that which is both key and typical is addressed. To go into more depth would require volumes, as have been written by professional economists.

Nevertheless, although short, this guide provides the reader with the basics of economics needed to make sound decisions on who to vote for at the voting booth.

One needs to possess a very basic understanding of arithmetic to grasp economics. This is especially true of understanding percentages.

ARITHMETIC AND RELATIVE POSITION

95% of what there is to know about economics can be understood through understanding basic arithmetic. Most important, a very basic understanding of the use of percentages will help the reader with his/her understanding of economics.

Many of us, however, have been out of school for a long time and, in that time, some have forgotten how to work with percentages. A one-page refresher on the character of percentages is provided in Appendix A. This should be all most readers need to grasp the concepts presented in this discussion guide.

It will not hurt you to look at Appendix A, even if you do not feel you need a refresher.

QUALIFIER

Definitions used in this book are designed to be simple. They are not meant to be collegiate. Thus, they are not exacting and all-encompassing in nature. But, they are close enough to more collegiate definitions and much easier for the reader to put into perspective.

Note that some of the definitions may be found to be a little complex. This is because there is no simple way to say some things.

Note also, the understanding of definitions as well as concepts tend to be circular in nature. We cannot understand what a wagon is if we do not understand what a wheel is; nor can we appreciate the purpose of a wheel without understanding what a wagon is. This means that two readings of select sections of a chapter will sometimes be required to fully appreciate the meaning of the chapter.

One more thing: **this guide is a working paper**. Several novel interpretations of economics are presented herein. As others critique these, new angles of thought may surface and will be incorporated into the guide. Your insights will be appreciated.

IF YOUR DISCUSSION GROUP HAS NOT COMPLETED THE "PENNY MONEY FLOW" EXERCISE IN APPENDIX B – YOU SHOULD DO SO.

Completing the exercise is not necessary – but, you will find it helpful.

The exercise demonstrates how government spending relates to the private sector income and how private sector spending relates to the government's revenue (i.e., tax collections).

It is assumed in the exercise, for simplicity, that one government exists (not federal, state and local). This government both spends money and collects taxes.

Prior to reviewing Appendix B, the reader may find it helpful to first review Appendix A - Percentages.

EXPLANATION OF CITATIONS

Many citations are used in this guide. The inclusion of a citation is not an endorsement of the citation.

On various points made in the guide, some parts of the citations provided the source, confirming support, or collaborating support of the point made. The whole of the citation may or may not be substantive. When citing an article or study: I am referring only to that part of a citation that relates to the point discussed in the text.

Additionally, I have provided conflicting citations, in some cases, to expose the reader to opposing points of view.

Citations appear both in embedded form (within the body of the text) and in Citation section at back of guide. Those that are embedded should be reviewed by the reader to help him/her develop a full picture of the point being discussed.

On completing each chapter or the full discussion guide – I believe the reader(s) will find it both interesting and educational to review the various citations and compare what is stated to what is stated in this guide.

CHAPTER 2 – Developing a Sound Foundation

Chapter 2 covers:

- The mindset of many voters
- Test of a citizen's readiness to do his/her civic duty at the voting booth
  - Problem review – relocation of a US business in whole or in part to a low-cost wage country
  - Problem review - shifting composition of household economic classes
- Federal Reserve's attempt to control the level of unemployment and inflation
- Basic definitions needed for an understanding of basic economics
- Key classes of economic units
- Money flow - government
- The tandem relationship – a very key point to understand
- Money flow exercise (similar to Penny Money Flow Exercise) of three government spending levels and two taxing levels
  - Pre-budget spending cut with an assumed tax rate of 20%
  - Post-budget spending cut with an assumed tax rate of 20%
  - Post-budget spending and revenue (tax rate) cut, with an assumed tax rate of 10%.
- Where does an economy come from?
- Questions for you to answer
- Appendix – Answers to chapter questions and questions for you to answer.

NOTE: Chapter 2 is a <u>study</u> – and - discuss chapter; all others are read – and - discuss chapters. However, all chapters should be read much as one would read a magazine article (perhaps this chapter twice). Very few of us, after reading a magazine article, could pass a test on the detailed content of the article, but we would have retained the concept of the article. This should be the reader's objective with this guide. The points put forth in this guide are items for discussion, not items to be memorized for earning a grade in economics.

The Mindset of Many USA Voters

Chuck, a friend of mine, is a veteran. He suffers medical problems due to Agent Orange exposure he experienced while serving in Vietnam. The damage manifested itself late in his life. He was, therefore, unencumbered in his career and was able to make a good life for himself and his family after leaving the military. Chuck retired as a CEO of a small publically traded software development company. Although he is in a financial position such that he can go to private doctors, he often uses the services of the

VA. Chuck feels that the VA doctors have greater experience in treating cases of ex-soldiers with Agent Orange issues.

Chuck discussed the experiences he had while in the waiting-room at the VA hospital. He told me how he began listening closely to the conversations of others. Many of the conversations focused on political and economic issues. The year was 2009, and understandably these were the hot topics of discussions at the time. He remarked that although many of the veterans were over the age of fifty, their conversations were identical to those they had when they were young soldiers, just nineteen or twenty years old. It was as if, he remarked further, at this early age they had formed an image in their minds of who they would be and what the world was about, and that mindset had stuck; unmoved by time and maturity.

Although one votes for a candidate, as said by one of my college professors, one is actually voting on political and economic direction, social issues, definitions of justice, matters of defense, and justification for war. Unfortunately, when we vote on issues many of us vote *not on the substance of the issues* but, in truth, we vote in our own image (conservative, liberal, libertarian, socialist, etc.) as defined by our mindset. It is a mindset many of us subscribed to in our later youth, and that has remained unchanged for many years thereafter.

Are You Ready to Vote?

I am not asking if you are dressed and have your car keys in hand, ready to drive to the voting booth.

Here we are addressing the issue of having invested the personal effort required to assess and understand the political and economic situations and forces that impact the quality of life of your family, friends, neighbors and fellow citizens.

To help you ascertain whether you are ready or not, I have developed a set of assessment questions that if not answered correctly will clearly demonstrate that you have a lot of work to do. Conversely, if you answer the assessment questions correctly, it is not necessarily true that you do not have a lot of work to do. Correct answers only indicate that you are further along in your thinking than are some others.

SECTION A

Warm-up Question and Answer:

Relocation of a US Manufacturing Operation to China (using 2017 corporate income tax rate)

Assumptions:

- 100 pennies represent the sales revenue of an American manufacturing corporation (Company X) that sells into the US domestic market

- 50% of each 100 pennies of sales revenue, or 50 pennies, is used to pay the wages of labor; the balance of the revenue pennies covers selling, administrative, materials, and overhead costs, plus profit

- Profit equals 5%, or 5 pennies, of every 100 pennies of sales revenue

- The effective USA corporate income tax rate (federal, 35%. and state, 5%, income taxes) is 40% of profits for this example, or 2 pennies out of every 100 pennies of revenue (40% of 5 pennies of profit equals 2 pennies)

- The Company will save 80% on wages if it manufactures its products in China. 80% equals a savings of 40 pennies out of every 100 pennies of sales revenue (80% X 50 pennies of wages). These savings are inclusive of all payroll taxes and benefit costs attached to wages in both the United States and China

- However, the Company will incur an additional cost for freight and other distribution costs of 3 pennies per sales revenue dollar if it manufactures in China. Currently, the Company's freight and other distribution costs equal 4% of revenue or 4 pennies out of every 100 pennies of sales revenue.

Question:

Will the Company relocate its manufacturing operations to China if the USA corporate income tax rate is reduced to **zero**? Before reading further – what do you think?

Logic:

The Company in question will save <u>40 pennies</u> on labor cost and pay an additional three pennies for freight and other distribution. This is a <u>net savings of 37 pennies</u> per dollar of sales revenue. The pre-tax profit will increase <u>from 5 pennies to 42 pennies</u> (5 pennies plus 37 pennies) per sales revenue dollar (100 pennies).

The USA tax on 5 pennies of profit is 2 pennies, if the operation remains in the US. The after-tax profit for a USA operation is 3 pennies per 100 pennies of sales revenue (5 pennies minus 2 pennies). **Due to the <u>great difference in the cost of labor</u>, the 2 pennies paid for US tax is insignificant to the review of the option of manufacturing in China**.

The after-tax profit, if the Company manufactures in China, is 25.2 pennies per 100 pennies (42 pennies minus the tax of 40% of 42 pennies) of sales revenue (following payment of repatriation tax – see section <u>Repatriation</u> of Chapter 7 for explanation; however, an understanding of the repatriation tax is not necessary to understanding this comparison).

Note, however, that **market pressure will push pricing down and the profits realized will be greatly reduced. The Company will not, therefore, realize the full financial benefit** of 25.2 pennies on 100 pennies of sales revenue. Refer to the discussion under Answer below.

Answer:

The Company will still relocate its operations to China. It does not make any difference whether the USA corporate income tax rate is <u>40% or zero</u>. The potential savings on taxes paid are very, very small as compared to the labor cost saved.

Additionally, **if the Company does not relocate** but the Company's competitors do <u>locate in low-cost wage countries, the Company will not be price competitive. Once this happens</u>, **the Company will go out of business and the employees will then become unemployed.**

Will the Company's domestic earnings increase as a result of the relocation to China? In the near term, possibly; but in the long term, as competitors also relocate, the Company's prices will be driven down by market forces. **Subsequently, the Company's domestic earnings will settle at approximately the same relative level (percentage) as before the relocation**. However, the Company will be more competitive internationally and may enjoy an increase in earnings from expanded international trade.

Discussion points: Discuss the previous answer with members of your discussion group, fellow congregation or club members, or with someone you meet while waiting for a bus or a train. What effect does the above answer have <u>on the quality of life for your family</u>?

If the labor savings were only 10 pennies and the new 21% top rate (passed by Congress, December 2017) was implemented 10 years ago; would there be a different outcome?

Is it both possible and probable that no US jobs would have been saved (i.e. not transferred overseas) if both the federal and state corporate income tax rates had been reduced to zero fifty years ago?

Assessment Questions:

Shifting of Population Through Economic Classes

At any given time a certain segment of the household providers is not employed. There are several reasons for this. A few of the key reasons are:

- The Federal Reserve Banking System in an effort to control inflation targets a selected unemployment level. This is discussed further in Section B of this chapter

- Less than 95% of the potential workforce is needed to provide the goods and services produced and procured by both the private and public sectors of the economy

- The level of goods and services procured (demand) is significantly limited by the country's distribution of both income and wealth; this has the effect of limiting the number of jobs available.

The nature of the effect of the economy on employment and non-employment is one of <u>relative position</u> – not of <u>absolute position</u>. (NOTE: herein, the term **non-employment** refers to all who could be and would be workers; not only those counted as unemployed by various government measures.) (NOTE also, to simplify – the retired portion of the population is ignored.) If we assume, for example, that in a given state of the economy 10% of the household providers are not employed then regardless of the size of the population 10% of the household providers will not be employed. In simpler terms, it is not 900 (an absolute position) of 1,000 household providers are employed and 100 are not employed; it is, rather, that 90% (a relative position) of the household providers are employed and 10% are not. For instance, if the population grew and there were then 2,000 household providers – then 10% or 200 would be non-employed. The opposite is also true if the population shrunk and there were 500 household providers – then 10% or 50 would be non-employed.

Now let's tackle the assessment questions.

In the assessment questions, for mathematical simplicity, the number of non-employed household providers is assumed to be 10%.

Pretend that a fictitious alien spacecraft jumped out of the movie theater screen and scooped up all of the non-employed household providers in America and their households. Once the craft had finished its task, there would only be employed household providers and their households remaining. But, for how long? Each economic layer of citizens depends on the layers below it to both maintain their level of employment and the size of their paycheck. Within the framework of the American economic system (as currently structured), the outcome for those Americans remaining on the planet would be far different from what most will imagine it to be.

Assessment Question #1:

Assumptions:

TODAY >>>

1. There are <u>100 million **household providers**</u>, in total, who are working Americans or who are receiving public support for help in providing for their households and themselves

2. These 100 million American household providers, on the average, provide for a household that includes 2.3 people (including other members of the household who, also, provide for the household)

3. Inflation is assumed to be zero, to simplify the exercise

4. No significant changes in <u>economic ratios</u> occur over a <u>ten year period</u> (i.e., the average amount spent per capita for food, clothing, housing, transportation, healthcare, interest, etc. remains roughly the same)

5. **Three months** is required for the economy and relative employment level (i.e., the percentage of could-be/would-be workers employed and not employed) to adjust after the occurrence of a significant change in the

economic environment (with or without a significant change in economic ratios). (NOTE: the economic environment is determined by many factors; but the two key factors are a change in the size or mix [retirees versus workers, children versus seniors, etc.] of the population, and a change in economic ratios.)

6. All public assistance programs remain in place, as is, for the <u>ten year period</u>

7. **10%** or 10 million of the 100 million American household providers are not employed. These individuals are drawing unemployment or are on disability or welfare or simply unemployed with no form of public support, etc. Most are on public support; this includes:

- Disability
- Veterans Benefits
- Unemployment
- Welfare
- Food Stamps
- Medicaid, and
- Other forms of non-employment support.

Question:

TOMORROW >>>

If this <u>10%</u> (10 million) and all the members of their households were to <u>disappear from the face of the earth tomorrow</u> (a significant change to the economic environment),

91 DAYS FROM TODAY; at 12:01 AM >>>

Three months after they disappeared – what would be the <u>approximate</u> number of household providers on public assistance or otherwise non-employed?

*Hint: Recall that **everything in economics is relative**. This is very true in the American capitalist system where non-employment is a relative number, <u>not</u> an absolute (definite) number. The form of non-employment could be "un-employed," "welfare" or some other class of non-working members of society (could be/would be members of the available workforce); but the number will be a relative number (a percentage of the whole) and will typically remain fairly consistent over near-long term spans of time (say 2 to 10 years).*

Therefore, it is the percentage -10% - that is important. The **total** number of household providers who will become non-employed has nothing to do with whether job candidates are able-bodied or disabled, highly motivated, <u>or anything else</u>. (There is very limited exception. The key exceptions are related to job skills, currently primarily in the medical field and a couple of vocational skills. These exceptions are typically related to the lack of an adequate supply of training versus a supply of workers. [Mufphy, Cait. **Is There Really a Skills Gap?** April 2014, Inc. Magazine, HTTP://WWW.INC.COM/MAGAZINE/201404/CAIT-MURPHY/SKILLS-GAP-IN-THE-LABOR-FORCE.HTML].)

Formulate your answer first – then continue reading.

Answer:

___90,000,000___ **Number of household providers remaining**
(100,000,000 (-) 10,000,000 = 90,000,000)

___9,000,000___ **Number of household providers non-employed**
(10% of 90,000,000 = 9,000,000)

Discussion points: Discuss the previous answer with members of your discussion group, fellow congregation or club members, or with someone you meet while waiting for a bus or a train. What effect does the above answer have on the quality of life for you and your family?

Assessment Question #2a:

To answer this question, you will need to refer to the assumptions and your answer for question #1.

Assumptions:

91 DAYS FROM TODAY (continued) >>>
At **11:59 pm**, 91 days from today the number of household providers non-employed, as referred to in assessment question # 1 (9,000,000) and the members of their households have disappeared from the face of the earth.

Question:

What would be the number of household providers remaining in the USA economy on the morning of day 92?

X = _____ **Number of household providers remaining**

(90,000,000 (-) 9,000,000 = X)

Assessment Question #2b:

To answer this question, you will need to refer to the assumptions and your answer for questions #1 and #2a.

Three months after day 92 (after the country's non-employment levels have adjusted) what will be the approximate number of household providers non-employed?

Y = _____ **Number of household providers non-employed**

(10% of X = Y)

Discussion point: Formulate your own answer first. Then discuss possible answers with members of your discussion group, congregation or club members, or with someone you meet while waiting for a bus or a train.

Explanations for the assessment questions are in an appendix to this chapter.

Tenth Percentile by Tenth Percentile

The population shift down through economic classes would not happen by everyone shifting down one class. The average income of each economic class would remain the same. But, a portion of the household providers in each class would move down. Most likely the greatest portion of those to move to the lowest rung would come from the second rung, but some people in each class would shift downward. Some would shift by one class, some by two, some by three, etc.

Let's call this shifting phenomenon the "crazy domino effect."

Think about a stack of 10 dominos. Now, imagine someone pulls the bottom domino from the stack. The whole stack, of the remaining 9 dominos, would drop down by the thickness of one domino. Should someone again remove the bottom domino, the whole stack of the remaining 8 dominos would drop down by the thickness of one domino. So far, everything makes sense.

However, if we try to form an analogy between the situations described in the assessment questions and a stack of 10 dominos – the outcome would not be the same. After the bottom domino was removed there would still be 10 dominos of the same thickness. But, excluding the thickness, the size of the dominos would have shrunk. There would now exist ten equally thick but otherwise smaller, equally sized, dominos. Starting with the domino at the top of the stack, some material of each domino would move down in the stack and provide the material needed to construct a new bottom domino. All of the material would not move from the higher dominos to the bottom domino. Some material would shift amongst dominos until both (A) the bottom domino was reconstructed and (B) all of the dominos in the stack were of equal size. **No matter how many times the bottom domino was removed ten dominos would remain, although smaller**. This is crazy – therefore, the "crazy domino effect."

If I were the top domino, I would not want the bottom domino to be removed from the stack. Further, I would want the bottom domino to be very secure in its position. This is true, as well, of every domino between the bottom domino and the top domino.

Discussion points - Members of US households with an income that falls into the lower 10th percentile have historically experienced shortened lifespans and are now experiencing a further shortening of their shortened lifespan. Who do you know within any of the 2nd through the top 10th income percentile who will take their place at the bottom? There is a moral saying that "you are your neighbors' keeper." Is there an economic perspective, in addition to the moral perspective, related to this saying?

SECTION B

The Federal Reserve's Attempt to Control Inflation

The real number of non-employed Americans is not, normally, 10%. 10% was used in the example to simplify the calculations. However, several times in USA history the number has been at or above 10%.

This number varies and is controlled to a large extent by the **Federal Reserve System**; commonly referred to as the Federal Reserve or the Federal Reserve Bank; although it is comprised of twelve regional Federal Reserve Banks.

The Federal Reserve Bank System (Federal Reserve; FR; Fed) is a quasi-government/private bank, whereas it is privately owned by commercial banks (many of the banks you drive by each day) but to a significant extent controlled by the Congress and Administrative branches of the government. The Federal Reserve is a non-profit corporation, and any profits it makes are turned over to the US Treasury.

An objective of the Fed is to control unemployment and inflation as a package. **- See citations. (This objective is known as the Fed's Dual Mandate**.)

The assumption it operates under is that **the primary source of inflation is wage increases**. **To this end, the Fed attempts to maintain a level of unemployment that is perceived to be needed to hold wage increases in line**. This is thought to be a number between 5% and 6.5%; but varies as the Fed management reviews and makes decisions regarding forecasted levels of inflation. (This may change if the downward trend in real wages and the upward trend in the importing of product from low-cost wage countries continue.) The Fed has several economic tools it uses for controlling unemployment and inflation. The options available to the Fed will not be discussed herein. The general public is familiar with the Fed's management of interest rates; therefore, interest rates will be used as an example. In brief:

a. If the unemployment rate is too high, interest rates are lowered. This is the interest rate the Fed charges member banks within the banking system; the individual banks then pass through lower rates to their potential customers as they determine is needed to be competitive with other banks. This action leads to an increase in borrowing, which leads to an increase in demand, which leads to an increase in the number of jobs available; or

b. If the unemployment rate is too low, interest rates are raised – this action leads to a decrease in borrowing, which leads to a decrease in demand, which leads to a decrease in the number of jobs available.

Why does an increase in borrowing lead to an increase in demand? "Demand" as defined in economics is a combination of the desire (need or want) for some thing and the ability to purchase that thing. Through borrowing citizens, both for personal and business reasons, attain an increased ability to purchase. Many citizens harbor a "pent-up demand" that they act upon when they can borrow at an interest rate they feel is reasonable; but, do not act upon when they when they feel the interest rate is unreasonable. In this latter case, one in which the interest rates are increased to a point considered unreasonable, the opposite happens – borrowing and demand decrease.

The Fed officials believe the practice of managing interest rates helps holds the unemployment rate to the targeted range as needed to control inflation.

SIDE NOTE: The interest rate charged by the Fed provides a signal to the banking system. It is significant, but not highly significant, in controlling the interest rates charged by your local bank. This is why the Fed has implemented QE, quantitative easing, and ZIRP, zero interest rate policy, and is reviewing NIRP, negative interest rate policy. How the system works will be reviewed in Discussion Guide 2.

The targeted unemployment rate is influenced by the relative number of people of working age in "other" types of non-employment situations not included in the reported unemployment numbers. These include those receiving welfare and seeking disability employment, or those said to have "given up," etc. but who in reality want a job. If this "other" group equals ½% of the total household providers then a stated target of 6% is really a target of 6.5%. This is true as most forms of non-employment provide downward pressure on wages and, thereby, downward pressure on inflation.

The Fed's current (as of August 2017) targeted level of inflation is 2%. Why not 0% or 1%. The discussion of this determination is beyond the scope of this basic guide. However, it is only important that voters know it exists so they can understand government and Fed decisions concerning unemployment. Voters do not have a need to participate, as citizens, in the determination of the inflation target. If, however, you are interested in learning more about the subject you can start with reading an article by Jeff Kearns and published by Bloomberg.com, January 2015. **- See citations.**

There are, however, factors other than interest rates which influence the levels of inflation and unemployment. Key amongst these are business cycles and demographic patterns. **– See citations.** Through the Fed's efforts to control both inflation and unemployment, the economic damage caused by both business cycles and demographic patterns is indirectly, to some extent, offset.

NOTE: All statements made in this guide related to job creation are subject to the limits established by the Federal Reserve for employment levels.

Here is Something to Think About

Discussion points: What, if any, do the Fed's practices related to establishing and maintaining targeted unemployment rates (5% to 6.5%) contribute to either long-term unemployment or the creation of a permanently unemployed class of American could-be/would-be workers?
Within the framework of your discussion(s), I suggest you consider how your answers:

- *Are influenced by the Fed's targeted unemployment rate relative to areas of the country that are experiencing economic growth versus those experiencing economic recession*
- *May differ for those who live in a sparsely populated rural area of the country versus those who live in a mid-size town versus those who live in a city*
- *May differ for workers who are 25, 35, 45, 55 or 65 years of age.*

This is a good question for you to discuss with your discussion group, members of your congregation or club, or with someone you meet while waiting for a bus or a train.

SECTION C

Basic Definitions You Need to Review

Note that definitions used herein are not meant to be exacting in the collegiate sense but are meant, <u>to the degree possible</u>, to be understandable. Also, there exist inconsistencies in the way various words and phrases are used in the media. Therefore, there may sometimes be an inconsistency between the meanings presented here and that you might read elsewhere.

Note, also that reviewing definitions is not the most exciting way one can spend one's time; however, it is necessary to do in order to allow the reader to follow the discussions in this guide, in the media, at political rallies, etc.

What is Economically Viable Conversion Labor?

<u>Economically viable conversion</u> labor is labor applied to some thing to change the character or placement of that some thing such that its usefulness to an individual, individuals or society is enhanced (subject to demand). The state of "usefulness" requires that there is a demand for the thing changed or relocated. (See the definitions for natural resources and demand below.)

To add clarity:

Eric lives in Nashville, TN. Eric decided to retire. He wanted a hobby that would pay for itself plus provide a little supplemental retirement income. He decided to carve duck decoys. Eric purchased a short piece of 4x4 and carved a decoy. Eric **changed the character** of the 4x4 from a piece of wood to a decoy.

Eric's sister and her family came to visit Eric and his family the week of the Baltimore, MD. wood carvers' show. Eric's friend Barbara, who he had met at a local carving meet-up and her husband attended the Baltimore show and took Eric's decoy to the show. The decoy sold for $425. Barbara **changed the placement** of the decoy. Both Eric and Barbara **applied conversion labor** to create a viable economic outcome.

To add additional clarity:

If Eric III, Eric's 8-year-old grandson, were to pour a bucket of water onto a spot of ground for no reason other than to create mud, the act of pouring water would represent conversion labor; the dirt was converted to mud, but this is not economically viable conversion labor. In fact, if Eric III tracked the mud into the house his mother would see this as destructive labor, not as economically viable conversion labor.

On the other hand, should Eric's grandson pour a bucket of water onto a spot of ground where a corn stock, intended for cattle feed, in need of water is growing, the act of pouring water would represent the application of economically viable conversion labor.

Throughout this guide the phrases "labor" and "conversion labor" refer to economically viable conversion labor.

What is a Natural Resource?

A natural resource is a substance found in nature that can be useful to man; it is the first ingredient in the development of "something." The substance can be hard in nature, such as coal or granite, soft in nature, such as water or fish, or a natural process such as wind or thought.

What is a Readily Available Natural Resource?

A readily available natural resource is one for which it makes sense to mine the resource as determined by the conversion labor applied versus the benefit derived from the effort. Typically such a resource is considered commercially viable to mine.

What is economics?

In simplified terms – economics is the study of what people do regarding the creation and exchange of goods and services of assumed value; including the systems employed by society to facilitate and govern such creation and exchange (condensed definition).

What are Needs and Wants?

Humans have needs and wants and the ability to apply conversion labor to natural resources such that their needs and wants to a degree are satisfied. Needs are human desires for necessities of human life such as a healthy diet and protection from the weather. <u>Wants</u> are human desires for things that are not necessities such as an expensive wristwatch or a sports car.

What is Economic Demand?

<u>Economic demand</u> is the total of the needs and wants within an economy for which the population of the economy has the means to procure those things desired. The means to procure requires that the population has both the abundance of readily available natural resources and the available conversion labor necessary to produce that which can satisfy demand or can be traded to satisfy demand. Further the available conversion labor must be effectively applied to production activities. It is important to note that the existence of desire does not constitute economic demand unless accompanied by the means to procure. The satisfaction of demand can be accomplished through consuming products produced within an *economic unit* or economy or by trading for products produced by other economic units or economies.

What is an Economic Unit?

An <u>economic unit</u> is:

1. A population group within an economy that applies conversion labor to resources, consumes the resulting product, and/or trades the resulting product with other economic units within an economy or within other economies. These types of economic units are normally such societal population groupings as households, businesses, industries, state governments, provincial governments, and central governments.

2. A population group within an economic unit, units, or an economy; or an economic unit or units within another economy(s) (can crossover other units and various economies) that shares particular economic characteristics; often defined for study (e.g. members of the population with household incomes between $80,000 and $120,000).

The population group can be just one individual or a group of millions of individuals. *NOTE: at some future point in time, as the global economy becomes one economy, the top side of the range of a unit defined for study will be the population of the planet earth.*

Economists often address the issue of the size of an economic unit by classifying it as either a **micro** unit or a **macro** unit. Micro units and macro units are, sometimes, addressed as microeconomies (household or business economy) and macroeconomies (the total economy overseen by a country's central government). Both are relative terms. Households and businesses and, sometimes, states and provinces are referred to as microeconomic units. Central governments and, sometimes, governments of states and provinces are referred to as macroeconomic units. Sometimes, a macroeconomic unit and a country's economy are treated, in discussion, as one-in-the-same. Based upon the framework of a discussion the terms micro and macroeconomic unit can be interchanged with the terms micro and macroeconomy.

For instance, the countries Libya, Greece, and Venezuela (often considered macro-economies) have populations of less than seven million, twelve million and thirty-two million people, respectively. The United States (a macroeconomy) has 330 million people. Within the United States, the states of North Carolina, Texas and California (microeconomic units within the framework of a macroeconomy) have populations of ten million, twenty-seven million and thirty-eight million respectively. When lined up in relative order the states of North Carolina, Texas and California are respectively larger economic units of a macroeconomy than are the Libyan, Greek and Venezuelan economies. As such, a "microeconomic unit/microeconomy" within one discussion framework can be a "macroeconomic unit/ macroeconomy" within another framework.

This guide uses a slightly different approach to defining micro and macroeconomic units. While size is a consideration – the focus is on the limiting and non-limiting behavioral characteristics of the economic unit (i.e., what an economic unit can or cannot do). The answer to the question of what an economic unit can or cannot do relative to other economic units is the basis for classification as mini (see next paragraph), micro, or macroeconomic unit.

The classification of a "**mini**" economic unit is used in this guide to distinguish between households and other economic units traditionally classified as "micro" economic units. This approach has been adopted because the economic perspective of a household is different from that of economic units such as a business or a town government (as a government sector entity; towns, cities, states, etc. have private sector business aspects, also). Two major differentiating factors that affect this perspective are:

- Commonly, households do not employ others from outside of the household except on an intermittent basis, and

- Households do not lay-off breadwinners of the household; this option typically does not exist for a household. (NOTE: in the case of states, cities, and towns – lay off government employees and/or lose population / i.e., Detroit.)

(Other factors are discussed in the section <u>What are the Key Classes of Economic Units</u>.)

Businesses, town governments, and many other economic units can expand or contract in size as the economic environment changes – households cannot.

The governor of a state can brag that his state has only a 5.7% unemployment rate versus a national rate of 7.7%. Typically, a household with one of two, or both of two, or one of one breadwinners unemployed has an unemployment rate of 50% or 100%; the members of the household aren't bragging.

In addition to establishing a classification of "mini" economic unit, this book establishes a unitized relationship between the economy of a country and that of its central government. The economy of a country and its central government typically work in tandem. (See section: <u>The Tandem Relationship – a Very Key Point to Understand</u>.) As such the economy of a country and its central government behave as almost one and the same. **The relationship provides the population of a country with the ability to manage the budget of the central government in ways that can expand or shrink the size of the country's overall economy.**

<u>Herein, often, the economic characteristics and behavior of a country and its central government are treated as one and the same</u>. Additionally, for ease of reading, the term "federal" is sometimes substituted for "central" as the USA has a federal type of central government.

Economist also often classify economic units as "types" that somewhat align with the classifications of mini, micro, and macro. A common classification system used is to classify economic units as "households, firms, and government." [Wikipedia – economic units, **http://en.wikipedia.org/wiki/Economic_unit**, as of 07/15/2015.]

One could construct a diagram of circles showing how the classifications of mini, micro, and macro interrelate with one another and with the types of household, firm, and government. While such an exercise would have value, it would add a layer of complexity to a guide designed to deliver basic information only. Therefore, we will follow the path of discussing only mini, micro and macroeconomic units.

What is an Economic Community?

An economic community, as the phrase is commonly used, is a variation of an economic unit, typically a subset thereof (e.g. business community, medical community); or a variation of economies designed to encourage trade between member economies (i.e., European (Economic) Community, Common Market for Eastern and Southern Africa, and Council of Arab Unity). However, some economic sub-sets of economic units are not economic communities. A study of the economic characteristics of single parents in America is a study of an economic unit that is a subset of the household economic unit and the US economy; but single parents do not function as an economic community (they are not organized for trade).

The phrase is used in different ways by different individuals; therefore, the reader or listener of this or that piece of information, where the phrase is used, needs to look to the context in which it is used.

Discussion points: What does it mean to members of your household if a breadwinner becomes unemployed? What does it mean to the economy of the state you live in if a breadwinner in your household becomes unemployed? What does it mean to the economy of the country if a breadwinner in your household becomes unemployed?

What can your employer or, if you own a business, your business do that your household cannot do as ways to reduce operating costs (expenditures – rent, utilities, wages, supplies, etc.)?

SECTION D

What are Key Classes of Economic Units?

If viewed from the <u>point of view of economic behavior</u>, there are three classes of economic units.

These are:

1. Minieconomic unit
2. Microeconomic unit
3. Macroeconomic unit

These line up closely, but not exactly, with the economic units of an economy as typically defined by many economists; but they are close enough and easier for the reader to put into perspective.

As mentioned in the section <u>What is an Economic Unit</u> there is a relationship between each class and specific formal and informal societal institutions, typically as:

1. <u>Mini</u>economic unit/household economies

2. Microeconomic unit/businesses, business-like institutions (non-profits, universities, etc.) and some economic aspects of governments of states, towns, cities, etc.
3. Macroeconomic unit/central governments and some aspects of governments of states, towns, cities, etc.

States, towns, cities and other local governmental functions exhibit to a degree both the economic behavioral characteristics common to microeconomic units and macroeconomic units. Wherein the source of revenue for a governmental unit is from "fixed" sources, to a degree, they behave as microeconomic units. Wherein the source of revenue for a governmental unit is from "relative" sources (those that vary with the level of spending within an economy) they behave, to a degree, as macroeconomic units. "Fixed" sources are those such as property taxes, vehicle licenses, and business licenses. "Relative" sources are those such as income taxes, sales taxes, and tariffs. "Fixed" revenue sources are more commonly found at the local governments (towns and cities) and "relative" sources (over 95% of US federal revenue) are found at the federal government. State government sources fall in between; but tend toward "relative" sources.[1]

The private sectors of states, cities, towns and other such locales reflect, within limits (beyond the scope of this book) the characteristics of the national macroeconomy. The section on page 27, <u>Reducing operating costs</u>, explains the private sector relationship to a greater detail.

> NOTE: *Comments herein apply only to the economies of most major modern countries with capitalist or somewhat socialist based economies. (The United States, Canada, and Mexico have capitalist based economies; Sweden, Germany, and England have more leaning to a socialist based economy than the USA – but currently, no major countries are fully socialist.)*

There are key similarities amongst these classes. These are covered by the definition of an economic unit as provided previously. More importantly from a voter's perspective, there are key dissimilarities amongst these classes. <u>Because there can exist a mixture of economic characteristics across the classes as related to local and state governments, to keep the discussion simple – we will focus on households, businesses, and central governments (**characteristics of local and state governments are too complex for a discussion of basic economics**)</u>. These will each represent their respective class. Within each respective class these differences are delineated for:

---

[1] A "fixed" source is one that remains constant, except for delinquent payments, as the income and transaction level (purchases) in an economy increase and decrease (robust economy versus recession or depression). A "relative" source is one that increases or decreases as the income and transaction level (purchases) in an economy increase and decrease.

- People
- Consumption and production
- Saving money
- Reducing operating costs
- Misdirecting money, and
- Expansion.

Additionally, a central government and a country's economy, to a large extent, work in tandem. The characteristics are, therefore, delineated where appropriate, also, for a country's economy.

People:

- Households (minieconomic units) cannot shed people
- Businesses (microeconomic units) can shed people
- Central governments (macroeconomic units) can shed people – but, are limited by the effect on the respective country's economy
- Countries (macroeconomies) cannot shed people (morally or effectively).

Consumption and production:

- Households (minieconomic units) consume
- Businesses (microeconomic units) produce for consumption
- Central governments (macroeconomic units) produce for consumption.

  Although there exist business-to-business consumption and business-to-government consumption, all such consumption feeds into the supply chain servicing eventual household consumption (note: even defense spending is a form of household consumption).

  Likewise, there exists government-to-government consumption and government-to-business consumption, and all such consumption feeds into the supply chain servicing eventual household consumption.

Saving money:

- Households can save money
- Businesses can save money
- Central governments, from a practical perspective, cannot save money (see the section of this chapter, Money Flow – Government for explanation). This is due to the form in which revenues are collected and the interrelationship with the respective country's economy

- Countries (imagine a personified national economy) cannot practically save money for more than a near-long-term period as needed to accumulate for investment. The expenditures of the economic units of a country add up to the economy of a country. If the rate of spending is slowed the economy of a country will deteriorate.

Saving money is accomplished by reducing operating costs (utilities, groceries, wages, repairs and maintenance, etc.) or forgoing "like to have" purchases.

Reducing operating costs:

- Households can reduce operating (expenditures for groceries, rent, entertainment, etc.) costs while maintaining a specified level of revenue (household income)
- Businesses can reduce operating costs (expenditures for labor, supplies, materials, maintenance, rent, etc.) while maintaining a specified level of revenue (sales revenue). However, as a collective group, from a practical perspective – the group behaves differently than an individual business. See discussion under the next bullet for central governments
- Central governments, from a practical perspective and typically, cannot reduce operating costs (see the section of this chapter: <u>Money Flow – Government</u> for explanation). This is due to the form in which revenues are collected and the interrelationship with the respective country's economy:

  o Governments that use "relative" tax assessment means for raising public revenue (i.e., USA income tax system type, state sales tax, value-added tax, flat-tax, etc.) cannot reduce operating costs (expenditures - wages, entitlement payments, repairs and maintenance, new equipment and facilities, defense, education, highway construction, social security, etc.) and maintain a specified level of public revenue. As operating costs (wages, entitlements, education, law enforcement, etc.) are reduced **– revenue, as a result of the cost reduction, at some high level of degree, is reduced; both for the government and private sectors. An informed citizenry can exercise control over the revenue and cost balance of the government's revenue/cost relationship as well as maintain both at a desirable level.**

  There is an explanation of "why" governments that use relative tax assessment means for sourcing revenue cannot reduce operating costs (i.e., budget cuts; a budget is the planned amount that an individual or organization plans to spend)[2] without experiencing a reduction in tax revenues in the section of this chapter, Money Flow - Government.

- o Private sector businesses, as a collection of businesses, make up the majority of the macroeconomy within a country (typically the private sector equals around 60% and the government sector equals around 40% [federal 20%; other 20%). While individual business within an economy can reduce costs (supplies, maintenance, software, etc.) while maintaining sales revenue, or even increasing sales revenue, **they too (like government), as a collective group**, cannot reduce costs and maintain revenue. **If all US businesses were to reduce operating costs to a significant degree within a short time frame, total business revenue would drop, and the country would experience a recession.** Why? Because business buy from businesses and people buy from businesses. A reduction in costs equates to, either or both of, a lower purchasing level of materials and supplies or labor. This factor equates to a lowered level of business revenue.

  There are limited direct means of control available to the citizenry for keeping the revenue and costs of the collective business community in balance and at a desirable level. The key direct control is the adjustment of import tariff levels. There are several key indirect means of control an informed citizenry can utilize. These include: raising or lowering Fed interest rates or reserve requirements, adjustments to tax code provisions, stimulus packages, increasing or decreasing general government spending as a balance to decreases or increases in general private sector spending, and taking actions to decrease or increase active or idle money within the system or to generally speed up or slow down circulation. [The private sector options will be discussed in Discussion Guide 2].

- Countries cannot reduce operating costs in total or the economy will weaken. However, countries can substitute new forms of costs for old forms of costs.

Misdirecting money:

- Households can misdirect where money is spent (buying a new red pickup truck, when the old truck is working well, as opposed to buying needed dental work

---

[2] Last week I went to the county fair. I planned to spend $40. The amount I planned to spend ($40) was my "budget." If I were a smart person I would have left home with only $40 in my wallet. But, I am not a smart person. I left home with $65 in my wallet. By the time I left the fair I had spent $49. My "actual" expenditures were $9 more than my budget.

for a child); once the money is gone there is <u>not any additional benefit to be had by the household</u>

- Businesses can misdirect money; once the money is gone there is <u>not any additional benefit to be had by the business</u>
- The governments (federal, state, local) of a country and the collective groups of the businesses and households of a country can misdirect money; but <u>economic benefits still are realized by the governments and the collective groups of businesses and households of the country</u>:

  o For instance, a government funds the building of an unnecessary airport expansion versus the needed extension of a highway – the country's general economy still realizes benefits in terms of employment and the downstream circulating money including tax recovery by the government.

  o If business "A" builds a manufacturing plant and, shortly after completing the project, business "A" goes into bankruptcy – business "A" does not realize any additional benefit. The country's general economy still realizes benefits in terms of employment and the downstream circulating money. The construction company, the companies that manufactured the machinery and equipment, the freight companies that hauled construction materials, machinery, equipment, etc. and several other companies that supplied the project all realized some benefit (up until losing some of the money due to the bankruptcy) as did their employees. Business "A" may have gone bankrupt; but, the collective businesses and the country's general economy realized economic benefits

  o If, as mentioned previously, a red pickup truck is purchased by a household instead of dental work there is the same downstream economic benefit for the community in terms of employment and circulating money.

Expansion:

- Households and businesses (mini and microeconomic units) expand based on individual achievement or/and within the framework of their parent macroeconomy

- Central governments (macroeconomic units) expand as the community deems necessary or in response to changes in the economic ratios or economic environment. This is the case, except to the degree of limitations set by the abundance of readily available natural resources.

  Macroeconomies typically (there are other less common reasons) expand when:

a. Money is moved from savings into expenditures at above a current normal rate (idle money becomes active money)
b. Credit use is expanded beyond current normal levels allowing participants in the economy to spend more than they previously were able to spend - **See citations**
c. A particular resource, which is economically readily available and needed, is discovered (this would have a minor impact in a country such as the United States; but a major impact in a country such as Haiti)
d. Other macroeconomies increase their demand for the goods and/or services of a particular macroeconomy
e. Native (excludes immigration) changes in demographic patterns favor expanded levels of working and spending; the key long-term pattern being natural domestic population growth
f. Planned immigration increases the domestic demand for goods and services (instead of exporting to people outside of the country, bring the people into the country and sell to them here)
g. A manipulation of the monetary system encourages international procurement of goods and services provided by a given economy.

Typical key drivers for moving money out of savings or for borrowing above current "normal" rates are: demographic patterns, some technological changes, disaster, some military actions, false economies, above normal availability of perceived investment opportunities, implementation of regulations, opening of foreign markets, reallocation of income from upper to lower income groups, and several minor drivers.

The money supply is increased in response to the demand for money as needed to support expansion of the economy; unless the credit markets (you buy on credit) are maxed out (as relates to sound investment opportunities: this has never happened in modern USA history for any given five-year period; however it does relate, to some degree, to unsound investment opportunities). The money supply is normally decreased, as a function of a slowing economy, as demand is contracted. However, in the recent recession – due to its depth – the Fed, through direct action, increased the money supply.

Discussion points: Same question as previously asked - what can your employer or, if you own a business, your business do that your household cannot do as ways to reduce operating costs?

If you or your employer/business (if you own a business) waste money does that help your household or employer/business's economy or hurt your household or employer/ business's economy? If you or your employer/business waste money does that help or hurt the USA economy?

This discussion guide focuses primarily on the federal government sector of the economy; as this is the aspect of the economy with the most identifiable and controllable characteristics that the voter has control over.

Discussion Guide 2 will provide more insight into the private sector and the relationship between the public and private sector.

SECTION E

Money Flow - Government

Under the section Reducing Operating Costs it is stated: Governments that use "relative" tax assessment means (i.e., USA income tax system type, state sales tax, value-added tax, flat-tax, etc.) cannot reduce operating costs (expenditures for education, defense, highway construction, law enforcement, etc.) and maintain a specified level of public revenue.

Why is this true?

In brief, the money the government pays out becomes revenue for businesses and households. These businesses and households pay taxes on the income they realize (the revenue minus costs = income) and make purchases (the "purchases" include paychecks for labor). The purchases these businesses and households make generate realized taxable income to the businesses and individuals they purchase from. These businesses and individuals pay taxes on their income and make purchases. This pattern of businesses and individuals realizing taxable income, paying taxes and making purchases continues until the total of the initial government expenditure has in large part been recaptured by the government. This is a **closed-loop, money circulation system**. Therefore, if the expenditure is not made (a government budget cut) a reduction in revenue received by the government (the taxes collected) will equal the amount of the initial expenditure not made (except for leakage). For instance, **a $100 government reduction in operating expenditures (budget cut) results in a $100 drop in tax revenues collected. <u>The net savings to the government and the community, as a whole, with minor exceptions due to leakage, will be zero (federal government budget cutting is a near zero-sum game – unless the government is competing with the private sector for employees and resources [this has not happened in America's history])</u>**. There are several forms of leakage; the two key forms are:

- The transfer of active money to idle money (i.e., savings, purchases of traded stocks and bonds, etc. that are not quickly put back into the economy [traded stocks and bonds – those purchased in the secondary market as opposed to directly from an issuing company or its agent]), and

- A negative international balance of trade (the USA imports more than it exports).

What else happens if the government does not make the expenditure?

- Individuals and businesses, within the economy, will not realize the level of private sector benefits of goods (TV's, video games, automobiles) and services (Internet, cell phone, barber) that would have been produced had the government spent the money, (therefore, a reduction in business revenues and profits), and

- There will be, as a result of not spending the money, a reduced need for workers in the economy. Therefore, the level of unemployment will increase.

The Congressional Budget Office (CBO) develops federal government budget projections and an economic outlook for the USA for the benefit of the US Congress. These two bits of information are developed in tandem. Why? There is no other way to do it. Because of the almost absolute level of interdependence of the government sector and the private sector (see Government Money Flow Exercise) it is not possible to project one without the other.

The economic outlook is a forecast which is not exactly a budget; but in essence is the total of the whole of the private sector budgets (if these budgets were developed objectively and all households and businesses developed a budget) and government budgets (federal, state and local).[3]

Although no one completes a budget for the total US economy; it helps (and is a practice used in this guide) to mentally picture a budget for the economy as a whole that is comprised of the total of all private sector and government budgets. Additionally, although it is "actual revenues and expenditures that work their way through an economy – it is customary to speak in terms of "budgets." The use of the concept of budgets simplifies discussions and allows for discussions of future events and outcomes related to economic decisions.

The Tandem Relationship – a Very Key Point to Understand

What is important to understand – <u>whether speaking to the subject of budgets or actual</u>

---

[3] The word "objectively" is used here because many households and businesses budget based on fantasized revenues and incomes. The CBO tries to work with a guesstimated reality.

revenues and expenditures- the government budgets/actuals **work in tandem** with and are **mutually dependent** with the budgets/actuals for the macroeconomy (the government and private sector economies of the USA) in which the government resides.

What does "work in tandem" mean, anyway?

The tires on a truck work in tandem when the truck is being driven on a straight section of highway. If the left tire travels 6" on the road - the right tire, also, travels 6" on the road; if the right tire then travels 18 feet on the road – the left tire, also, travels 18 feet on the road. The left and right tire move together; they move in tandem. ("Tandem" – working or occurring in conjunction with one another. *Webster's*.) Additionally, if the tires do not work in tandem the truck will swerve.

What does "dependent" mean, anyway? Dependent means – determined or conditioned by another. (*Webster's*.). "Dependent" is a form of the word "dependence." Dependence means – the quality or state of being influenced or determined by or subject to another. (*Webster's*.)

FYI: In government talk, it is common to speak in terms of "budgets." It is not often that the word "forecast" is used. A budget is a forecast (estimate), usually very detailed, that is compiled once each year; whereas, that typically spoken of as a forecast is an update to a budget, typically of less detail than a budget, reflecting expected variations in "actual" revenues and/or expenditures from that depicted in the budget. "Actuals" are the actual revenues collected (taxes, license fees, tolls, etc.) and actual expenditures made (rent, wages, facilities, fighter jets, computers, etc.).

Forecasts, also, are often made for purposes other than those related to a budget. For instance – a forecast can be made of expected birth rates or energy consumption.

The important thing to remember is that the federal government's expenditure and revenue (tax) system works as a closed-loop system. If expenditures increase, the loop goes up, both expenditures and revenues increase – plus the private sector's revenues increase and the level of unemployment drops (subject to Fed limits). If expenditures decrease, the loop goes down, both expenditures and revenues decrease – plus the private sector's revenues decrease and the level of unemployment increases. The money always flows around in a loop.

Money Flow – Government Exercises

Following is a brief explanation of the above explanation based upon tracking the money flow of government expenditures and relative taxation through the economy using pretend, but representative, situations as examples. There are three alternate scenarios examined.

As you read the examples, you should think back to the <u>Penny Money Flow Exercise</u> in Appendix B and the discussion on <u>Shifting of Population Through Economic Classes</u>.

Examples:

In these example exercises,

Key Assumptions are:

- Bob and Sue are government employees; <u>who represent the whole US Government</u>

- Jim, Jane, Mary, and George are four of eight private sector workers, <u>who represent the whole US private sector</u>; all four are self-employed; all in a service industry (this is done for simplicity)

- For simplicity a flat income tax rate of 20% is used (this is for example only; it is not a statement in favor of a flat tax system); income taxes are paid the day the income is received

- There are no other government income taxes at the local, state or federal levels

- Again for simplicity, there is no one in the US economy unemployed at the start of the exercise

- The other four private sector workers are not directly included in the exercises

- BUT, in the beginning

  In all three scenarios, eight (8) private sector workers provide **all** of the private sector goods and services needed to satisfy the needs and wants of all ten (10) workers (2 government workers, 8 private sector workers) and their dependents <u>and</u> workers who become non-employed and their dependents.

  NOTE: This is approximately the same as the real-life ratio whereby roughly 16% of the USA potential workforce works in some type of government job and less than 80% of the workforce works in some type of private sector job. Those (the less than 80%) private sector workers provide all of the private sector goods and services demanded by 100% of the household providers (both those in the workforce and those who are non-employed or retired) and their dependents. **There are no additional workers required to produce goods or services unless the level of demand changes**. If a government worker is laid off and, subsequently takes a private sector job for approximately the same pay, the total level of demand in the economy will not increase. Therefore, there will not be a need for any additional private sector workers. Therefore, if the ex-government worker takes a private sector job; either some currently employed private sector worker will need to be laid off or an unemployed private sector worker will need to remain unemployed - as the position will be filled by the ex-government employee.

NOTE ALSO: It is **important** to recognize that **less than 80% of USA workers** are required to produce 100% of the private sector product required by all USA residents. This is in a robust economy; the average is below this. This is a function of the design of the American capitalist system and technology. **Unfortunately, many in politics and economics look at the level of unemployment without looking at the level of possible private sector employment.** This has led to the development of highly irrational employment and other economic type proposals by various congresspeople and some presidents.

I refer to this twisted logic as the <u>water bucket syndrome</u>. The first question to ask relative to employment is "how big is the bucket"; where the "bucket" is the number of jobs the economy can support (the number of jobs that can be available in the economy at any given time). What determines the number of jobs the economy can support? Demand. What determines demand?

- Business cycles
- Demographic population expansion or contractions
- Demographic mix (for instance, the relative number (i.e., %) of seniors in the population versus the number of teenagers)
- Federal Reserve practices related to controlling the levels of inflation and employment
- Consumer confidence, and
- Etc.

The size of the bucket (number of jobs the economy can support) is not in any way, shape, or form determined by the willingness, the level of personal determination, the level of an individual's education, or anything else of citizens who need to work. (NOTE: the "fit" to the jobs available is influenced by the available supply of workers with the right education or experience. But, the "need" for a worker is not determined by the supply of workers with the required type of education or experience.)

Some politicians and economist think it is possible to fit seven gallons of water (the total potential workforce) into a five-gallon bucket. God did not provide man with a five-gallon bucket that will hold seven or even only six gallons of water. God did provide man with the means to build a bigger bucket – but only through increasing demand.[4]

What do Jim, Jane, Mary, and George do?

1. Jim installs software and fixes computer viruses
2. Jane is a house cleaner; she uses the customer's supplies
3. Mary is a masseuse
4. George is a gardener/handyman; he uses the customer's supplies

Scenarios:

We will explore three scenarios related to government spending and the private sector effect:

1. Bob and Sue work for the government (and represent the whole government) and **the tax rate is 20%**. This scenario shows the way things are prior to a government spending budget cut. [Scenario 1]

2. Sue is laid off as the result of **a 50% budget cut in government spending** and not replaced, and **the tax rate remains at 20%**. [Scenario 2]

3. **Sue is laid off as the result of a 50% budget cut in government spending** and not replaced. Additionally, **the tax rate is reduced by 50%, from 20% to 10%** [Scenario 3].

The money flow for each scenario is followed through two business days in this chapter (Monday and Tuesday). If you are so inclined, you can work it through as many days as you wish. Also, the money flow is followed through further in Appendix D.

_____

[4] Some congress people and some Presidents are guilty of trying to fantasize their political positions into reality. The same people repeat this same practice over and over again. They never catch on – it doesn't work. The American voters need to assess a candidate's ability to work with reality so that people are elected who can develop sound solutions that benefit the community as a whole.

Scenario 1:

The transactions for Scenario 1 are as follows (See Schedule 1):

- On **Friday** both Bob and Sue each receive a government issued paycheck for $100 gross amount; the IRS takes $20 of tax from each paycheck; the net paycheck amount for both Bob and Sue is $80

- Bob and Sue cash and spend their paychecks on **Monday**
    1) Bob hires Jim for $80 to fix a computer virus problem
    2) Sue hires Jane for $80 to clean her house

- Jim and Jane pay the 20% tax to the taxman, $16, and spend their after-tax paychecks, $64 ($80 - $16), on **Tuesday**
    1) Jim hires Jane for $64 to wash the windows in his house
    2) Jane hires Mary for $64 to fix her sore back

Review Schedule 1 to follow the money flow by transaction for each of the three scenarios.

The money flowing from Bob and Sue Government Employee's paychecks will continue to flow through the US economy until all (all, except for leakage) of the initial tax outlay (Bob and Sue's paychecks) has been recovered through the payment of taxes on the income generated. This will happen reasonably fast (the majority in less than two years and the balance over the next one to three years).

Excluding leakage, as the money (originally $200 paid to Bob and Sue Government Employees) continues to circulate it will create approximately $1,000 of private sector, after-tax income.

How do we know this? The answer is we simply run out the numbers representing the circulation of the $200. This is done in part through the review of Scenario 1 and Schedule 1 discussed herein and in full in Discussion Guide Appendix D.

Leakage comes in many forms. The two primary sources are (a) the transfer of active money to idle money and (b) a negative balance of international trade (trade deficit) (including exported military operations). Both of these factors remove money from the US active economy. (See Appendix F for a more detailed explanation of leakage.)

The effect of leakage is probably less than 5%. However, the development of a substantive estimate would be a project for some very smart economists.

Scenarios 2 & 3:

The transactions for Scenarios 2 & 3 are the same for transactions flowing from Bob Government Employee's paycheck. Sue Government Employee's job was eliminated due to the budget cut. Therefore, all transactions in the private sector that would have come about as a result of the money flow from Sue's paycheck are eliminated from the US economy.

Excluding the effects of leakage, as the money continues to circulate it will create approximately:

Scenario 2:

$ 500 of private sector, after-tax income, and

Scenario 3:

$1,000 of private sector, after-tax income.

SCHEDULE 1 - GOVERNMENT MONEY FLOW EXERCISE EXAMPLES - THREE SCENARIOS:

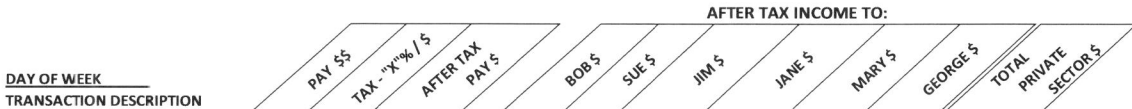

AFTER TAX INCOME TO:

DAY OF WEEK / TRANSACTION DESCRIPTION	PAY $$	TAX - "X"% / $	AFTER TAX PAY $	BOB $	SUE $	JIM $	JANE $	MARY $	GEORGE $	TOTAL PRIVATE SECTOR $

SCENARIO 1 - PRIOR TO CUT IN GOVERNMENT OPERATING COST BUDGET
INCOME TAX RATE ASSUMED TO BE 20%:

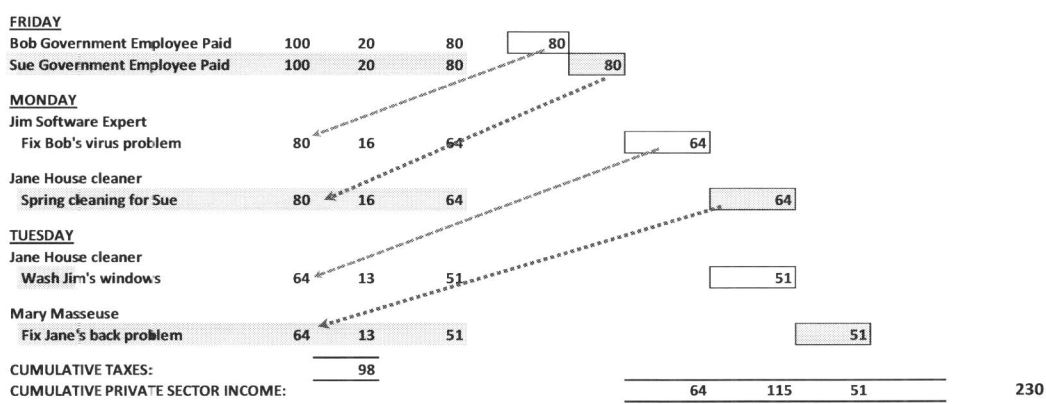

FRIDAY										
Bob Government Employee Paid	100	20	80	80						
Sue Government Employee Paid	100	20	80		80					
MONDAY										
Jim Software Expert										
Fix Bob's virus problem	80	16	64			64				
Jane House cleaner										
Spring cleaning for Sue	80	16	64				64			
TUESDAY										
Jane House cleaner										
Wash Jim's windows	64	13	51				51			
Mary Masseuse										
Fix Jane's back problem	64	13	51					51		
CUMULATIVE TAXES:		98								
CUMULATIVE PRIVATE SECTOR INCOME:					64	115	51			230

SCENARIO 2 - 50% CUT TO GOVERNMENT OPERATING COST BUDGET
INCOME TAX RATE ASSUMED TO BE 20%:

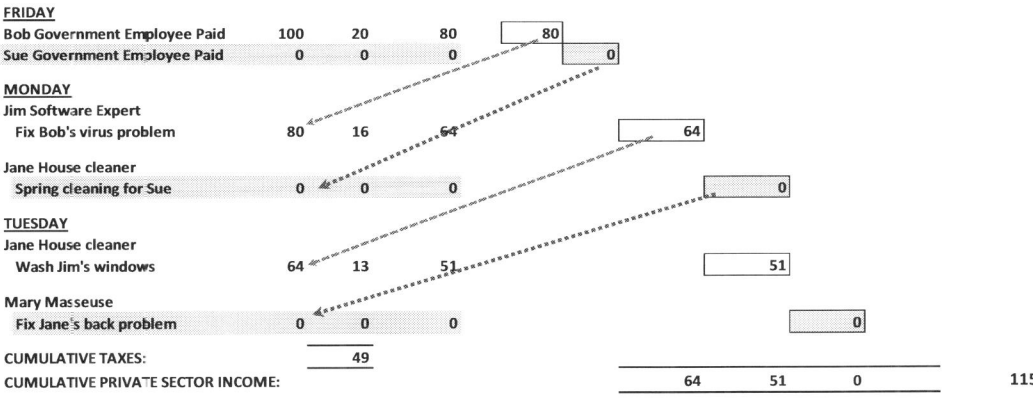

FRIDAY										
Bob Government Employee Paid	100	20	80	80						
Sue Government Employee Paid	0	0	0		0					
MONDAY										
Jim Software Expert										
Fix Bob's virus problem	80	16	64			64				
Jane House cleaner										
Spring cleaning for Sue	0	0	0				0			
TUESDAY										
Jane House cleaner										
Wash Jim's windows	64	13	51				51			
Mary Masseuse										
Fix Jane's back problem	0	0	0					0		
CUMULATIVE TAXES:		49								
CUMULATIVE PRIVATE SECTOR INCOME:					64	51	0			115

SCENARIO 3 - 50% CUT TO GOVERNMENT OPERATING COST BUDGET
INCOME TAX RATE ASSUMED TO BE 10%:

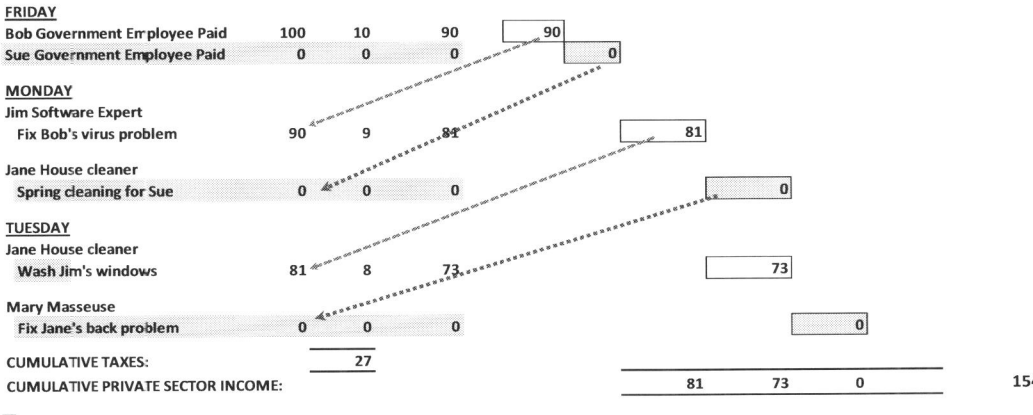

FRIDAY										
Bob Government Employee Paid	100	10	90	90						
Sue Government Employee Paid	0	0	0		0					
MONDAY										
Jim Software Expert										
Fix Bob's virus problem	90	9	81			81				
Jane House cleaner										
Spring cleaning for Sue	0	0	0				0			
TUESDAY										
Jane House cleaner										
Wash Jim's windows	81	8	73				73			
Mary Masseuse										
Fix Jane's back problem	0	0	0					0		
CUMULATIVE TAXES:		27								
CUMULATIVE PRIVATE SECTOR INCOME:					81	73	0			154

Transactions highlighted flow from the paycheck given to Sue Government Employee.

To recap, once the money flowing through the economy completes its circulation the result is a $500 reduction in after-tax private sector income in Scenario 2 and an unchanged after-tax income, $1,000, in Scenario 3; as in Scenario 1 (prior to government spending cut). The private sector after-tax income effect is **negative** under Scenario 2 ($1,000 versus $500) and **zero** under Scenario 3 ($1,000 versus $1,000). The best of the alternative scenarios 2 or 3 for budget change is Scenario 3; this alternative, however, accomplishes nothing as it simply brings the private sector income back to where we started in Scenario 1.

The community is best off, economically, with the original situation presented in Scenario 1. Although, mathematically, in Scenario 3, the private sector remains at the same level of income, the government sector income drops, which means the country's unemployment levels increase. (Appendix F provides an example of a cash flow including leakage. This appendix is a bit more complicated than the balance of this book. It is not a necessary read; but is provided for those who wish to take a more complete look at how the system works.)

The question is "what is the financial advantage to the community of cutting the government's operating budget?" The answer is – except for a rare situation, one which has never happened in US modern history, the community realizes **no** financial advantage from reducing government spending. If government spending is cut the private sector income will be reduced by a much greater amount than the spending cuts. If taxes are reduced proportionately to the level of spending cut there is still no advantage (i.e., both taxes and spending are cut by 50%, [proportionately] as depicted in Scenario 3). Until government spending results in creating a situation in which government is competing with the private sector for labor or capital (i.e., the level of taxing is slowing needed private sector investment) a cut to government spending will have either no effect or a negative effect on the economy and a negative effect on employment.

Why a negative effect on employment? The private sector demand under Scenario 3 was reinstated to its original level per the mathematical exercise. But, prior to the government budget cut, only 80% of the workforce was required to provide for 100% of demand as supplied by the private sector. This includes the $1,000 of pre-budget cut private sector demand depicted in Scenario 1. Therefore, there is no need for Sue in the private sector. Her after-tax earnings will disappear and therefore not circulate through the economy. She will need to either move in with mom and dad, who will now split their demand three ways instead of two or join the others who left the planet on the fantasy spaceship.

There is the option of reallocating government spending to provide a better outcome in terms of meeting community needs. (Not discussed in Discussion Guide 1).

However putting history aside, should there arise a situation in which the government was competing with the private sector for employees or that monies were not available to support sound private sector investment opportunities (versus some unsound investments that were supported prior to the 2008 economic meltdown and are continuing to be made in 2017) there might be an advantage to cutting government spending.

Did the payroll tax cut holiday (the employee's share was cut from 6.2% to 4.2%) help spur the economy and help strengthen the economic recovery from the 2008/09 recession? Yes. Does this fact contradict the statements made above? No. What happened is the payroll tax cut was financed by additional government borrowing and simply converted idle money to active money. This act grew the economic activity by forcing (not a bad word here) the community (government) to borrow beyond its then current normal borrowing level. It was the act of borrowing and spending that grew the economy – not the actual payroll tax cut itself. The effect on the economy would have been approximately the same had the government simply borrowed the money and distributed it to the workers and left the payroll tax rate stay at 6.2%. Eventually, under traditional government finance practices – this money will need to be repaid. At that time the repayment will slow the economy, thereby, in the long term, offsetting the boost to the economy resulting from the cut. There may be a way to eliminate some of the debt without slowing the economy; however, this discussion needs to take place at higher levels of government and finance.

What happens under Scenarios 1, 2 & 3 to the number of people unemployed? Under:

> Scenario 1: Per the assumptions, no one is unemployed under Scenario 1
> Scenario 2: 2 persons, Sue plus someone else who loses a private sector job or, if a business owner, goes out of business and joins the unemployment rolls, because of the drop in market demand, and
> Scenario 3: 1 person, Sue, is added to the unemployment roll.

However, Sue is an aggressive individual, and she has saved a lot of money. Therefore, Sue will try to take your job or the job held by your son or daughter for pay that is less than any of you are earning, OR, if you are a business owner, Sue may start a business that competes with your business and possibly put you out of business.

From the perspective of job creation – no jobs are created by either a reduction in government spending or a balanced tax cut (meaning the budget cut and the tax cut proportionately are the same). However, **jobs are lost**.

Discussion points:

a.   *Do you want Sue to take your job?*

b. *If there are any business owners in the group, – do you want Sue to open a business that competes with your business?*

c. *Of those discussion group members who are employees, – do you want Sue to open a business that competes with your employer's business?*

SECTION F

Where Does an Economy Come From?

An economy develops as the result of the application of economically viable conversion labor (herein "conversion labor") to a readily available natural resource.

Conversion labor is labor applied to some thing to change the character or placement of that some thing such that its usefulness to an individual, individuals or society is enhanced.

<u>Economy</u> herein (expanded definition) refers to the system and activities of related economic units that govern the realizations by the population (an individual and/or group(s) of individuals) of the satisfaction of needs and wants (consumption) by managing:

- The allocation of various natural resources in line with both the availability and the relative level to which each is readily available (scarcity) as is each required to satisfy needs and wants of members of the economic units

- The application of conversion labor to the natural resources, including various forms of conversion labor as natural resources unto themselves (architects, electricians, college professors, ministers, lawyers, comedians, and others), in a way directed toward satisfying the needs and wants of members of the economic units, and

- The trading of the products of the conversion labor applied to natural resources amongst the economic units of the economy or with members of other economies.

SECTION G

Questions – for You to Answer:

Questions provided in this guide are not of the nature of "test" questions but are provided as issues for discussion. To help with the discussion process, answers are provided for chapters two and three. The reader does not need to agree with the answers, only consider them; there may be other answers. The reader is on his/her own for chapters four and beyond.

Mark all answers that are reasonably correct; if an answer is not correct, for discussion purposes develop a relative answer that is correct, or at least more correct.

1) If import tariffs were changed so that goods from China (apparel, stereo equipment) and services from India (telephone help lines, engineering design, etc.) and other low-cost labor nations are not competitive with goods and services produced in America:

   a. There would be more jobs available in America

   b. American wages, as measured in real income (purchasing power), would go up

   c. US domestic prices of goods now manufactured in China would go up considerably

   d. Planned legal immigration would be increased to place downward pressure on American wages

   e. Planned legal immigration would be increased to provide needed workers to accommodate the domestic expansion of the domestic economy

   f. Illegal immigration would be increased to place downward pressure on American wages (as a side issue: what American employers benefit from "illegal" as opposed to "legal" immigration)?

   g. Although wages would increase for those American workers whose earnings are now in the lower 50% of earnings – the price of goods and services now imported would increase to a level such that the "real income (purchasing power)" of this group would decrease.

2) Controlling inflation is important to:

   a.   Senior citizens on fixed incomes

   b.   Lenders such as banks and mortgage companies

   c.   Workers who find themselves unemployed due to Fed actions taken to control inflation

   d.   All Americans

   e.   My friends and I are going to develop a way to control inflation other than through Fed management of unemployment levels and interest rates.

3) The total number of household providers who will become non-employed has nothing to do with whether job candidates are able-bodied or disabled, highly motivated, <u>or anything else</u>; there is very limited exception as related to job skills, currently primarily in the medical field and a couple of vocational skills. (These exceptions are typically related to the lack of an adequate supply of training versus a supply of workers.)

   a.   Joe is the type of irresponsible person who stays out late drinking on work nights, is tardy for work a lot, and absent a lot (probably to go fishing). Everyone who knows Joe calls Joe lazy. Joe is terminated from his job because of tardiness. Because Joe exists, in the example used in Assessment Question 2b the number of non-employed will be 10% plus 1.

   b.   Rick is a highly motivated individual. Rick becomes unemployed when the company he had worked for files for bankruptcy. Because Rick exists, in the example used in Assessment Question 2b the number of non-employed will be 10% minus 1.

   c.   There is a lot of nonsense perpetuated by many in the news media, many politicians, some economists, and people who like to hear themselves talk related to the ability of the non-employed to find work

   d.   If the Federal Reserve would set their interest rate, (the rate they lend at to banks) at 2% and keep it there, everyone who wants to work would have a job.

   e.   50% of the people in prison are grandfathered when marijuana is legalized. When these people are released the Fed will not need to take any action related to interest rates.

CHAPTER APPENDIX

Answer to the Warm Up question discussion points

The number of jobs lost would probably be the same. This is true if the labor cost savings is 40 pennies or only 10 pennies on the sales revenue dollar.

If corporate income taxes were reduced today or had been reduced 50 years ago – it is both possible and probable that no jobs will/would have been saved (i.e. not transferred to low-cost wage countries).

The savings in taxes paid is diminutive (too small to matter) when compared to the labor cost savings realized by relocating to or sourcing in a low-cost wage country.

Another question for the group > why do some politicians represent that American jobs would be saved or the number of jobs would be increased if corporate taxes were lowered?

Answers to Assessment Questions:

The purpose of these particular assessment questions was to facilitate the reader's understanding of a very important basic economic fact about the American capitalist system as it is currently (2018) designed to operate. The number of people in each economic class of Americans, as measured by earnings, except those at the lowest level, is dependent on the class below it to enable the relative <u>number of people</u> at each level to be maintained in the economy.

Assessment Question #1:

Logic:

The total of American household providers is stated to be <u>100 million</u>. The non-employed portion of this group is <u>equal to 10%</u>. This means that <u>10 million</u> household providers are not employed.

If these 10 million household providers and their household dependents were to disappear from the face of the earth, there then would be 90 million American household providers left.

After the economy adjusted for the drop in demand caused by the absence of those who disappeared would any of the 90 million workers left become non-employed?

Answer:

Absolutely, **10% would be non-employed**. Why? Because, in the American capitalist system, non-employment is a relative number, not an absolute number. The form of non-employment could be "un-employed," "welfare" or some other class of non-working members of society; but the total would equal **10%** or 9,000,000 household providers.

Can this be changed by lowering the tax rates of relative taxes (i.e., income taxes, sales taxes, etc.) and government spending?   No. Can this be changed by implementing changes to tariffs? Maybe. Can this be changed by effectively encouraging the population to spend rather than save money? Yes.

Discussion points: Is the above information consistent with your understanding from your reading of the body of the chapter? If not, discuss this answer with members of your discussion group, your congregation or club, or with someone you meet while waiting for a bus or a train.

Assessment Question #2a & b:

Logic:

The total of American household providers as adjusted under Scenario #1 above is 90 million. The non-employed portion of this group is equal to 10%. This means that 9 million American household providers are not employed.

If these 9 million household providers and their household dependents were to disappear from the face of the earth, there then would be 81 million American household providers left.

After the economy adjusted for the drop in demand caused by the absence of those who disappeared (the economy requires 3 months to adjust) would any of the 81 million workers left be non-employed?

Answer:

Absolutely, <u>10% would be non-employed</u>. Why? Because in the American capitalist system, non-employment is a relative number, not an absolute number. The form of non-employment could be "un-employed," "welfare" or some other class of non-working members of the community; but <u>the total would equal 10%</u> or 8,100,000 household providers.

Can this be changed by lowering the tax rates of relative taxes (i.e., income taxes, sales taxes, etc.) and government spending? No. Can this be changed by implementing tariffs? Maybe. Can this be changed by <u>encouraging</u> manufacturing businesses to invest in America? Prudent business people will invest where it makes the best economic sense to invest. **Encouragement has nothing to do with it**. Will <u>some non-prudent business people</u> invest based on encouragement in the form of special tax breaks? Yes, but within those companies of adequate size to meaningfully impact the economy, there is a shortage of non-prudent business people; additionally such individuals tend to lead short business lives. However, <u>some prudent business people will take all of the tax breaks governments are willing to give them; but this will not encourage them to make non-prudent investments</u>. The investments will be made based on their own merit, with or without tax breaks. There are a few investments to be made (typically in the area of redevelopment work) that may need government help to generate a practical financial return. These are so few and far between that many Americans will never see one.

Currently, <u>due to the extreme differences</u> in labor costs, it often makes the best economic sense for business people to invest overseas. Note that in some countries it is not unusual that a family of six lives in one room and shares a bath with other families; whereas, in the USA typically a family of six has a home with multiple rooms and at least one bath. Due to this difference in lifestyle, workers in some countries can afford to work for lower wages than those currently earned by American workers.

Questions – for You to Answer – Possible Answers:

1) If import tariffs were changed so that goods from China (apparel, stereo equipment) and services from India (telephone help lines, engineering design, medical care, etc.) and other low-cost labor nations were not competitive with goods and services produced in America:

   a. Maybe. Imports would decrease, thereby, creating more jobs for Americans. However, most likely, American wages would increase and, thereby, cause a price rise in USA exports which would subsequently decrease and eliminate

American jobs. Some very sharp economists need to analyze this issue and develop a best estimate answer.

b. Maybe. As mentioned in the answer to "a" above, the drop in export-related jobs might offset the increase in jobs related to the tariff increases. If there is a "wash" such that there is not a change in the employment situation; there may be a drop in real income. If more jobs are created than lost (not a wash) a probable increase in wages will push up purchasing power. To the degree, this wage increase will offset the, to be expected, increase in prices is difficult to determine. However, there most likely would still be a decrease in purchasing power. Again, some very sharp economists need to answer this question.

c. Yes

d. Probably. Some business leaders would put pressure on the government to bring this about.

e. Probably. Manufacturing employment is now 9% of the non-farm payroll in the USA. In 1977 it was 22% of the non-farm payroll. While there is a high level of non-employment in the country – there would still not be enough people to fill the returning manufacturing jobs. Keep in mind that the hamburger flipping jobs will not go away. In fact, the number may increase. Plus there would be an increase in service jobs.

f. Probably. Many Congress members have objected on this basis or that to the e-verify system that allows employers to check to see if a work applicant is legal (if the employer knowingly hires an illegal immigrant he/she will be fined). Some of the objection bases may be smokescreens put up to block prosecution of employers who want to use illegal immigrants as a means of pushing down the cost of labor. What has been your congress members' stance on e-verify and why?

g. Very unlikely, but possible. Americans purchase a mixture of goods and services, some that are produced domestically and some that are imported. The balance of domestic versus imported purchases for an individual would determine the degree to which his/her real purchasing power decreased, increased or remained unchanged. Some very sharp economists need to analyze this issue and develop a best estimate answer, preferably by household income deciles (classed by 10% groupings of the total population).

2) Controlling inflation is important to:

    a. Yes.

    b. Yes.

    c. Mixed. Those who within a reasonable period land a job are better off in the long term if inflation is controlled. Those who experience long-term unemployment or join the permanently non-employed class of Americans would most likely prefer to live with high inflation if it meant they could have a job.

    d. Mixed See the answer to "c," above.

    e. The citizens of this country are counting on you. In fact, I will be very disappointed if you do not come up with a solution.

3. The total number of household providers who will become non-employed has nothing to do with whether job candidates are able-bodied or disabled, highly motivated, or anything else; there is a very limited exception as related to job skills, primarily in the medical field and a couple of vocational skills. (These exceptions are typically related to the lack of an adequate supply of training versus a supply of workers.)

    a. No. It will still be 10%, and it will include Joe.

    b. No. It will still be 10%, and it will include Rick.

    c. Absolutely.

    d. No. There have been times in recent history when the FR (Fed) interest rate has been below 1% and unemployment has been high. Key other influences, besides the Fed interest rate, include, but are not limited to, business cycles and demographic patterns. In managing interest rates the Fed is attempting to offset the economic damage done by the other factors that also influence inflation and unemployment. The current (as of, November 2017) Fed objective is to keep inflation at 2%. This will be to a degree a function of both the interest rate and the unemployment rate.

    e. Yes, the prisoner release will have a very minor effect on interest rates. Probably not immediately, but the freed prisoners who are looking for jobs will be taken into consideration along with others looking for jobs relative to employment and inflation related decisions.

CHAPTER 3 - Basic Economic Relationships

Chapter 3 covers:

- Where does an economy come from?
- Development of an economic perspective
- What is money?
- The relationship amongst supply, demand, and cultural views.

Where Does an Economy Come From? / Conversion Labor and Readily Available Natural Resources

An economy develops as the result of the application of economically viable conversion labor (herein "conversion labor" or "labor") to a readily available natural resource.

Conversion labor is labor applied to some thing to change the character or placement of that some thing such that its usefulness to an individual, individuals or society is enhanced. (Recall from Chapter 2, the story of Eric and his grandson Eric III.)

A natural resource is a substance found in nature that can be useful to man; it is the first ingredient in the development of "something." The substance can be hard in nature, such as coal or granite, soft in nature, such as water or fish, or a natural process such as wind or thought.

To become useful to man a natural resource must be extracted from its natural state. Whether the extraction of the resource is through activity such as farming and called agriculture, through invention and called thought, or through digging and called mining – the extracted resource is said to be mined. A *readily available natural resource* is one for which it makes sense to mine the resource as determined by the conversion labor to be applied versus the benefit derived from the effort and the relative scarcity of the resource. This act of balancing the application of effort and natural resource supply against output is referred to as the development of an *economic perspective*.

An Economic Perspective

This section follows an example of the development of an economic perspective.

The country of BlueGreen has an abundant supply of coal and oil. The coal is very deep underground and the oil is located at a convenient depth for mining. BlueGreen is in a very cold part of the world. The population cannot survive without heat.

George, a citizen of BlueGreen, has available to him the latest technologies for both mining coal and oil. George determines that <u>to heat his home for two weeks,</u> he will need to spend <u>sixteen hours per day for four weeks</u> digging coal. George determines that to heat his home for two weeks he will need to spend only <u>eight hours every other week pumping oil.</u>

The option of using coal is not available to George. George's family, along with George, would freeze to death before George mined an adequate supply of coal for keeping warm for two weeks. However, the option of using oil **is** available to George; as by using oil he will not only be able to heat his home, but he will have time to:

- Apply his labor to changing the character or placement of other natural resources, or

- Mine oil to trade for other goods and services produced by others.

In the country of BlueGreen coal is **<u>not</u>** a readily available natural resource and oil **is** a readily available natural resource.

Should George or others develop the level of technology for coal mining as is needed to allow George to mine coal by applying a sensible level of labor, coal would be reclassified to a readily available natural resource. This does not necessarily mean the coal will be mined; it means, only, that it is now, from an economic perspective, reasonable to mine the coal.

It may still be cheaper (less labor required and/or more abundant supply) to use oil than coal for heating. Therefore, the coal may be a dormant readily available natural resource.

The country of YellowGreen manufactures steel. The people of YellowGreen need coal for making steel and may be willing to trade steel, which contains iron ore and conversion labor, for coal from BlueGreen.

George may determine that by employing the above-mentioned level of improved technology <u>three eight-hour days of working at digging</u> coal is necessary for heating his home for two weeks. Therefore, George will stick with oil for heating his home. However, George may find it beneficial to work for two eight-hour days every other week digging coal to trade for steel and steel products. Should this be the case, the coal will be reclassified from a dormant to an active readily available natural resource.

George and his neighbors will look at the total of BlueGreen's known supplies of both oil and coal and determine how much of each they can afford to use for trading with people in other countries for steel products, bananas, telecom services, etc. They will need to make certain that BlueGreen has an adequate supply of coal and oil as is needed to support the citizens of BlueGreen in the future. Additionally, they will establish a safety buffer to hold to cover the unexpected. They will only mine for trading purposes a portion of BlueGreen's readily available natural resources as has been determined can be traded at a low risk of running out of supply at home. The resources they decide to mine for use and trade over time, but are not yet mined, plus those they hold as a buffer, represent their *reserves*.

Discussion points:

Adam mines copper ore from his property. He uses the latest and greatest mining and processing technologies. Adam trades the copper for food, supplies, energy, etc. Adam has two copper veins on his property.

The first requires Adam to work three forty hour work weeks to mine an adequate supply of copper to feed and otherwise support his family for one month. Adam, therefore, can mine enough copper in three five-day work weeks (fifteen (15) 8-hour work days) to trade as required to support his family's consumption (supplies, food, energy, etc.) for 30 days. This equates to one day of work for two days of livelihood (30 days of support divided by 15 workdays).

The second vein, which Adam does not now mine, would require eight weeks at sixteen hours per, every day, for Adam to mine enough copper to feed and keep his family for four weeks (two double shift days of work for one day of livelihood).

As of March 24th, Vein #1 will run out of copper after fifteen (15) 8-hour shifts of mining. He has enough copper on hand to support his family until the end of March. Adam's only alternative for supporting his family is to mine vein #2; Adam has no alternative means of supporting his family.

If Adam starts working sixteen hours a day on April 1st – will <u>Adam and his family be able to survive (live) for an additional six months</u>?

Was the copper in vein #1 a readily available natural resource? Is the copper in vein #2 a readily available natural resource?

DO NOT READ THE DISCUSSION BELOW UNTIL AFTER YOU HAVE ATTEMPTED TO ANSWER EACH OF THE ABOVE QUESTIONS.

Logic:

Read through lightly and follow the logic – do not try (unless you love arithmetic) to follow the numbers.

1) *Adam can now provide 30 days of support for his family by working 15 eight hour shifts mining copper from vein #1.*

2) *Therefore, starting with April 1st if Adam mines vein #1 sixteen hours per day (two 8 hour shifts), in 7½ days he can produce enough copper to support his family for 30 days, which is the end of April.*

3) *He will then start mining vein #2 in the middle of the eighth workday of April.*

   The April production from vein #1 will support his family until the first of May; therefore, he will produce but not use copper from vein #2 until May 1st.

4) *From the <u>middle of the eighth workday of April until the end of April</u> Adam worked 22½ sixteen hour work days (45 shifts). In this time he produced enough copper to provide <u>for his family's livelihood for the first 11¼ days of May</u> (recall vein #2 requires two sixteen-hour days of work to provide for one day of livelihood).*

5) *During the first 11¼ days of May, working vein #2, Adam will produce enough copper to support his family for 55/8 days. Adam's family will now be able to survive for a total of 167/8 days in May. (Convert 11¼ to 112/8; 112/8 days + 55/8 = 167/8 days.)*

6) *During the 55/8 days Adam will produce enough copper to support his family for one-half (½) of 55/8 days, or 213/16 days. Adam's family will now be able to survive for a total of 1911/16 days in May. (Convert 167/8 to 1614/16; 1614/16 + 213/16 = 1911/16 days.]*

7) *During the 213/16 days Adam will produce enough copper to support his family for approximately 16/16 days. Etc.*

Adam's family will have no means of surviving after May 23rd.

In Genesis, man is told to be "fruitful and multiply." Using Genesis as the standard:

- *Adam could support his family with the copper available in vein #1; therefore vein #1 was a readily available natural resource.*

- *Adam cannot support a family with the copper available in vein #2; therefore vein #2 is not a readily available natural resource. (With vein #2 as the sole means of supporting his family Adam could not be fruitful and multiply.)*

However, putting Genesis aside, a man with a wife and no children who can work sixteen hours a day, seven days a week at vein #2 could provide only for his wife and himself. Or, a single man who can work eight hours a day, seven days a week or the same number of total hours but in a different number of days could support just himself. Using either of these measures as standards vein #2 is possibly a readily available natural resource.

In your opinion is or is not vein #2 a readily available natural resource? What standard did you base your opinion on?

The value of the reserves is determined through a review of the expected future cash flow to be derived from mining the reserves or from expected royalties to be paid by mining companies. The expected cash flow represents the future ability of the holders of title to the reserves to directly use or trade for other types of readily available natural resource and/or conversion labor (labor to change the character of or placement of some thing that is useful to man) as desired for satisfying needs and wants. This type of discussion is beyond the scope of this guide. This is OK, as a voter does not need to know how to determine the value. He/she only needs to know that the value represents the ability of the reserve to directly or indirectly satisfy future economic demands of the holders of title. However, should you wish to learn about the process of valuation you can find various papers via the Internet by entering "valuation of _____ deposits." (A good place to start is with a West Virginia state paper on coal reserves available at:
 http://www.wvpolicy.org/downloads/CoalReserveTaxationPrimer-FINAL-5-19-09%20-%20FINAL.pdf.)

The title to reserves represents a component of potential economic wealth.

In capitalist economies this title rests with an individual(s). In communist economies this title rests with the community as a whole. In socialist economies this title for "select" (special) resources rest either with individuals or with the community as determined by a small group of citizens, the citizenry as a whole, or somewhere in between. The title for those resources not considered "select" rests with various individuals as in a capitalist economy
.
"Select" resources are typically defined in terms of either those:

- That are basic to production of a wide variety of products (such as iron ore and oil),
- Whose logistical position limits the level of competition needed to allow market forces to control pricing (such as utilities), or
- With strategic security advantages (such as uranium and titanium).

Why are non-security issue resources designated as select? At times in history owners of certain resources have engaged in unfriendly takeovers of downstream businesses. The weapon used to get their way has been to withhold supply of the resource. Additionally, those with title to particular select resources can run the price up, and the buyers will have no recourse but to pay (i.e., consumers of heating oil). To prevent such situations from developing some communities take title to such resources.

In socialist economies the businesses engaged in the first level of conversion from natural resource to useful material (iron ore to steel, crude oil to fuel oil), also may be controlled by the community.

NOTE: Communities, in countries such as the United States, often use trade laws to control the issues mentioned above. For instance, in the US there are laws against predatory pricing and some types of schemes for selling below costs; two practices previously used by larger companies to drive smaller competitors out of business.

Although natural resource reserves are a component of wealth, wealth does not truly exist until labor has been applied to a resource to render it useful to man. Resources are a fact of nature; <u>all realized economic wealth comes through the application of conversion labor</u>. The trading of one form of converted natural resource for another form of converted natural resource is accomplished through the application of additional labor. The collective activities of applying conversion labor to natural resources, directed to changing the character or placement of said resources to provide some things that are required or desired in some form or another by man, and the systems that govern such activities, including the output and consumption of such output, is called an "economy" (condensed definition).

The term "collective" can be defined in many different ways. It can refer to all conversion activity taking place in a particular state or province, a country, a group of countries (European (Economic) Community), or many other groupings as someone analyzing an "economy" may choose to define that which will be included in an economic unit or community. For the most part, the determination of what to include or not include within an economy that one is addressing is up to the individual directing a discussion on or about a particular "economy."

Money

To this point, we have discussed the economy and wealth in terms of conversion labor and natural resources with only limited mention of money.

To understand a macroeconomy one must first forget the concept of money and think only in terms of conversion labor only (labor applied to create or relocate some thing useful to man). Once one understands conversion labor, it is necessary to introduce the concept of *money* to facilitate further discussions about the macroeconomy.

What is money? The definition of money is somewhat complex, and the uses of money are varied. In this guide, a simple definition is used. If the reader wishes to develop a higher level of understanding of the concept of money he should refer to several papers available on the Internet or textbooks on economics.

Money is a **record** of the value of the "means" to complete an exchange for title to natural resources and/or units of labor applied to changing the character of or changing the placement of some thing useful to man. This "means" accrues, from a macro-economic perspective, to individuals or to groups of individuals in recognition, by the participants in an economy, of his/her/their own conversion labor performed or to be performed. For instance, John applied three hours to building a chair; Mary applied one hour to planting and harvesting the wood for the chair; and Andy applied one hour cutting the lumber from which John built the chair. "This means accrues" simply signifies that, at least, some members of the community are willing to pay John, Mary, and Andy for their labor as will be reflected in the price some are willing to pay for the chair. Based on this community perceived value, a bank will be willing to lend money to John, Mary and Andy until the chair is sold at which time John, Mary or Andy could repay the bank.

The land (the natural resource) and other natural resources used in processing the wood from seed to lumber also carry a value that is recognized by the community as providing the "means " to complete an exchange. The "record of means" (money), however, follows the labor performed or to be performed. The natural resource value is an "implied value." The character of the natural resource "implied value" will be covered in Discussion Guide 2.

Money is used:

- In exchanging all or portions (partial values) of a particular resource or labor for all or portions of another and probably different particular resource or labor

- For immediate exchange or delayed exchange

a. Immediate exchange can be accomplished through:
   - Immediate satisfaction (i.e., the full amount is paid upfront) or
   - Satisfaction over time (debt)
b. To the extent that the act of exchange is delayed the value of the resource and/or labor is stored (saved). Note that the act of saving value enables the lending of value; thereby, facilitating investment.

- As a standard of value for items not yet subjected to exchange (e.g., Joe discovered oil on his land, he is worth millions; the painting by Janeu Pennlies is worth at least $100,000).

Anything acceptable as a substitute for the direct exchange (barter) of natural resources and/or conversion labor can be money. However, typically when speaking of money we speak of legal tender – that which is officially recognized by the community.

The use of money as a standard of value for natural resources that have not, yet, been exchanged creates confusion as to the basis of money. Money does not arise (come into being) within an economy because a mountain is discovered to contain copper, coal or gold deposits. It is introduced into the economy by the US Treasury or the Fed only as a record (think of it as a symbol) of a right to value earned by the application of labor or the anticipation that labor will be applied. It is possible for a function in an economic system (i.e., central bank – Treasury or Fed) to create money in anticipation of some future application of conversion labor; however, this should only be done on a short to a sensible long-term basis. This is necessary to protect the integrity of the money (avoid over employment leading to runaway inflation). The creation of money in anticipation of forthcoming applied conversion labor helps grow the economy.[5]

Money can take many forms such as cash, checks, drafts, electronic record, etc. All of the forms, other than cash, are expressed in terms of cash. NOTE: In the study of economics the term currency can have different meanings. The term sometimes is used

---

[5] Barbara owns farm land she inherited from her dad. Her dad paid $50,000 ($394,400 in 2017 constant dollars, 2017 value) for the land in 1964. The value of the land, today, as farm land, is $200,000. Joe finds Barbara's land has a good coal deposit. Barbara does not have the ability to make the financial investment necessary for mining the coal. Barbara sells the land to Joe for $600,000. Joe needs to buy $1,000.000 worth of equipment to start up the mine. Joe has the coal deposit and the land assessed. The assessment value is $800,000. The local bank lent Joe $900,000 to buy the land and equipment. Joe puts up his personal money for the balance. The bank lends $400,000 on the land and $500,000 on the equipment. The loan is payable over ten years. The $400,000 lent on the land is based on the anticipation of the application of conversion labor and the farming value. The $500,000 is lent based on the recognition of the natural resources and conversion labor required to manufacture the equipment that Joe buys.

to mean only government issued notes and coins – <u>cash</u> and at other times to mean all types of medium of exchange (cash, checks, drafts, etc.). All of the forms provide a means of exchange of the value of title (designation of whoever owns something) to a natural resource(s) and/or units of conversion labor (labor directed to creating or relocating some thing). Wait! You're thinking the car I own is not a natural resource and I have title to it. The car you own, however, is comprised of several natural resources (primarily petroleum, natural gas, sand, aluminum and iron ore) to which labor has been applied.

Money does not come into the economy (rise) as each valued unit of labor is worked. Money, as is the case with government issued currency (cash), can be reused many times (think about how many times the quarter in your pocket has exchanged hands). Therefore, the supply of money needed for supporting an economy is less than the cumulative value of applied labor. (For instance, if you do something for me for a dollar you can use the dollar [ignoring taxes for discussion sake] I pay you to pay Andrea to do something for you for a dollar. Andrea, in turn, can use the same dollar to pay Tony to do something for her for a dollar, etc. The same dollar bill supported at least three transactions that gave recognition to labor applied by at least three people: you, Andrea and Tony. Therefore the system needed only to provide a one dollar bill to recognize three-plus hours of labor.) This re-use of money is called *money circulation*. The needed supply to support the conversion labor worked is managed for the community by the USA Treasury and the Federal Reserve.

The objective of these organizations, as it relates to money, is to balance the overall supply of money, in all forms (including cash) with the supply or anticipated supply of conversion labor and the implied value of the first level of mined natural resources (this latter issue will be covered in Discussion Guide 2).

Governments must be able to exercise control of that which is used as money. Otherwise, the supply of money could be extended beyond the value of the labor it represents (legally or illegally counterfeited).[6] Ideally, money is designated to be an item that is difficult to replicate and, yet, inexpensive to produce (e.g., a twenty dollar bill that has threads running through the paper that can be detected by holding the bill up to a light). "Difficult to replicate" such that a government can exercise control over how much is produced and "inexpensive to produce" such that it does not absorb (dilute) the value of the labor and implied natural resource value that it is to represent. To this latter point, it would not make sense for a man to work two days to produce an

---

[6] Money may be, and by some countries has been, created legally but disproportionately to the level of conversion labor or anticipated conversion labor within an economy. This act creates, in effect, legally counterfeited money which is introduced into the economy through pay increases for civil servants and other means - leading to high levels of inflation.

item of currency that will represent only one day of labor. An item of currency that is relatively expensive dilutes the value of the conversion labor it represents. NOTE: There exists an option of employing cash that is expensive to produce, but that will last for thousands of years. Such cash would be used to facilitate thousands of transactions; therefore the currency cost per trade (dilution) would be low. For several reasons, no country has exercised this option.

In today's world checks, drafts and electronic records fall a little shy of the goal of being difficult to replicate, but they do meet the goal of being inexpensive to produce.

Supply, Demand and Cultural Views

The concept of the value of a resource or unit of labor is determined by a mixture of scarcity (supply and demand), and, although not always logical, cultural views.

In most countries, most of the time, the value of natural resources and conversion labor is determined by the market balancing of supply and demand (market forces). In most countries, some of the time, cultural views override the issue of supply and demand, and the value is fixed informally by the community or formally by the community (government). For example, based upon cultural concepts of morality, the community in China formally fixes utility prices at low rates and the community in England formally sets the salaries of most medical doctors.

Heart surgeons are scarcer than are brick layers; therefore, it is understandable that to a reasonable degree, the labor of a heart surgeon has a higher value than that of a bricklayer. The earnings of heart surgeons and bricklayers, to a significant degree, reflect the market balancing of supply and demand.

On the other hand, a member of a school board made a snide comment referring to the fact that investment bankers earn more money than school teachers. Obviously, in this individual's mind, people with the ability to teach school are scarcer than are people with the ability to do investment banking. He may or may not have been correct. In either the worst or best case the level of scarcity is probably equal. However, being fair to investment bankers, some investment bankers sometimes need to work a year or more between commission checks. There is both a stress component and a risk component to working as an investment banker as opposed to working as a school teacher. These components must be compensated for or no one will be willing to take on the task of investment banking. However, there is a limit to what is reasonable compensation. Reasonable compensation might be that which is three to ten times the earnings of a school teacher; but it is not twenty to thirty times the earnings of a school teacher. Yet, some investment bankers do enjoy extremely high incomes. **- See citations.** That portion of compensation that goes beyond the point of "reasonable" exists due to the influence of cultural view. To again be fair to investment bankers, the same can be said for <u>some</u> attorneys, plumbers, public company CEOs, and those in several other occupational groups.

Recap

Conversion labor, readily available natural resources, and money all interrelate with one another to enable the existence of an economy within a particular community. What is <u>key</u> to the well-being of such an economy is the existence of readily available natural resources to which labor can be applied. Additionally, the development of an economic perspective and a system for managing the use of the natural resources and the conversion labor bring about an enhanced realization of economic benefits to a community.

The level of scarcity of each particular resource or unit of labor typically determines its economic value. However, sometimes the value is set by cultural views.

Within limits, the members of a community can trade the products of their particular natural resource(s) and labor with one another by trading in kind (barter). You would make a table and I would make a wheel barrel; you would want my wheel barrel and I would want your table; assuming we each desired the other's product <u>equally</u> we would trade. However, exchanges would need to be of equal value (you could throw in a bushel of apples to even up the value – if I wanted apples) unless we adopted a medium of exchange that allowed us to <u>trade partial values</u>. If in fact, I felt – and you agreed –

- That my wheel barrel was worth twice as much as your table, and

- The economic system provided a medium of exchange (money) that could accommodate partial values

- I could sell my wheel barrel to someone else and use half (a partial value of the wheel barrel) of what I received to buy your table.

This medium of exchange is called money.

Questions:

Mark all answers that are reasonably correct.

1. An "economy" can result from the:

   a. Initiation of exchange of goods within a particular community.

   b. One person on an island in the middle of nowhere can create an economy by applying viable conversion labor to some thing.

   c. Application of labor to create some thing useful for fulfilling a want or need.

   d. Discovery of a natural resource.

   e. The US economic system owns me; I do not own the system.

   f. I own the US economic system; it does not own me.

2. Macroeconomic "Wealth" (i.e., the wealth of a country) comes from:

   a. The discovery of a natural resource.

   b. The application of labor to a natural resource.

   c. Taking title to a readily available natural resource.

   d. In a capitalist system, the transfer of community-owned title of a readily available natural resource to an individual (change from government to private ownership).

3. Personal "Wealth" comes from:

   a. Discovering a natural resource.

   b. The application of conversion labor to a natural resource.

   c. Taking title to the financial benefits to be derived from a readily available natural resource.

   d. Inheriting title to a readily available natural resource.

4. Title to natural resources can be held by:

   a. Individual members of a community that operates a capitalist economic system.

   b. A dictator of a community that operates a communist economic system.

   c. Either by individual members of a community or by the community as a whole for a community that operates a socialist economic system.

   d. All members of a community that operates a communist economic system.

   e. A dictator of a community that operates a capitalist economic system.

5. "Money" is:

   a. Cash.

   b. Cash, checks, drafts, electronic records and other items of exchange used to facilitate the transfer of title to natural resources and conversion labor between individual(s).

   c. A representation of the value of gold, whether or not gold backs it.

   d. Stated in terms of cash if it is not in the form of cash (i.e., a check for $150).

Discussion points: Before reading more of the discussion guide, discuss with members of your discussion group, fellow congregation or club members, friend, neighbor, relative or someone you meet while waiting for a bus or train, the ramifications your answers to the question(s) above might have on the USA economy and society. Then write down your conclusions as formulated in answers to the questions. Next, think about the ramifications that the answers have on the quality of life of your family.

Additional Discussion

How do the means of title to natural resources currently affect the lives of you and your family as the USA economic system operates? How would the treatment of the title to natural resources impact the lives of you and your family if the USA employed a different economic system? How does the assignment of different values to different types of labor affect the lives of you and your family (i.e., the value of an hour worked by a lawyer versus an hour worked by a bus driver versus an hour of labor worked by you)? What job types are paid, in your opinion, a disproportionate wage (overvalued/under-valued) due to cultural view in relation to what you are paid for your job type due to cultural view?

A whole list of questions could be compiled of the above type that you should be asking yourself based on the information covered in this chapter. You should be asking yourself these questions so that you can form substantive opinions before the next time you vote for a candidate; who may or may not agree with the opinion(s) you have developed.

Discussion points: Formulate your own answers to the questions above, first. Next, come up with some other questions you should be addressing. Then discuss possible answers, to the above questions and any you come up with, with members of your discussion group, fellow congregation or club members, relative, friend, neighbor, or with someone you meet while waiting for a bus or a train.

CHAPTER APPENDIX

Answers to Test Questions:

1. An economy can result from:

   a. Yes, an initiation of exchange represents an economic activity in process.

   b. Yes, it is possible to have a one-person economy.

   c. Yes, this is part of the definition of what constitutes an economy.

   d. Technically, no; but yes and no. Yes, the potential to develop an economy or an upgrade to an existing economy exists because of the discovery; however, an economic effect is not realized until conversion labor is applied.

2. Macroeconomic wealth comes from:

   a. No, all wealth comes from the application of labor; until conversion labor is applied wealth is not realized. The discovery represents a potential source of wealth. Recently, large gold deposits were discovered in Haiti. These deposits represent an opportunity to significantly upgrade the economy of Haiti.

   b. Yes, if there is demand, this leads to the production of some thing that will satisfy the economic demand. See the answer to question 3a for further discussion.

   Recall this guide when using the phrase "conversion labor" means "economically viable conversion labor." Recall, also, this guide when using the phrase "labor" means "economically viable conversion labor." (Unless otherwise stated.)

   c. Technically, no; as above in "a," conversion labor must be applied for wealth to be realized. However, this can happen instantaneously with taking title. For instance, if farmland is being worked at the instance that title is transferred some wealth may be realized almost immediately.

   d. No and Yes. Either the community or an individual(s) can arrange to apply conversion labor to a readily available natural resource. However, there is an underlying tenet of capitalism that the community (government) should not compete with private enterprise. This means that the community will restrain itself from applying conversion labor; and thus, the potential wealth available through the mining of a particular resource is greatly enhanced by the transfer of title to an individual(s).

3. Personal wealth comes from:

   a. No, all wealth comes from the application of labor; until conversion labor is applied wealth is not realized. The discovery represents the <u>potential</u> to realize wealth. First the resource must be needed; secondly, it must be readily available; and thirdly it must be favorably situated logistically.

   Although the discovery may increase the wealth of an individual, when converted, it is possible that it will not increase the wealth of the country. For instance, if you discover and mine a limestone deposit and I own a limestone mine in close proximity to your limestone mine, my realization of wealth may decrease as yours increases. This is so because an increase in supply does not necessarily relate to an increase in demand. Without an increase in demand the effect on the macroeconomy may be neutral.

   b. Yes, if there is demand for your product.

   c. Yes. Economic colonialism (Neo-colonialism), as opposed to occupational colonialism, is practiced by super powers throughout the world today. Herein, the wealthy of a superpower country capture the cash flow advantage of a third world country's output.

   d. No. The same logic as discussed in answer number "1" above applies here. However, if the title is for a resource such as a working mine or farm the realization of some wealth can be almost instantaneous with taking title.

4. Title to natural resources can be held by:

   a. Yes.

   b. No. The community holds all such titles. However, there have from time to time been rumors that such dictators hold title. If these rumors are true, the country in question does not have a pure communist economic system. It has a mixed communist/capitalist system. This is true simply because some person (the dictator) holds title natural resources.

   c. Yes.

   d. Yes.

e. Yes. Throughout the world, several such dictators hold title to natural resources.

5. Money is:

a. Yes. Cash is a form of money.

b. Yes, this statement represents the underlying basis of what money is.

c. No. <u>Money</u> is a **record** of the value of the "means" to exchange for title to natural resources and/or units of conversion labor applied. Further, "cash" could be anchored in a commodity such as gold, but there are no means by which checks, drafts, electronic transfers, etc. can be directly anchored in a commodity. The government could back all forms of currency with a promise to redeem any form of currency in gold if requested to do so. This means would indirectly anchor checks, drafts, electronic transfers, etc. in the commodity. This latter approach would work only for international transactions. If domestic citizens redeemed currency for an anchor commodity domestically the government would lose control over the commodity. More importantly, there is no relationship between the conversion labor worked or anticipated to be worked and the volume of any commodity available to be mined.

d. Yes.

CHAPTER 4 – Applied Wealth

Chapter 4 covers:

- Accumulation of personal wealth
- Determination of earnings distribution.

Accumulation of Personal Wealth

I have not been able to identify any particular documentation of sources of wealth in America. Therefore, I have listed, not in order of rank, key sources that I have identified. These are:

- Land grants (primarily during colonial and early America times)
- Overseas money sources (primarily during colonial and early America times)
- Invention
- Innovation
- Earnings
- Investment
- Luck
- Unethical or criminal activities

Invention, earnings, and investment are self-explanatory sources of wealth. A short discussion of land grants, overseas money sources, innovation, luck, and unethical or criminal activities is provided below. (NOTE: wealth from any of these sources can be passed on to beneficiaries.) This is followed by a discussion on the determination of earnings.

Land Grants

Members of royalty and gentry were awarded land grants of significant size during the colonial period. These grants ranged in size of 20,000 to over a million acres. After the revolution, many colonial period land grants were recognized in whole or in part. There, were also, both during the colonial period and the early independence period, small land grants (from one (1) acre to three hundred and fifty (350) acres), awarded to soldiers and bonded servants who had completed a seven-year servitude period to various landowners. Additionally, the USA government awarded land grants for specific purposes. The most notable were awarded to railroad companies to pay for their development of railroads. **- See citations.**

The large land grant holders would sell or lease land to raise capital that would be used for building roads, canals, factories, plantations, etc. After the American Revolution most land grants remained intact; but, some land grants were rescinded. Although a land grant may have been rescinded, a family's wealth in the form of factories, toll bridges, barges, construction companies, etc. typically remained intact.

The early system of granting major land titles was similar to that followed historically throughout the world of taking lands from the inhabitants by force, transferring title to the crown, which in turn subsequently transferred title to others. The transfer to others was based on the assumption that the others would develop the property and, thereby, generate the basis of tax revenues for the crown. In fact, some, but not all, large land grants were conditional such that the designated owner had to develop within a set time (say twenty years) a targeted source of wealth for the crown or lose title to the land.

The wealth which came by way of large land grants was so enormous that it has allowed select families in the United States to maintain a significant position of wealth even today.

Overseas Money Sources

Some colonial immigrants from well to do British or European families did not receive land grants; but did have the ability (due to family relationships) to entice overseas investors or lenders to finance projects in the new country. This ability to own a piece of the American pie early on was far more financially advantageous than that financial advantage realized by typical investors today. Like the land grant holders, these immigrants built businesses that gave rise to tremendous wealth that has passed down through many generations.

Innovation

Innovation is the knack to effectively put to work something that one invents or something that was invented by someone else, perhaps invented a long time ago.

The Starbucks coffee chain is a good example of innovation at work. Starbucks management team did not invent coffee, coffee machines, water heaters, or anything else. They took what already existed and put it to work in an effective manner that produced significant sales revenue and profit.

Luck

If you find readily available copper ore deposits on your land tomorrow, without much effort, you will probably begin to accumulate wealth.

Unethical or Criminal Activities

A number of people accumulated a lot of wealth selling toxic financial assets or engaging in predatory lending practices in the five-year period prior to the 2008 financial crises.

Determination of Earnings Distribution

This section includes discussion that is swayed by opinions; including my own.

There are seven key determinants, I have identified (there are probably others), of how high earnings in most macro-economies are distributed. These are:

- Family economic class
- Salesmanship
- Relationship
- Ability
- Chemistry
- Supply and demand
- Cultural momentum.

The above order does not have a particular meaning as I have not found a way to obtain the information needed to stratify the determinants.

Family Economic Class

Winston Churchill's mother went about "shamelessly exploiting her extensive contacts in society to further his career" (Churchill the Unruly Giant by Norman Rose).

Thirty years ago I completed a management review of an 800 employee division of a Fortune 500 company. The management conditions of the division were not pretty to look at. The root cause, at the division level, was that the Division President, John, was in way over his head. I found that this individual had no qualifications for the job. My boss met with two corporate officers to discuss the problems and possible solutions. Replacing the President was, of course, the number one solution. I was informed that John (not his real name) was a member of the Bodine family (not the real family name); the most prominent family in southern Tennessee (not the real state). Therefore, the position of Senior Division Vice President would be created, and a competent individual would be brought into this position to shore up the President.

I have, throughout my career, come across several "Johns." "Family," in these United States of America, often does play a major role in who gets what position and at what paycheck.

Whereas "family" is and should be a determinant of income in private companies – it plays a surprisingly large role in publicly traded companies, civil service organizations, public universities, and other institutions.

Salesmanship

Salesmanship takes on several forms:

- Persuasiveness - the ability to get people to "buy" into the concept that one is worth a high price, whether or not this is the case
- Likeability – being a person that others like to associate with, and
- Manipulation- finding weak targets in a community or an organization and playing their weaknesses to one's advantage. Within an organization, this often takes the form of brown-nosing and/or grand-standing.

Relationship

One individual in a group through some means secures a high-income position in the community or an organization and pulls others with whom he/she has a relationship up the ladder with him/her. This can take many forms. A few examples are:

- Sue, Nancy, and Bob grew up in the same neighborhood
- George and Jim were in the army together
- Barbara and Mary were in the same sorority.

Ability

- Joe is a great baseball player, and he earns a lot of money

- Howard is highly analytical and earns a lot of money analyzing investment opportunities
- Dick is a great residential building contractor and earns a lot of money based on his skills.

Where "ability" is visibly attached to an individual in the community's eye, ability plays a major role in the earnings of the individual with a high level of ability. However, most individuals with a high level of ability are employed within the framework of an organization. Within such a framework often their ability is overshadowed by the effects of family, relationship, salesmanship, and chemistry.

High income and positions of economic influence typically go hand and hand. From the economic perspective of the community, it is beneficial to have high levels of ability, high income, and economic influence go hand and hand. The "family" approach and several other approaches not related directly to ability often lead to significant economic inefficiencies to the detriment of an affected community.

Chemistry

We all have a tendency to hire and promote in our own image (in fact, most of us vote in our own image). Some in high earned-income positions tend to clone themselves when pulling people up through an organization. This is human chemistry.

Supply and demand

In some cases, the demand for the services offered by individuals in certain jobs is greater than the supply of individuals qualified to perform the services. This situation leads to a rise in what people are willing to pay for the services offered. Currently, in many parts of the country, the cost of dental service provides a good example of this determinant.

Cultural momentum

The concept of a cultural momentum determinant is introduced in this text. Cultural momentum allows individuals in certain job classifications to earn a higher income than that which they would earn should their earned income be based upon the relative challenge of their position, the contribution of their position to society, and supply versus demand. Cultural momentum is a driver for both high earned income and relatively higher earned income as measured by the earned income of others who do not work in a particular job classification. The two key classes of cultural momentum are:

- Historical practice, and
  - Often anchored in the occurrence of a historical shortage of supply
- Shared "delusions of grandeur" within a subgroup of a society. **- See citations (Exceptional citation – BBC, Brain Surgeon video).**

Three hundred years ago a small portion of the population was highly proficient at reading and writing. Of those who were, probably the two most significant groups were medical doctors and lawyers. Although in the modern world, people such as nuclear engineers, electrical engineers, physicist, chemists and a few others perform more intellectually challenging tasks than half of the medical doctors and the majority of lawyers, these two groups have tended to hold onto their relatively high paychecks. This can be attributed to historical practice which was, at one time, based upon a shortage of supply. NOTE: due to current trend lines in the makeup of graduating medical doctors "shortage of supply" may soon support those earnings that are above what may currently be reasonable. Therefore, the cultural momentum of medical doctor earnings will be replaced by the realities of supply and demand. **– See citations**

Conversely, we could say that most nuclear engineers, electrical engineers, physicists, chemists, etc. have not commanded their true worth from the economy. If the only comparison were to doctors and lawyers this could be true and would represent negative cultural momentum. But if we compare to accountants, air controllers, electricians, farmers, landscapers, etc. such career positions appear to earn close to a reasonable pay (maybe a little low still). In several such technical fields there is a shortage of supply, but this is not typically reflected in paychecks. This is due to lack of or negative cultural momentum.

Lawyers are guilty of falling into two determinant groups – the historical practice and subgroup delusions of grandeur. To this latter subgroup, delusions of grandeur, we can add:

- CEOs and board members of major corporations **- See citations.**
- Senior level civil servants (primarily those in management and professional roles) **- See citations.**
- Senior financial services managers and senior financial sales types, and **- See citations.**
- Perhaps, others of which I am not aware.

"Delusions of grandeur" is a typical trait of individuals with personality disorders. However, groups of individuals can share in a delusion that their particular subgroup of society is by some means greater, more intelligent, more capable, or in some other way has more value than that found to be the case with most members of other subgroups. Some such groups have found ways to leverage their delusion onto the backs of others. In doing so, the whole of the group benefits financially.

When select citizens take out more from the economy than can be logically justified relative to that which others take out, they do so at the expense of the others. Said practices can lead to compromised wages for the others, smaller dividends, lower stock appreciation (your retirement savings or pension fund), etc. Summed up, a great quality of life for some and a compromised quality of life for many.

Cultural momentum is such a strong force that it often significantly overpowers the basic economic tenet of supply and demand. For instance, there is an abundant supply of individuals in the USA that could do an equal or better job than that done by current CEOs and board members of the Fortune 500 corporations. The overly high paychecks these CEOs enjoy are a product of cultural momentum. Side note: the concept of boards of directors exercising proper fiduciary responsibility, in several areas including executive pay, is not working.

Keep in mind that in a practical sense – all wealth comes from the application of conversion labor. This includes your family's labor and your labor.

Questions:

Mark all answers that are reasonably correct; if an answer is not correct, develop a relative answer that is correct, or at least more correct.

1) Recently through the news media, many in the private sector have become aware that many in the civil service sector (town, city, county, state, federal) (chiefly professionals and management) are paid wages that are considerably above those for similar jobs in the private sector. Plus, these individuals are receiving healthcare benefits and healthy pensions that are significantly better than those of most who are or will be retired from the private sector:

   a. For the United States to remain competitive in a global economy, private industry must attract those job candidates who are best able to compete. If the current situation continues, these individuals will seek employment in the civil service sector. To prevent this from happening, either a significant proportion of the employees in the private sector must receive a 30% increase in pay or a majority of those in civil service management and professional positions must receive a 30% decrease in pay.

b. If the current earned income relationship continues between the civil service sector and the private industry sector the economy will weaken, unemployment will rise, and many people, both those employed in civil service and those employed in the private sector, will find it difficult to earn a living.

c. Regardless of that which is stated in the department's job specifications, there are fewer than 500 positions in the Social Security Administration that might require a college degree, and there are none (from the top job on down) that require a master's degree.

d. There are less than 50 positions in your state's Department of Motor Vehicles that, regardless of what is stated in the job specifications, truly require an individual with a college degree.

e. The relationship of pay levels between the civil service sector and the <u>private sector</u> will not impact the global competitiveness of the United States.

2) In consideration of sources of personal wealth:

a. Families that today enjoy the benefit of a major colonial land grant have earned their wealth as have other citizens.

b. The wealth of major land grant beneficiaries was earned not by the beneficiaries, but by the soldiers who risked their lives to conquer the Native Americans.

c. People who have accumulated their wealth through unethical or criminal activities should have streets named after them if they donate some of their wealth to building a public library or a wing of a hospital.

d. In addition to civil action available to an inventor who has his/her invention stolen by others, the public should make such stealing a criminal offense. Legal action against the offender(s) should be prosecuted at public expense.

3. As related to the determination of earnings (if you need to, put your ego in a locked drawer while you answer the following question):

a. If the average Fortune 500 CEO had the ability to score at the 95th percentile or above in critical thinking skills, there would be at least 10 million Americans who could do these CEOs' jobs as well or better than the incumbent CEOs. Therefore, the rule of supply and demand in this situation is not working.

b. A Social Security Administration employee interviews SS applicants and completes the appropriate forms. Although he/she does other tasks, all of these, also, are simple. Therefore, the SSA should require individuals in this particular person's job to have a college degree.

c. Unreasonably high paychecks for government employees lead to higher taxes – both income taxes and property taxes.

d. CEO pay at public corporations has gotten out of hand.

e. None of the above.

CHAPTER 5 – Types of Economic Systems

Chapter 5 covers:

- Five key aspects that differentiate economic systems
- Systems types
- Benefits and disadvantageous of the system types.

There are many types of economic systems in our world. Additionally, there are many types of theories regarding economic systems. Various countries practice various economic systems, often based on a combination of more than one economic theory. Economists, typically, when defining the various types of systems do so by looking at what they see without separating the chaff from the grain. What they see, in most, if not all cases, are economic systems interlaced with political and cultural characteristics common to particular economies. This issue becomes a significant issue in the development of definitions of capitalism, socialism, and fascism. This issue is a root cause of much confusion.

Herein we keep it simple. Definitions are provided for six types. The definitions of socialism and fascism will not align with many definitions – but, they do align with those provided by the professor in my college economics class. These are the clearest definitions I have come across.

Key Differentiating Aspects of Economic Systems

Five key aspects that differentiate economic systems are:

- The method of determining title to natural resources and the means of production and distribution
- The method for determining the direction and development of the economy (command-driven versus market driven)
- The degree of regulation
- The degree of alignment with the needs of the greater citizenry for a good quality of life, and
- The degree of compatibility with a democratic political system.

System Types

Unfettered Capitalism (Un-tethered) – a system free of any regulation by the community or else wise; the title to natural resources and the means of production and distribution is held by various individual members of the community (as individuals or groups of individuals – e.g., partnerships and corporations). Additionally: (A) it is purely a market driven system and (B) there is no attempt by the community to align the design of the system with the need of the general citizenry for a good quality of life.

Laissez Faire Capitalism – a system free of regulation except for those necessary to protect property rights, prevent theft, and prevent aggression. **- See citations (Wikipedia).** Various individuals hold title to natural resources and means of production and distribution. As with Unfettered Capitalism, Laissez Faire Capitalism is (A) a market driven system and (B) there is no provision for providing a good quality of life for the general citizenry.

Regulated Capitalism – a system regulated by the community, to a degree, as is perceived by the community as necessary to protect members of the community from economic and personal harm and to accommodate certain political and cultural ideologies and values. Regulations in line with cultural ideologies and values are intertwined with the economic system. Therefore, the same type of economic system can transcend the boundaries of various countries, but the regulations will not be consistent country to country. The title to natural resources and the means of production and distribution is held by various individual members of the community (as individuals or groups of individuals – e.g., partnerships and corporations). Regulated Capitalist systems are (A) market driven systems and (B) typically exhibit some provision for providing a minimally acceptable quality of life for the general citizenry.

Fascism - Most, if not all, economists are not fully clear as to the exact nature of fascism; as the key champions of the concept, Mussolini and Hitler, appear themselves to have been somewhat unclear [http://en.wikipedia.org/wiki/Economics_of_fascism].This having been said, fascism combines an extreme form of capitalism with a form of tight regulation. The political system based on the rule of a plutocracy is interlocked with the economic system; as such title to productive resources remains with individuals. The system is not focused on the well-being of the members of the community. Some have said that fascism is based upon "corporate rule" of the community. This is not exactly true. Hitler and Mussolini used the term "corporate" to designate a political structure versus rule by groups of business people who have come together and incorporated. However, the effect is the same as the few control the rest. The concept is that the few know what is best for the community and will thus plan and provide for the community.

The theme of "fascism" is used today to market select products such as belt buckles and tattoos to a limited group of people. Beyond this, there is not a lot of buy-in to the concept of fascism. The answers to the questions of:

A. Whether fascism is command driven or market driven is unclear, however, many hold the opinion that it is a mixture, and
B. As to the quality of life of the general citizenry – possibly, the quality of life of the general citizenry is not a point of focus.

Socialism – a system wherein title to select natural resources and downstream means of production and distribution is held by the community; whereas the balance of the resources and means of production and distribution are owned by individual members of the community. The sectors of the economy owned by the community are tightly regulated. The sectors of the economy owned by individuals are regulated in a manner similar to that found under a regulated capitalist system. Some economists have described Socialism as a cross between Capitalism and Communism. Socialist systems are (A) a combination of both command-driven (a central committee plans and schedules development and production to meet needs and wants as conceived to exist by the committee) and market-driven systems. In practice, most socialistic systems (B) attempt to provide a minimum, yet decent, quality of life for the general citizenry as a whole. It is necessary to temper this goal based upon the level of the readily available natural resource base per capita of a country.

Communism – a system wherein title to all natural resources and means of production and distribution is held by the community. Depending on the purity of the definition employed by a country, individuals may own non-productive land on which their house sits and the retail stage of distribution. As such, the majority and perhaps all of the sectors of the economy are tightly regulated. In a pure communist economic system, every individual is guaranteed a job (citizens may be required to re-locate). Communist systems can be (A) command driven, market driven, or a combination of the two. In practice countries tending toward employing communist systems have primarily been command driven. The communist economic system is (B) heavily directed toward providing a good quality of life for the general citizenry. It is necessary to temper this goal based upon the level of the readily available natural resource base per capita of a country. A resource-rich country could provide a high standard of living for the general citizenry, and a resource-poor country could provide only a poor standard of living for the general citizenry.

All of the above systems, in theory, will work with any of the various political forms of government; from a democratic type of system to a dictatorship. However, in reality, some are not compatible over an extended period with a democratic political system. Below a limited discussion is provided, of the benefits and disadvantages to the citizenry as a whole, for each type of economic system.

Benefits and Disadvantageous

Unfettered capitalism:

Benefits –

The market is the best determinant of what should or should not be produced. This rule applies to all aspects of an economy. Those in business leadership positions who are best suited to manage will survive, and those who are not best suited will fail. These two aspects of unfettered capitalism theoretically provide society with the most effective means of satisfying needs and wants.

Labor is willing to do what the employer wants when the employer wants it done; sometimes without regards for worker safety. This fact provides the employer with the means to produce at a higher level of productivity and, thereby, sell his product at a lower cost. In the USA and Europe children age 5 – 14 were often employed outside of the home in deplorable situations prior to regulations (primarily in factory and farm work) against such practices being implemented in the 1940's. **- See citations.**

Disadvantageous –

Man cannot be trusted to compete fairly. As demonstrated in the USA prior to implementation of trade laws, those most corrupt survived better than those less corrupt or honest, with little or no regard to those best able to manage. This problem has raised its head again with the repeal of laws such as those against proprietary trading.

The inevitable outcome of an unfettered capitalist system is the eventual mega-conglomeration of businesses. This leads to the development of an aristocracy in agricultural based societies and plutocracy in industrial based societies. **An aristocracy or plutocracy cannot coexist with democracy**. Politically an unfettered capitalist system in the US would eventually lead to rule by a few (plutocracy) or to dictatorial rule.

In today's world under the structure of unfettered capitalism, labor, in developed markets (e.g., USA, Canada, Germany, etc.), would have an extremely weak market position – with the options of increased immigration and offshoring production, an oversupply of labor exists. Labor would, therefore, be willing to work for marginally substantive wages which equates to a very low quality of life and a much-shortened lifespan.

A weak labor market would lead to low wages which in turn leads to a weak domestic demand. Therefore, the capitalists would focus on supplying the well-off members of the worldwide society at a detriment to the domestic community. Eventually, as all worldwide markets are developed, the labor cost would increase as supply and demand for labor balances out, to the degree that readily available natural resources in a particular part of the world allow for balancing. The time at which this would happen is at least 200 years out. Therefore, the majority of the citizenry of advanced economies would experience a drop in quality of life, and subsequently a lag in recovery, for at least 200 years.

Laissez Faire Capitalism:

Benefits and Disadvantageous -

The benefits and disadvantageous are the same for Laissez Faire Capitalism as for unfettered capitalism; with the theoretical qualification that aggression is controlled (aggression in claiming title to productive assets). While this may be true of physical aggression, it is not true, in the real world, of economic aggression. Before the establishment in the USA of trade laws (regulations), major corporations who had clout with vendors strong-armed the vendors into cutting off supplies of smaller competitors. Once the smaller competitor could not produce due to lack of materials, the larger competitor stepped in and forced the smaller competitor into submitting to acquisition, or the smaller company went out of business. Additionally, predatory pricing and bid-rigging were used by larger companies to put smaller companies out of business. **- See citations.**

After implementation of trade laws the incidence of these practices was greatly reduced in the USA.

Regulated Capitalism:

Benefits -

As in unfettered capitalism, market forces define and drive the economy.

Irresponsible and just plain bad people have existed since the time of Cain and Abel. Under regulated capitalism control by the community over business practices is expanded to provide a reasonable level of protection to the community as a whole and possibly individuals (both as businesses and individual people) from the ill effects of irresponsible business management practices.

Most Americans will agree that based on the experience in the USA from the 1940's through the early 1980's regulated capitalism and democracy worked very well together.

Disadvantageous -

The degree of regulation can go "over the top." Bureaucrats can generate regulations for the sake of regulation. Conversely, needed regulations can be (and often are) effectively weakened (as has been the case with the USA banking system regulation definitions and enforcement).

Socialism:

Benefits –

The community owns businesses that are basic to the well-being of the community. This fact helps to protect the community from failed businesses, bankruptcy, in such key areas as utilities, steel production, and mass transportation.

The community and businesses that operate downstream from the key businesses are protected from price gouging and other unethical practices that might occur if the community-owned businesses were privately held.

As in capitalism, that portion of the economy not owned by the community is market driven; thereby, satisfying the needs and wants of the community in an efficient manner.

Socialism is the economic system that is the most compatible with a democratic political system. However, creeping privatization of community-owned productive assets, in some countries, is systematically weakening this relationship.

Disadvantageous -

The command-driven portion of the economy may miscalculate that which is needed to satisfy the needs and wants of the citizenry (This point, while often cited, is not a major issue). This could lead to inefficiencies in production. Therefore, the community would realize less benefit for a level of applied labor than would be the case with a market-driven approach directed by fair and honest businessmen.

As in regulated capitalism, the degree of regulation of the private sector businesses can go over the top.

Fascism:

Benefits -

Fascism unites the people of a country behind economic goals and objectives. The citizenry is conditioned to focus on the economic needs of the country as a whole as defined by the leadership. Theoretically, this leads to a higher level of production efficiency. The alleged efficiency with which Hitler and Mussolini built their countries' infrastructures and militaries is pointed to as proof of this efficiency.

Disadvantageous -

Fascism is not compatible with democracy, and it is highly subject to corruption.

Communism:

Benefits -

Communism is based upon the system operating creed of "from each according to his ability; to each according to his need." All workers, in the purest form of communism, are guaranteed a job and all are paid equally. Those who have above normal needs, predominantly physically and/or mentally disabled and elderly, are provided with extra support as are their families such that their quality of life, to a reasonable degree, is the same as that of those without above normal needs.

The communist economic system provides a barrier of protection from exploitation at the level of near slavery in countries where the abundance of readily available natural resources per capita is low. In such situations, under a capitalist system, the people become the major resource to exploit.

Those who support the communist approach argue that, contrary to the claims of those who favor capitalism, the combination of command/market driven economy is more efficient than the pure market driven economy. They point to high levels of unemployment, bankruptcies, infant mortality rates, and life expectancy patterns found when a capitalist system is applied to a country with limited readily available natural resources.

Disadvantageous -

Once I heard a man say that "for communism to work, we would all have to be as perfect as Jesus Christ."

Members of a community who hold a high level of self-interest (greed) will constantly try to undermine the system to the detriment of the community. Others with weak personal constitutions will see that the options these people offer will benefit them personally, although to the detriment of the community and often of members of their extended family, and will join up with those who wish to undermine the system. This latter group does not envision how the disadvantageous of undermining the system might backfire on them within their own lifetime. **- See citations.** It is difficult and probably impossible for the community to hold these forces in check and the system will eventually fail.

Due to the above mentioned economic/political stresses, it is not reasonable to expect communism and democracy to work smoothly together for an extended period of time.

Questions:

Mark all answers that are reasonably correct.

1. There are many types of economic systems in our world; what can be said about these varieties?

   a. Most and possibly all countries employ a combination of systems.

   b. "Fascism" while possible in theory, today is used primarily as a marketing theme for selling belt buckles and other products to a small portion of the population.

   c. The definitions of socialism and fascism used in this guide do not align with definitions used by many economists; but the author believes them to be more understandable than most others.

   d. Without the regulatory benefits of trade laws in the USA small businesses will be abused by larger businesses, as has historically been the case.

2. Five key aspects differentiate the various economic systems from one another

    a.   The method of determining title to natural resources, the means of production and distribution.

    b.   The degree of compatibility with a democratic political system.

    c.   The degree of regulation.

    d.   The method for determining the direction and development of the economy (command-driven versus market driven).

    e.   The degree of alignment with the needs of the greater citizenry for a good quality of life.

3. Based on what you know about the USA economic history

    a.   All American business people can be trusted to compete fairly.

    b.   Some American business people cannot be trusted to compete fairly.

    c.   In a global labor market, American labor cannot compete with third world laborers who, in some cases, live in a mud hut.

    d.   Many American small businesses would be economically defenseless without adequate regulations to protect them from such practices as forms of predatory pricing (underpricing small business "A", thereby, putting it out of business; then moving on to underprice small business "B" putting it out of business; etc.).

    e.   None of the above.

CHAPTER 6: CURRENT ISSUES -Welfare Payments

Chapter 6 covers:

- Impact on the economy of reduction in welfare payments
- Recommendation to complete the Penny Money Flow exercise with 200 pennies instead of using the original 300 pennies
- What should a welfare support system look like?

As most readers already knew, but regardless as addressed in Chapter 2, the Federal Reserve in an effort to help control inflation maintains a targeted percentage of the workforce at a non-employed status. Until one of you can come up with a way to control inflation through a different means, there will be a segment of the workforce, by design and by law, which will be non-employed. **- See citations (Law).**

Also discussed in Chapter 2 was the fact that if all the non-employed and their dependents were to disappear from the face of the earth some of the members of the employed workforce would need to become non-employed (there would be a shift between employed and non-employed status for a segment of the population) in order for the Federal Reserve to meet its non-employment targets.

Most citizens receiving financial allocations from welfare programs are members of the class of non-employed citizens. A reduction in financial allocations to those on welfare (both in relative and absolute terms) has in-some-part a similar effect to that of non-employed citizens disappearing from the face of the earth (see discussion in Chapter 2). It does/will lead to additional members of the employed workforce being reassigned by the system to the non-employed group. Why?

- If a reduction in the allocation is accompanied by a reduction in taxes, then personal and business savings will increase. As a result, (1) "active" money will be reclassified as "idle" money and this will create a drag on the economy and (2) there will not be an increase in market demand. The demand previously created by the welfare recipients will simply be transferred to others and subsequently diminished as savings increase.

- If there is not a corresponding reduction in personal taxes at the lower middle-class income brackets, then business revenues will drop in response to a drop in market demand (lower income for welfare recipients means a lowered level of demand for the goods and services provided by businesses). As a result, either business profits will be reduced or workers will face a wage reduction or layoff. It is both possible and probable that a reduction in welfare payments will generate a downward economic spiral.

You can see the effect of lowering the allocation to the welfare recipients by redoing the Penny Money Flow Exercise (Appendix B) with 200 pennies and then comparing the outcome to that of your previous exercise using 300 pennies.

What should the system to support welfare recipients look like? This is for each citizen to determine. It is not only about "being thy neighbors' keeper" or "doing unto others as you would have them do unto you." It is, also, about maintaining a strong economy (high level of demand) so your children and you can be employed. As a community, we have adopted an economic system that limits what we can do. We are limited significantly by our need to control inflation. You, as a responsible citizen, must define the degree to which support can be offered without causing inflation to go wild. Against this backdrop, you must recognize that morally the community must provide adequately for its neighbors regardless of what might happen with inflation. This is a difficult balancing act. This is why the politics of economics is not easy. (NOTE: This is why God gave you big shoulders.)

Question:

1. A reduction in welfare payments will:

    NOTE: As you think through the choices provided below – think back to the section on the <u>Shifting of Population through Economic Class</u> *and on the* <u>Government Money Flow</u> *example involving Bob and Sue. Relate the reduction in welfare payments both to the option of reducing welfare payments and not reducing taxes and reducing welfare payments and reducing taxes.*

    a. Increase the number of jobs available in the community.

    b. Encourage "freeloaders" to look for work; this will be a benefit to my family as a "freeloader" <u>will not displace one of my children or grandchildren</u> in the workforce. (Should the latter in fact happen, my child or grandchild will end up on welfare [take the place of the ex-freeloader who will now be employed].)

    c. Accelerate the rate of early death for those living below the poverty line. - **See citations.**

    d. Cause market demand to increase and non-employment to decrease – even if the Federal Reserve's management feels that the situation with inflation is threatening to get out of hand.

e. Result in a reduction in taxes collected (review 200 penny version of Penny Money Flow exercise; if you completed it).

f. Result in a reduction in taxes collected; but also in private sector revenue – the resulting reduction in private sector revenue will significantly weaken the economy.

g. Motivate the members of my congregation to figure out a way the USA economic system can accommodate true full employment without causing runaway inflation.

h. Discourage single women from having children.

i. None of the above.

CHAPTER 7: CURRENT ISSUES - Investment Shortfall, Idle Money, Repatriation, and Job Creation

Qualifications: this chapter addresses direct economic issues only; primarily as related to tax issues. It does not address government actions related to environmental and safety regulations, etc. that may or may not affect the level of investment in America.

Additionally, the tax laws are being changed as this guide is being published; therefore, the narrative herein is of a transitional character. It may be rewritten, to a limited degree, once the IRS provides its interpretations of new laws passed.

This version focuses on the before (i.e. 2017 laws). This allows the reader, especially those reading the guide several years after the new tax laws are implemented, to understand where the country came from and where it went to. This provides the reader, also, with a basis needed to determine what to expect from the relative changes to the corporate tax structure and rates.

Chapter 7 covers:

- Background material on investment shortfall, idle money, and repatriation
- Why American corporations are not investing more in America
  - o Good investment opportunities are hard to find
  - o Many USA companies are focused on expanding internationally
- Have US Corporate tax rates discouraged investments in America?
- Do US corporations have the money needed to invest more in America?
- Would Corporations have invested in America and created American jobs if another Repatriation Tax Holiday was declared?
- Descriptions of three typical overseas investment actions.

Background Material on:
- **Domestic Investment Shortfall,**
- **Idle Money, and**
- **Repatriation**

It has been, is being, and will in the future be claimed and reported by some that American companies are not investing in America because of high US corporate tax rates. (This will be less true, but still somewhat true, under the new, 2018, corporate income tax rate cap of 21%.) At the same time it has been, is being, and in the future will be claimed and reported, sometimes by some of the same people, that American companies would invest more in America should the community provide a tax break (post 2017, perhaps in the form of tax credits) for bringing profits from overseas operations into America. Are these claims in any way rational?

Domestic Investment Shortfall

Current data accumulated by the US Department of Economic Analysis and published in chart form by the Federal Reserve suggest that companies did, in the year 2017, invest in America. In fact, 2015 represented a record year for investment in non-residential business assets (in current dollars; more on the constant dollar effect in Discussion Guide 2). Further, following the 2008 financial crash the year 2012 matched the previous peak set in 2008. New records were set in each of 2013, 2014 and 2015. Investment in 2016 dipped a little, but 2017 may set a new record. Following is a list of recommended charts, published in FRED (Federal Reserve Economic Data) by the Federal Reserve, you will want to view (do searches on the following phrases):

- Private Nonresidential Fixed Investment – FRED

- Gross Private Domestic Investment: Fixed Investment: Nonresidential: Equipment - FRED

- Real gross domestic product: Gross private domestic investment: Fixed investment: Nonresidential: Intellectual property products: Software – FRED

The above-mentioned charts vary in the form in which the information is presented, and you would need to learn the meaning of each form to fully understand each chart. However, even without an investment in learning the full meaning of the charts, the charts can be easily viewed as a means for completing a general assessment of how trends in domestic investment levels are tracking.

Over the last thirty years, the nature of this investment has changed significantly. A significant and growing portion of the investment today, for instance, is in software (as opposed to manufacturing plants, office buildings, construction machinery, etc.). This feature may be part of the reason the public feels the level of investment is inadequate. There are other changes that have taken place that may or may not influence public perception as well. NOTE: Political propaganda, also, influences public perception in this area.

From a different perspective, as of November 2017, the reported unemployment rate, although the labor force has grown, is at a sixteen year low, 4.1% (the "real" unemployment is higher – but declining). If the investment in America had not been adequate there would not have been places for the increasing number of employed Americans to work. They landed jobs; therefore, the investment has been adequate.

NOTE: The "real unemployment rate" (referred to as U6 in government reporting) reflects unemployment problems centered primarily in rural America.

The public relates investment in America with job creation in America. For most of our existence, this is the way things worked.

Sticking with software investment as a subject; let's pretend that your cable company invests $25 million in a software package. This package is designed to enable your cable company to locate its customer service center in India. This investment enables your cable company to globalize its operations. The $25 million of investment was invested in America, but the jobs were created in India.

This writer looked for studies that in a substantive way analyzed the effect that investments in America made to enable globalization (transportation, communication, warehousing) has had on employment in America. I was unable to find anything – but, I will keep looking.

Idle Money - Domestic

Estimates of domestic-based companies' excess idle funds for non-financial type US businesses range from $1.7 trillion to $2.4 trillion. **- See citations.** I have seen, also, estimates that approximately 1/3 of the excess is held in the US and the balance in overseas subsidiaries. This, the 1/3, plus normal depreciation and amortization, plus annually generated additional corporate free cash flow, are more than enough money to cover any domestic investments US businesses may wish to make in America; should they wish to make any additional investments.

There are published estimates as high as $7 plus trillion of excess idle corporate funds. Estimates in the $1.7 trillion to $2.4 range are more common and I have used these herein. NOTE: "funds" are somewhat different than "profit."

Repatriation (based on 2017 corporate tax laws)

NOTE: Reminder – the top corporate income tax rate in the US in 2017 was 35%; this is reduced to 21% under the 2018 changes to the tax laws.

Repatriation provisions may or may not, in some form or another, remain as part of the 2018 tax laws. It was proposed in Congress that the US would change from:

- Taxing corporations based in the US a US tax on overseas profits, to
- Not requiring any additional tax over that paid to the country hosting a portion of the company's operations. This constitutes an adoption of "territorial tax" versus "country of residence tax."

The laws are new and it will be several months before they are fully understood. As this was a significant issue addressed in the new laws – it is important that US citizens understand where the US came from so as to be able to assess the expected benefits to be derived from the changes. The benefits to be assessed include whether or not jobs will be created.

Definition of Repatriation - Profits earned in a foreign country that one wishes to bring into the borders of one's own country. For example, a corporation in the United States may repatriate the profits earned by a French subsidiary. Repatriated profit may be subject to special tax rules. **[http://financialdictionary.thefreedictionary.com/Repatriated+Profits]** (**It has been proposed that US repatriation taxes be eliminated**.)

How did this work?

Pretend, in 2017 or prior years, you are the CEO of an American international company that has a subsidiary in China, a country which regulates money exiting its economy. Your business has a sizable loan from a Chinese bank, which requires you to do the majority of your banking with the same bank. Regardless, you could still get a sizable portion of your money out of China and into the US. China's corporate income tax rate is 25% (China has a special 15% rate for electronics manufacturers). We will assume you wished to transfer a pre-US tax amount of $10 million out of China and that it would be taxed at the full US federal rate of 35% (does not include "state" tax rates). The US would give you credit for the 25% tax you paid to China and require a tax payment of 10% (35% US corporate income tax rate minus (-) 25% China corporate income tax rate = 10 %).[7]

How much excess overseas profit, belonging to American international corporations, is there? The number is possibly over $2 trillion. **[http://blogs.reuters.com/david-cay-johnston/2012/07/16/idle-corporate-cash-piles-up/]**.

---

[7] If you owned or managed a US subsidiary (business) in China that manufactured socks or broomsticks your corporate tax rate would be 25%; but China has special tax rates for select businesses. For instance the tax rate for businesses engaged in electronics is only 15%.

If an excess cash situation did not exist domestically it "**might be**" of value to the community to provide a tax break to entice corporations to bring the profits into the US. However, it is far more likely that corporations will invest in America based upon the merits of various investment opportunities, with or without tax breaks. Should a US corporation that is short on domestic money identify a good domestic opportunity, it will bring money from foreign operations into its domestic operations without the enticement of a tax break. Why "might be?" Prior to 2018, corporations could bring money into the US, but there were limits on what could be done with the money. See the section in this chapter, <u>Do US Corporations have Money Needed to Invest More in America if They Want to Invest More in America</u>?

Why are US Corporations not Investing More in America?

Why, because:

- Finding good domestic investment opportunities is difficult, and
- Many US companies are focused on expanding internationally.

Finding Good Domestic Investment Opportunities is Difficult

I was a member of two different teams chartered to review the financial return on investment of the domestic <u>internal capital investment programs</u> (process upgrades, new manufacturing plants, new product introductions, etc.), but not the external capital investment (primarily acquisitions), of two Fortune 500 manufacturing companies. One of the businesses is in foods and chemicals, and the other is in heavy equipment.

The CEO of one of the companies had completed a rough cut analysis of his company's internal CapEx program (capital expenditure program) and he found based on a three-year period with a one year lag that:

- The total of returns projected for the <u>profit improvement projects</u> included in the CapEx programs was greater than the company's profits; yet,

- The company's profits had not changed.

The CapEx program reviews were completed, also, on the basis of the latest three-year period allowing a one year lag.

The one year lag allows time for the projects to move through the respective start-up curves (time to get all of the kinks out) and, thereby, be fully operational for the period under review.

Both companies had a return on investment for their profit improvement CapEx programs that was, significantly, below the then current personal savings account interest rate. They would have had a higher investment return had they left their money in the bank. There are several reasons for this which I will not cover here; but in summary, **it is very hard for companies to come up with good investment ideas**. This is particularly true for US investment <u>due to the wage difference between US wages and those of some other countries</u>. Companies try and try again, but most of the time, effort and money spent are spent running in place. Why does the world move forward? Because there are thousands of companies trying and now and then one hits a home run. (Due to the number of companies trying this could be 1,000 to 10,000 home runs per year here in the US; but the ideas behind the home runs are sometimes implemented overseas.)

Many US Companies are Focused on Expanding Internationally

There are many reasons that companies focus on expanding internationally. For instance, Japanese companies focus on producing and selling automobiles in America. Three key perspectives on this subject are:

- A company has a strategic plan to invest in developing countries, assuming the return on investment would be much higher than in countries with mature economies (like the US, which has a mature economy). The company will need to sell in such countries at a lower price than possible if producing in the US. If it produced the product in the US at the US wages the company's product pricing would not be competitive. Therefore, to sell into low wage countries, a company has to produce in low-wage countries.

- Management of a US company believes the company's product features will have a competitive advantage over the competitors in nations that are developed. It wishes to produce in or near the markets to be served. Additionally, the company wants to produce at the lowest cost possible; typically, this means paying the lowest wage and distribution costs possible. These requirements eliminate the US as an option. What about "automation;" can't US producers be competitive through automating production? Automation is for sale. The businesses producing in foreign countries can buy the same automation equipment as can businesses producing in America.

- A company has a patented product that it can produce and sell both in countries with developing or mature economies without fear of competition. It wishes to produce in or near the markets to be served. More importantly, the company wants to produce at the lowest cost possible; typically, this means paying the lowest wage and distribution costs possible.

Discussion point: What alternatives, if any, would the companies exercising any of the above three options have for investing in America?

Have US Corporate Tax Rates Discouraged Investments in America?

BUT, as mentioned previously, companies are investing in America. There appears to be an issue with the character of the investment make-up. This requires study by some very sharp economists.

Twenty-five years ago I was thinking of starting up an accounting and tax practice focused on servicing small businesses. A friend of mine, Gary, had done so four years earlier. I spent three days with Gary at his practice to learn the ropes. Both Gary and I had worked in Fortune 500 businesses; both had held positions as division officers. My wife and I owned a small retail business; however, I had very few business discussions with other small business owners. Gary, in the course of his briefing, made this statement "what you need to understand is that there are three things most people who own small businesses (50 or fewer employees) do not understand – business, economics, and taxes." As the years passed, I came to realize that there are three things some CEOs of large businesses do not understand – business, economics, and taxes. Yes, most are fairly knowledgeable, but some are way out in the weeds.

It is from these people, who do not understand, that the public hears a pot load of non-substantive rhetoric about why American businesses are not investing in America.

Keep in mind the lesson learned on the third page of Chapter 2 - <u>Section A, Warm-up Question and Answer</u>, when comparing investment alternatives between low-cost labor countries and the US, the income tax bill becomes diminutive (too small to matter). As to investment determinations that consider the domestic alternative only – corporate tax rates at times have been higher and these did not discourage investment in America.

Do US Corporations have the Money Needed to Invest More in America if They Want to Invest More in America?

As discussed previously, American businesses have a significant excess of money available domestically. Additionally, if they have good investment opportunities, they can free up money earned by their foreign subsidiaries for investment in America. It is very unlikely that adding more money domestically on top of too much money domestically will in any way lead to increased investment in America. **- See citations.**

What will be the effect – of tax relief designed to encourage US Corporations to bring the money from overseas profits into the country? Will the money be used to invest in America and create jobs for Americans?

A review of the 2017 versus 2018 situation

There were (2017) two aspects faced by an American company that had overseas earnings and wished to use some of these earnings for investment in America or for other reasons:

- What a corporation was not allowed to do with the money unless US corporate repatriation taxes were paid, and
  - An American company could bring money from profits into the United States to do as the company pleased without paying repatriation tax, <u>except</u> for some actions that were prohibited unless the tax was paid.

- Bookkeeping entries.

If you were the CEO (Chief Executive Officer) of an American company, key actions you would <u>not</u> be allowed to undertake in America, before paying repatriation related taxes, with money earned overseas includes (but is not limited to):

- Invest domestically in your company (build facilities, buy equipment, buy software, etc.)
- Initiate a buyback of outstanding company shares of stock by the company, itself (treasury stock), and
- Issue dividends to your company's stockholders from the money earned overseas.

  To learn more about the things a corporation could do with overseas earnings see: https://www.americanprogress.org/issues/tax-reform/report/2014/01/09/81681/offshore-corporate-profits-the-only-thing-trapped-is-tax-revenue

  - A corporation could bring money into the US for other purposes.

Here is the deal – even though you reported (for accounting purposes) your profits overseas, you deposited some of the money from the overseas profits in a US bank. Yes, you were allowed to do this without paying the US corporate income taxes due. In fact, you could use the money from your overseas profits to buy US Treasury Notes, stocks of other US corporations, bonds of other US corporations, etc.

If a US corporation could bring money from profits earned overseas into America and deposit the money in a US bank or use the money to buy stocks or bonds of other companies, etc. what effect would repatriation of the overseas profits have on American jobs?

Obviously, if the money is in a US bank it is available to lend to other US businesses. While a direct investment by the company would create US jobs, the money lent based on the bank deposits made will have created jobs – if there is room in the economy for additional jobs. The jobs created by commercial lending need to be netted against the jobs that might be created by a company making a direct investment of its overseas profits in America. Therefore, there may or may not occur a net increase in the number of American jobs created if the company were to make a direct investment. **This is true both under the old and new tax laws.**

What part did bookkeeping entries play in the non-payment or payment of US taxes for repatriation? A bookkeeping entry was the trigger that necessitated the payment of the tax. If the entry is not made – no tax is due.

Your overseas subsidiary has its own set of accounting records. It is in the financial statements developed from these records that the subsidiary shows a profit for the subsidiary. If you did not wish to pay repatriation taxes on these profits, for tax purposes, you simply allowed them to sit on the books of your subsidiary. Keep in mind, you could still bring the money related to the profits into the US; you were simply restricted in what you could do with that money until you paid repatriation taxes. If you decided, for tax accounting purposes, to bring these profits into the US your accounting department simply deducted the profits from the books of the foreign subsidiary and added these profits to your domestic corporation books. It may be a little more complex than this – but, not much; basically your foreign subsidiary issued a dividend to its parent company. This action triggered the requirement for your company to pay the required US corporate income taxes. Once this was done your company was allowed to do everything with the money earned overseas, it was allowed to do with the money if the profits had been earned in the US. This includes investing in your own company in the US.

Based on the country's experience with the 2004 repatriation tax holiday – No.

The US government in response to demands from some business CEOs and others implemented a repatriation tax holiday in 2004. Corporations still had to pay a repatriation tax – but it was limited to 5%. If in 2017 you wanted to repatriate $10 million (pre-tax) and your tax difference due was 10% - your tax would be $1 million. However, you would only have to pay a US tax of $500 thousand, 5%, on the $10 million (pre-tax), you wanted to repatriate in 2017 if a similar tax holiday had been declared. (NOTE: 5% is used for simplicity. The actual cap was 5.25% and the determination of the tax due was based on a complex calculation.)

Pretending you did transfer the same amount back in 2004, how much did you invest in the US? The answer is typically none of it. **- See citations.**

We (US citizens) can look to the year 2004 to understand why you want tax relief on your company's repatriated foreign earnings. This is equally true under the 2017 and 2018 corporate tax laws.

Why (as in 2004), if you do not need the money for domestic investment, did you want to avoid the restrictions and taxes on money earned at overseas subsidiaries and brought into the US? Recall that the two other key restrictions placed on money brought into the US and not officially repatriated. The money could not be used to:

- Purchase treasury stock – a company buys its own stock to lower the number of shares on the market and, thereby, increase the share value, and

- Issue dividends to the company's stockholders.

You wanted tax relief so you have more money with which to purchase treasury stock or to distribute as dividends; not money to invest in America.

Purchase Treasury Stock

Treasury stock is stock a company buys of its own shares held by the company's stockholders. The purchase of treasury stock by a company lowers the number of shares held by stockholders, and therefore profits are divided amongst fewer shares than would be the case had the company not re-acquired the shares. This action results in a higher profit per share than would have otherwise been the case and the value of the company's remaining publicly held shares increases.

Part of your CEO bonus is based on stockholder value enhancement (i.e., an increase in the value of shares). You, therefore, wanted to use the repatriated money for the company's repurchase of some outstanding shares. Once these shares were repurchased, the earnings of the company would be divided amongst fewer shares. As such, the earnings per share would be higher and the price of the shares will increase in market value.

Issue Dividends

You wanted to increase the payout of your company's dividends to stockholders; of which you are one.

To the degree that those receiving dividends spend the money they receive they will stimulate the economy. To the degree, they invest in traded stocks and bonds (those purchased in the secondary market [aftermarket]) or deposit money in a bank they may or may not stimulate the economy. To the degree, they invest directly (personally or through Initial Public Offerings or Follow-on Offerings via purchasing a company's shares) in hard or soft assets (bricks and mortar, machinery, software development, etc.) (primary market) they will stimulate the economy. Most stockholders do not use dividends to invest in brick and mortar, machinery, software development, etc.; so if this does happen it will be to a minor degree. **If** the economy is stimulated it will be only to a minor degree and _if_ jobs are created this, too, will be only to a minor degree.

Discussion point: Continuing to assume you are the CEO of an international corporation, other members of the community (including your relatives, neighbors, and members of your congregation or club) will need to pay more in taxes, now or later, had the US government given you a 2017 repatriation tax holiday. What could you have given them in return that you would not give them anyway if they had supported another repatriation tax holiday? What will you give them in return for the new (2018) 21% tax cap on corporate profits?

Descriptions of Three Typical Overseas Investment Actions

The following discussion is not super complicated, but it is a little complicated. As has been the case in a couple of other sections of the guide – it is necessary only that the reader grasps the concept of the business action contemplated. It is not necessary for the reader to dig into the details.

Staying with the theme that you are the CEO of an American international corporation, three possible overseas investment actions you might have taken under the 2017 tax laws are listed below:

- Building facilities in low-cost wage countries, Action 1
- Contracting with overseas companies located in low-cost wage countries, Action 2
- Locating all or, more typically, a portion of a corporation's headquarters overseas for the purpose of lowering corporate income taxes, Action 3.

These actions are still available to you under the 2018 tax laws; but the format of your tax strategy will be different.

Think for a moment, as in **Action 1**, you have the option of:

- Building a manufacturing plant in the US that will cost you $1 million to build and will generate, for you, a profit of $100 thousand a year, or

- Building the same manufacturing plant in Vietnam at the cost of $600 thousand (because of lower Vietnamese wages) but that will generate, for you, a profit of $300 thousand a year (because of lower Vietnamese wages).

Which option will you pick? It doesn't matter how low your US corporate taxes are – you will build your plant in Vietnam not in the US. The difference in labor costs is so great that <u>the difference in corporate income tax rates is insignificant</u>. When the corporate tax rate in Vietnam was significantly lower than in the US (now, 21% US and 20% Vietnam), you would have had your Vietnamese subsidiary overbill the US Company so that profits in the US are lowered and those in the foreign subsidiary are increased. The 2018 tax laws make it unnecessary for you to overbill the US Company – nothing of benefit to the majority of US Citizens happens.

Discussion points: Since the US lowered its corporate tax rates, will Vietnam lower their rates? Why? What would be different if the Vietnam rates were again significantly lower than the US rates?

You may be able to contract your work, as stated in **Action 2** listed above, to a manufacturing company in China (Apple iPad) and not need to build a plant. The wages in China will be less competitive than those in Vietnam (China's wages are more than double those of Vietnam's). By contracting with a Chinese company, therefore, you may only earn $200 thousand per year, but your investment may be less than $50 thousand (initial travel costs and legal fees for setting up the contract). In this situation your earnings are:

- Double what they would be should you produce in the US
- A $100 thousand less than they would be should you build your own plant in Vietnam, and
- Your investment is only $50 thousand.

If your Company is in the electronics business where, due to the fast-changing technology, your product may be obsolete in three years– you do not want to risk building a plant. Therefore, contracting the work to a Chinese company is your best option. Again, <u>no matter how low US corporate tax rates are</u> contracting with a Chinese company is your best option.

Under the 2017 tax laws, you would not have had the Chinese contractor bill your US Company for the product. You would have had them bill your Chinese subsidiary which you set up for just this purpose. Your Chinese subsidiary would then bill your US Company at over inflated prices. This practice lowered profits at the US company where corporate income tax rates were higher, 35% cap, and increased profits at your Chinese subsidiary where corporate income taxes were lower, 15% cap (NOTE: China has a special tax rate of 15% for high-tech companies. The standard rate is 25%).

Within the framework of the **3rd type of action**, you are a business person who owns a business in the US, and you wish to transfer as much of your corporate profits as possible to Ireland. You will still <u>produce in the US and deliver your product to the US market;</u> and use the US infrastructure to support your business (paid for by your neighbors and I / US taxpayers). You decide to relocate your corporate headquarters to Ireland. So why do you want to relocate your headquarters? Because on trading profit (in US language – profit earned from an active business activity versus a passive business or investment activity such as real estate) the corporate income tax rate is 12.5% in Ireland. In the US the 2017 tax rate ranged from 25% to 35% and in 2018 the tax rate is capped at 21%. (The US 2017 tax rate schedule applied to profits over the first $50 thousand, which is tax-free.)

Within the same framework, you must establish business practices, whereas you can keep your business in the US but <u>file the principal portion of your income as having been earned in Ireland</u>. What you are going to do is sell your patents and trademarks to your Irish company. Then your US Company will pay inflated royalties to your Irish company for the rights to use your patents and trademarks. You will then deposit the profits from both your US Company and your Irish company in a US bank (to the degree allowed by Ireland).

At this time it is unclear as to the tax laws change effect as related to the above type of situation. I will research it after the IRS has completed its interpretations of the new laws. At that time we can assess whether the new laws bring any benefit to the majority of the US taxpayers.

Review of Medtronic's Deal (US Corporation Move to Ireland)

For a bit of fun, review and then discuss the following articles for a picture of a real-life corporate relocation to Ireland, as in the 3rd type of action discussed above:

http://www.startribune.com/business/263385221.html Medtronics

Medtronic's deal, plan to move base to Ireland rekindle tax debate

- Article by: **JIM SPENCER** , Star Tribune
- Updated: June 17, 2014 - 5:34 AM

http://www.wsj.com/articles/medtronics-irish-jig-not-as-easy-as-it-seems-1403220286
Medtronic's Tax Inversion: Not as Easy as It Seems

Merger With Covidien Provides Address in Ireland, but Tax Implications Are Complex

By
JOSEPH WALKER
June 19, 2014, 7:24 p.m. ET

http://www.wsj.com/articles/medtronics-irish-jig-not-as-easy-as-it-seems-1403220286

Discussion points: A US company manufactures textile products in China. Under the old tax laws, the CEO might have inflated profits at the Chinese subsidiary and understated those in the US for the purpose of lowering taxes paid. Now that the US has a tax cap of 21% the CEO will want to do the opposite. This means China will, relatively, collect less tax revenue in the future than in the past on US owned companies. What might China do to offset this loss?

By setting the cap at 21% - has the US initiated a race to the bottom? Keep in mind that the tax bill for the US company is insignificant when compared to the cost savings realized.

Assuming the new tax laws have eliminated the repatriation tax requirement, in its entirety– how will this affect job creation in America?

CHAPTER 8: CURRENT ISSUES - Education and Welfare to Work

Chapter 8 covers:

- Will uplifting the educational level of Americans create jobs?
- There exist some career fields in which there is a shortage of qualified candidates of which education is a component of qualification
- Putting welfare recipients to work <u>will not change the **total** number of Americans employed</u>.

General Review

From the perspective of the community, there is a social (moral) aspect to providing higher education (college) to all citizens and the opportunity to transition off of welfare dependence to those on welfare. There is another discussion guide planned, to address social issues of the US community. This guide, however, focuses only on the economic aspects of these issues.

When politicians address free or low cost higher education – they are typically speaking of a college education. Many jobs do not require a college education; but – in today's world - do require more advanced training than that now offered in high school. Excluding STEM type of graduates (science, technology, engineering, and math) there may be an excess of college graduates as compared to job market demand at this time and for the near-long term.

However, there appears to be job market demand for employees with higher technical and trade skills than currently being provided via the high school system. This, possibly, should be the free or low-cost education requirement to be first addressed.

NOTE: Should we add a year to high school, which will focus on STEM and trade skills only (except for an additional course in economics)? If we were to do this, it must be required that no additional hours of classroom or home study would be devoted to any subjects that are not STEM or trade skill related throughout the entirety of the students' K-13 school program.

NOTE, also: Programs of apprentice, journeyman (person – nowadays), and master career development, paid for by the employer, are re-appearing. This is a good thing for America and should be formalized by the government. The structure of a formal program should ensure that employers cannot hire immigrants to drive down labor costs using the excuse that American job applicants are not qualified.

Additionally, from the perspective of the community that which is covered, herein, regarding education is true today and probably for the next twenty years – some of what is stated may need to be changed twenty-one years from now.

Three key things create jobs – (1) the combination of availability of readily available natural resources and conversion labor, (2) demand, and (3) anticipated demand.

There is confusion attributable to myopic perception.

John and Barbara came from a poor American family that lived in a poor neighborhood. John and Barbara obtained advanced educations and landed good jobs. Therefore, many people relate the availability of "good jobs" with "good education." However, the good jobs were not created because John and Barbara obtained an advanced education. The good jobs were created by demand or anticipated demand. Someone else with the right education would have landed the jobs if John and Barbara had not obtained good educations.

Most likely, the someone-else who landed the jobs would have been an American. It is not a typical situation, but it sometimes happens that there is not an American with the required education or training to fill a job requirement. If this is true, then in very rare cases an employer may need to fill a job with a foreign individual. If in such an instance a John or Barbara were available to fill the position, it would have been filled with an American; but, the job would not have been created because an American had the right education.

I recently reviewed a forecast that projected American worker shortages in electrical engineering, accounting, science and medical fields (a different forecast disputed the projected shortage of electrical engineers). It would be good for Americans and America if students studied for careers in these areas. Then job openings would be filled by Americans. Note, some Americans, in fact, hold the opinion that student loans should not be underwritten or funded by the government unless the student is pursuing an education in a career area forecasted to experience a shortage of qualified workers. Note also, some employers hire foreign workers (especially in science and engineering fields) not because of a lack of qualified Americans but to put downward pressure on wages. - **See citations.** (The H-1B program, [temporary work permits for high tech type immigrant workers] may be creating a shortage of American high-tech types – by depriving American workers of needed experience.)

Let's pretend that lots of Americans who do not now have an advanced education obtained an advanced education. Would this fact change the targeted unemployment (and, effectively; the total non-employment) number as determined by the Federal Reserve? No, it would not. The average and median pay of Americans would not change because America now had a better-educated workforce. Would the average income of each 10th percentile income group change (that of those in the lowest 10th percentile and in each 10th percentile above)? No, it would not. Most likely, all that would happen is many people who have obtained an advanced degree would be working in low-wage jobs.

What about putting people on Welfare to work? Would that change the percentage of the workforce that is non-employed? No, as stated previously the Federal Reserve's target for unemployed / non-employed members of the workforce would stay the same. All that would happen is that someone who is now working and subsequently lost their job might lose the opportunity to land a new job to an ex-welfare recipient. The number of available jobs would not change and pay levels would not increase; however, the pay levels might **decrease** due to the **increase** in the number of workers competing for the jobs.

This is a good point at which to consider something stated in chapter 2:

> *Unfortunately, many in politics and economics look at the level of unemployment without looking at the level of possible private sector employment.* *This has led to the development of irrational employment and other economic type proposals by various congresspeople and some presidents. As mentioned previously, I call this the water bucket syndrome. Some politicians and economists believe seven gallons of water (the available potential workforce) will fit into a five-gallon bucket (number of jobs available). God did not give man a five-gallon bucket that will hold seven gallons of water or even just six gallons of water.*

Job retraining, higher education, welfare to work initiatives and any other efforts to uplift the American workforce are good economics if these initiatives focus where there is a shortage of qualified applicants for particular jobs. Such initiatives enable the American worker to be more competitive with immigrants that might be brought in by employers. However, the foreign worker will have both educational qualifications and experience, whereas, the newly graduated machinist or chemist will not have experience. If Americans do obtain the needed education to fill those very few jobs where there might be a true shortage of labor supply; then there will need to be some controls implemented to limit the immigration of individuals who would compete for these jobs.

Unfortunately, a significant portion of most initiatives, such as job retraining, higher education, welfare-to-work, and prison diversion, amount to no more than "robbing Peter to pay Paul." A job will be filled by Paul, a welfare recipient, and poor Peter, who had a steady job for fifteen years before his employer went out of business, will remain unemployed.

Questions:

Mark all reasonably correct answers.

a. Although higher education programs and sometimes the "welfare to work" program are often good for particular individuals, such programs will not benefit the community unless (subject to Fed employment actions to control inflation)

  a. Demand for goods and services are increased domestically.

  b. Demand for goods and services are increased internationally in products that can be produced at a competitive cost in the US by workers earning a fair wage.

  c. Demand for goods and services are increased; but the system needs to be changed such that the demand increase does not lead to inflation.

  d. The design of the American economic system is changed. Otherwise, the relative number of citizens with high, middle and low incomes will remain the same, even if all citizens hold Ph.D.'s.

b. If every American child came from a good home, had good role models, and attended good schools:

  a. The average wage for each income quartile would increase.

  b. The median wage (the wage smack in the middle) for each income quartile would increase.

  c. There would be more jobs in the economy.

  d. There would not be any long-term unemployment.

  e. Everyone who wanted a job could find one.

  f. The Federal Reserve System would no longer need to balance the level of national employment and inflation.

g. All of the above.

h. None of the above.

Before reading more of the discussion guide, discuss with a friend, neighbor, fellow congregation member, civic club member, relative or someone you meet while waiting on a bus or train, the ramifications your answers to the question(s) might have on the US economy and society. Next, think about the ramifications that the answer will have on the quality of life for your family.

CHAPTER 9: CURRENT ISSUES - Minimum Wage

"Thousands of lights were burning on the green branches, and gaily-colored pictures, such as she had seen in the shop-windows, looked down upon her. The little maiden stretched out her hands towards them when--the match went out. The lights of the Christmas tree rose higher and higher, she saw them now as stars in heaven; one fell down and formed a long trail of fire." —from "The Little Match Girl" [http://www.online-literature.com/hans_christian_andersen/.

Chapter 9 covers:

- Introduction
- A Word about "real wages"
- What we think we know
- Developing a basis for weighing the pros and cons
- Inverse Domino Effect (IDE)
- Pros and cons of an increase in minimum wage
- Discussion of pros and cons
- More on what we know
- Recap of key points.

Introduction

President Obama proposed (HR 1010) raising the minimum wage to $10.10 per hour. This was to be implemented in steps starting in January of 2015 to be fully implemented by 2017. The federal minimum wage as of December 2017 is $7.25 per hour.

The issue of minimum wage is one that should be with you at all times. This is true; whether you are reading this guide before or after a new minimum wage schedule is implemented. Why is this true?

- The minimum wage levels affect what you and your children earn or will earn, even if you or your children earn or will earn over $100 thousand a year, and

- Every eight to ten years a new schedule is implemented. Therefore, if you are reading this guide after the latest implementation you are, also, reading it before the next new schedule is enacted.

Be aware that a minimum wage schedule does not only directly impact those earning the minimum wage but, also, all of those earning below the final top wage (e.g. $10.10 per hour under Obama's proposed program) when the final tier goes into effect.

A Word about "Real Wages"

Definition:

Real Wages: Wages adjusted (discounted to constant dollars) to accommodate the rate of inflation determine whether or not a wage increase provides an increase or decrease in purchasing power. For instance, if inflation increases this year by 3% and your wages increase by only 2% you will experience a decrease in purchasing power of approximately 1%. If your household income is $40,000 per year your purchasing power will be reduced by approximately $400 (1% of $40,000.)

What We Think We Know

What we think we know about the minimum wage workers and their households:

a. Per the University of California-Irvine economist David Neumark, about half of the people working minimum wage jobs come from households that are above the poverty line. 45 % of minimum wage earners lived in households earning $63,000 or more. **- see citations (Jacoby).**

   These are working spouses (full and part-time), people holding second jobs, working children living at home, etc.

b. Per Martin Rafanan, co-chair of St Louis Workers' Rights, according to the Bureau of Labor Statistics, 48 percent of the jobs by the year 2020 will be low paying McDonald's type, low-wage jobs. **- see citations (Jacoby).**

c. Dr. Joseph Sabia of San Diego State University found that over the past twenty years:

   - Each 10% rise in the minimum wage has reduced employment for less educated young adults by 2.3%.
   - Further, in tight labor markets (prime age male unemployment exceeds 8%) the employed, prime age (25-54) male drop-outs drop by over four percent**. - see citations (Sabia).**

d. Since it was established in 1938, the federal minimum wage has not kept pace with inflation. In real dollars, the peak value of the federal minimum wage was in 1968, when the wage was set at $1.60. That would be $10.56 in today's economy, well above the current $7.25.

- From a consumer's point of view, the average cost of a loaf of bread in 1968 was 22 cents, accounting for **14 percen**t of an hour's pay at the $1.60 minimum wage. The average cost of a loaf of bread in 2012 was $1.88, which accounts for **26 percent** of an hour's pay at the current minimum wage. - **see citations (Mejeur).**

Shortly I will list both pros and cons offered by individuals and organizations that support raising the minimum wage and those who are opposed to raising the minimum wage.

First, however, to properly consider the pros and cons the reader needs to establish a basis for evaluation of the arguments offered.

Developing a Basis for Weighing Pros and Cons

What is your position regarding wages? Below I discuss several points of consideration that represent common issues for all people. Readers may each have other points they want to consider – these will be too many for discussion in this guide. Therefore, I have stuck to those which I consider to be both basic and common.

In your consideration of each point, relate the point back to the fact that someday your position may affect your child or grandchild.

- A man/woman should be paid a fair day's pay for a fair day's work.

- The minimum fair day's pay is one that allows a man access to a healthy diet, adequate clothing, transportation, good healthcare, adequate shelter, adequate job training, etc.

- The minimum fair day's pay is one that allows a man plus his spouse and two children to have access to a healthy diet, adequate clothing, transportation, good healthcare, adequate shelter, adequate training, etc. This would allow mom the option to stay at home with the children while they are young (family values issue).

- The community should address social issues such as disabilities, single moms, age discrimination, etc. separately from wage issues. The opposite also is true. Wage issues should be addressed separately from social issues. Therefore, each man or woman desiring work is unto himself/herself a business. The relationship between an employer and a worker or a potential worker is a business to business relationship. This would include agreed to wages as long as those wages met a minimum of the community's definition of fair pay.

- To require a man to work for less than a fair day's pay/a living wage is to enslave such a man.

- A relationship between a fair day's pay and a living wage does not exist. Some work performed is simply not worth rewarding with a living wage. In such situations, less than a living wage is fair pay.

- If the community is not willing to pay the price for a good or service that enables an employer to pay employees a fair day's pay for a fair day's work – the members of the community are not entitled to the particular good or service provided.

- An employer who cannot accommodate paying workers a fair pay should go out of business.

- The approximate average manufacturing wage (based on various sources) in China is $2.67- $3.00 per hour (garment workers earn less than $1.50 per hour) and in India $1.47 - $2.00 per hour. American workers do not wish to compete with this and should not compete with this.

- We now live in a global economy; it is, therefore, reasonable that business owners will bring immigrants from China and India to compete with Americans for low-wage jobs.

- The market should determine what a man is paid; this includes the global market.

- A fair day's wage should be something more than "adequate." The principle of adequate pay should apply only to those who are out of work or unable to work and are receiving public assistance.

- The advantage of "competition" is that it drives down prices of goods and services. The disadvantage is that it drives down wages. The capitalist system, operating within the framework of a global economy, will by design push down the real dollar earnings of American workers. This factor is the nature of capitalism, and it must be controlled by the community. If it is not controlled, the system will wreak havoc on the livelihood of 99.9% of the citizens (actually, all of the citizens eventually – but the top .1% as measured by income and wealth may not experience significant effects for 100 years).

Discussion point: What thoughts does the discussion group have on any of the points listed above?

There is something else we need to know before evaluating Pros and Cons of an increase to the minimum wage.

Inverse Domino Effect (IDE)

This is a phenomenon that I call the "Inverse Domino Effect (IDE)," which is like the commonly noted "ripple effect" but more defined.

There exist in the workplace concepts of pay hierarchy. A supervisor earns more than the hourly workers he supervises. A first level manager earns more than the supervisors he manages. A senior manager/director earns more than the first level managers he supervises. A junior vice president earns more than the senior managers/directors he supervises, etc.

Within various organizations, there are various, formal or informal (company culture), guidelines as to how much more a supervisor should earn relative to a subordinate; a first level manager should earn relative to a supervisor, etc. Let's pretend for the sake of discussion that the national average is that a supervisor should earn 20% more than a subordinate and that a first level manager 20% more than a supervisor.

There exists in the workplace, also, a sense of grade (sometimes formalized in union contracts). An employer will pay two hourly jobs at different pay rates, typically based on the level of skill set. Using a manufacturing environment as an example – a maintenance person will typically earn twice as much as a janitor and a tool and die maker two and one-half times as much. The wage difference is based not only on the market worth of the position to the employer but also to the perception of relative worth held by those holding particular positions – say a perception of relative worth as held by a group of tool and die makers. Throughout my forty year career in manufacturing, I have had forty or fifty semi-skilled to highly skilled hourly workers remark to me as to the adequacy of their pay. Never has anyone said "my abilities are worth 20% of the CEO's abilities; it is always in effect – the janitors or the dockworker are paid <u>only</u> $4 per hour less than I am – I need to be paid more." This "worth" perception is often incorporated into union contracts and is very often (perhaps always) adopted in non-union shops. It's a cultural facet that the union leaders and the employers buy into this "worth" perception.

If the minimum wage is raised, based upon history, there will be pressure in all organizations to increase earnings for those in the managerial hierarchy (per our assumption above – 20% at each organizational level) and those in the grade hierarchy. Again, historically, these pressures have resulted in actual wage increases. There are two significant issues that arise:

- These increases promote inflation, and

- The workers who were working for or near minimum wage at the time of the directed minimum wage increase end up in time almost, <u>as measured in real wages</u>, right back where they started. <u>The cost of a loaf of bread, as measured in percentage of one hour paid, may increase by as much or more than the increase in minimum wage rates</u>. I have used the word "almost" because to the extent that they purchase less expensive foreign-made goods they do pick up some real income (purchasing power) advantage.

How does an attempt by the community to provide workers with a minimum fair pay possibly promote inflation? Most workers receive an annual increase that to a significant degree accommodates inflation. Does this fact not, in itself, promote inflation? The answer is "yes" to the latter question. However, the nature of the implementation of minimum wage adjustments is more likely to have an upward influence on inflation than the normal wage increases afforded most workers. The minimum wage adjustments in recent history have hit the economy with significant kicks. The 1978 adjustment was a 45% increase spread over a four (4) year period; 1990 was a 27% increase spread over a two (2) year period; 1994 was an 11% increase; and 2007 a 52% increase spread over a three (3) year period. These hefty kicks more likely draw attention to the increases than do the normal cost of living type adjustments most workers receive annually. Without the benefit of study and only the benefit of logical supposition, these kicks should be expected to have a noticeable influence on the IDE. This factor would lead to inflation above that which would otherwise be expected.

What would be the effect on the economy of incorporating an annual cost of living adjustment in the minimum wage guidelines? Almost nil, most other workers (non-minimum wage workers) already realize an annual pay increase that typically represents an adjustment for inflation. (NOTE: in the last twenty years this increase has been for slightly less than the increase in inflation.) Therefore, except for the initially directed minimum wage increases (the increase is implemented in steps); there would not likely be an effect on the inverse domino effect. The future minimal minimum wage increase would simply flow along with the increases realized by other workers.

Discussion points: What has been the experience at organizations where members of the discussion group work? Are there jobs where group members work that pay minimum wage? What has been the effect on non-minimum wage jobs when previous minimum wage increases have been imposed – (a) those that paid $2.00 over the minimum and (b) those that paid $8.00 over the minimum?

Pros and Cons of an Increase in Minimum Wage

Following are arguments of pros and cons from various papers published by economists and others who have an interest in and write on such matters. These are noted in the discussion as well as a list is provided in the Citations section of the guide. The pros and cons I have listed appear to be those with, at least, some substance. Some that appear in some papers are pure nonsense and are not discussed in this chapter.

I have listed the relevant pros and cons followed by a discussion of each.

PROS:

1. An increase in the minimum wage raises the standard of living for impoverished workers. **- see citations (Doyle).**
2. Additional income (as provided to minimum wage earners) would be spent by consumers and would ripple through the economy if overall budgets for salaries were increased under a gradual increase in the minimum wage. **- see citations (Doyle).**
3. Minimum wage increases put more money into the economy since low-income workers are more likely to spend their higher wages than are their higher paid counterparts who are more likely to save them. This increased demand for goods and services tends to stimulate the economy, which in turn, leads to job creation. **- see citations (Mejeur).**
4. Government expenses for social programs aimed at the poor would be reduced. This might result in slightly lower taxes for other Americans. **- see citations (Doyle).**
5. Slightly more revenue for the government would be generated from payroll taxes for social security. **- see citations (Doyle).**
6. Minimum wage increases shrink the gap between low-wage and higher-paid workers, lessening income inequality, both within individual businesses and in the larger economy. **- see citations (Mejeur).**
7. *Higher minimum wages reduce turnover* among low-wage workers. Lower turnover rates are a net positive for businesses, since high turnover increases training costs and results in lower productivity. **- see citations (Mejeur).**

CONS:

1. Possible layoffs to workers at employers with a fixed compensation budget *(NOTE: Non-profits, governments, etc.).* **- see citations (Doyle).**
2. It results in job losses. Labor costs are the largest share of the budget for many businesses. Mandatory increases in hourly wages mean that businesses will be forced to cut jobs or reduce hours to maintain their bottom line. That could mean no income or reduced income for low-wage workers. **- see citations (Mejeur).**
3. Employers might hire fewer workers in the entry level jobs needed to begin a career. **- see citations (Doyle).**
4. Provides an incentive for employers to invest in automated processes, technology, and machinery to increase productivity rather than human resources. **- see citations (Doyle).**
5. Prices might be increased to offset higher labor costs. **- see citations (Doyle)**
6. For small companies, already stressed owner/operators might take on more responsibility. **- see citations (Doyle).**
7. Wages for higher paid workers might be suppressed, and salary increases might be lower for those not impacted by a higher minimum wage. **- see citations (Doyle).**
8. There are better ways to address poverty, such as income tax credits for low-income workers or tax policies that encourage asset development and savings for low-income families. **- see citations (Mejeur).**
9. Increased labor costs result in lower profits for businesses. Lower profits mean that businesses have less money to put back into their enterprises for job creation and business expansion. **- see citations (Mejeur).**
10. Lower profits also mean less money is available for dividend distributions.

Discussion of Pros and Cons

PROS:

1. An increase in the minimum wage raises the standard of living for impoverished workers.

This is true only for a short time as inflation eventually wipes it out. It would probably be true permanently if, after a <u>fair jump</u> in the minimum wage, there was a cost of living adjustment included in the minimum wage guidelines. Historically, this has not been the case. Therefore, the real income (ability to buy a loaf of bread) of the minimum wage workers decreased as inflation drove prices up, but Congress did not adjust the guidelines. The extent, however, to which it is true, depends on what happens to the wages of others and subsequently to the rate of inflation. Should there be a compression of the organizational hierarchy wage differentiation or the job grade wage differentiation (as discussed above under Inverse Domino Effect) the immediate and long-term standard of living would be improved in terms relative to that of other workers.

The key word above is "relative." Under the umbrella of an economy that in the last seventeen years has, as a result of both globalization and greed, delivered a declining real wage for over 90% of Americans the actual standard of living may not improve – at least not much. - See citations.

2.   Additional income (as provided to minimum wage earners) would be spent by consumers and would ripple through the economy if overall budgets for salary were increased under a gradual increase in the minimum wage.

This statement aligns with the discussion in the section Inverse Domino Effect. Should salary and wage budgets overall be increased inflation will be increased. Although the amount of money rippling through the economy would increase the actual level of purchasing power would not; therefore, the trading of goods and services would not be increased. Therefore, there would not be any economic benefit ripple.

3.   Minimum wage increases put more money into the economy since low-income workers are more likely to spend their higher wages than are their higher paid counterparts who are more likely to save them. This increased demand for goods and services tends to stimulate the economy, which in turn, leads to job creation.

This could be not true, a very little bit true, or a whole lot true.

To the extent that resulting inflation offsets the increase – it will not be true; as there would not be an increase in real wages. Should an increase in real wages for the working poor be financed from wage compression at the lower levels of the organizational hierarchy or between labor grades it would be a very little bit true. This is because the minimum wage workers would spend their income faster than other workers and would have a lower propensity to save. In other words "active money" would become slightly more active. Should an increase in real wages come, to a large extent, from compression of CEO wages (possible on a case by case basis, but generally not possible[8]; but used here for the sake of example) and profits then the statement (#3,

---

[8] Why is compression of CEO wages not a possible way to finance an increase in minimum wage? Because although in the aggregate CEO's are significantly overpaid, this is not necessarily the case on a company by company basis. A CEO earning a disproportionately high wage may head up a company that has few or no minimum wage type employees. Conversely a CEO of a company that has an abundance of low wage jobs may not be overpaid.

PRO) would be a whole lot true. This is because the potential idle money would, to a large extent, be diverted from idle to active money.

However, should the number of jobs created push the unemployment level down past the targeted unemployment level set by the Federal Reserve (FR, Fed) (typically 5% to 6.5 %) the Fed would increase interest rates. This action would slow the economy and eliminate jobs.

4. Government expenses for social programs aimed at the poor would be reduced. This might result in slightly lower taxes for other Americans.

This would not be true to the extent that the resulting inflation offsets the increase in minimum wage. The community would need to increase the payments made through social programs, or the beneficiaries of the programs would suffer a significant reduction in real income/quality of life. Many of these individuals, from a moral perspective, are already living in an unsustainable situation as indicated by declining life expectancy. - **See citations.** Additionally, unless there was wage compression (a minimal wage increase, no wage increase, or a wage cut) to offset the minimum wage increase those organizations that operate on fixed budgets would need to cut back on employees. This would need to be done regardless of the effect on the quality of delivery of their goods and services. Therefore, there would be some increase in the level of unemployment as a result of the increase in the minimum wage guidelines. These factors, if anything, would drive up costs for the community and subsequently drive up needed tax collections. This needed increase in tax collections may be covered to a significant degree by inflation; as wages and profits go up, in inflated dollars, so does the level of income and sales taxes collected. However, to the extent this is not the case, such as with property taxes and license fees, there would need to be an increase in tax levies or an increase in government borrowing.

As with the subject of real wages, the subject of the effect of the minimum wage increase on unemployment would be hard to determine. This is because the forces of globalizing the economy and greed will continue to negatively impact employment levels at the same time as the minimum wage raise is transitioning to full implementation.

There is an assumption in this statement, also, that a reduction in government expenditures on a particular program might lead to a reduction in taxes. This may or may not happen.

5. Slightly more revenue for the government would be generated from payroll taxes for social security.

This is true in dollars and cents, but it will be offset by inflation should the community decide it is necessary to increase social security payment levels to accommodate the inflation.

6. Minimum wage increases shrink the gap between low-wage and higher-paid workers, lessening income inequality, both within individual businesses and in the larger economy.

This could be true if there were a way to make it happen. Historically, it has not been true. The gap would temporarily lessen but then expand as the Inverse Domino Effect set in and spurred inflation.

7. Higher minimum wages reduce turnover among low-wage workers. Lower turnover rates are a net positive for businesses, since high turnover increases training costs and results in lower productivity.

Most prudent business people have already weighed the issue of wage level versus the cost of turnover and have adjusted their wages paid appropriately. However, there are many non-prudent business people. These people have gone through their business life complaining about turnover, but not making the connection between wage levels and turnover incidents. To some degree, therefore, this statement would be true. However, this would be the case only until the Inverse Domino Effect took hold. After that, the wage differentiation would be back to where it started and so would the level of employee turnover. An inclusion of a COL adjustment in a minimum wage guideline would help make this statement truer than it would be otherwise. This is because the gap between wages paid for minimum wage jobs and other jobs would not, again, widen as it has in the past due to inflation.

Discussion point: Review the "pros" relating your discussion back to your "basis for weighing pros and cons."

Which bases aligns with which "pro" and which do not. How does your matching of the "pros" to your basis affect your thinking?

CONS:

1. Possible layoffs of workers at employers with a fixed compensation budget.

This is true as discussed, previously, under PROS statement number four (4). This could be counteracted by compression of the wage differentiation within such organizations. Historically, this has not happened.

2. It results in job losses. Labor costs are the largest share of the budget for many businesses. Mandatory increases in hourly wages mean that businesses will be forced to cut jobs or reduce hours to maintain their bottom line. That could mean no income or reduced income for low-wage workers.

This statement is taken from a different paper than that referenced in CON number one (1). Therefore, there is some overlap of the concept expressed.

Although in meeting after meeting, even without the issue of an increase in the minimum wage on the table, business management holds discussions on cutting jobs or reducing hours not just to maintain the company's bottom line but to improve it, it very rarely happens. Management sometimes dictates mandatory cuts, but over time most of the time, the headcount and the hours reappear at the old levels. Why? Because output, whether goods or services, is a function of time and motion. Those management teams that have the ability to effectively manage time and motion have already done so. The implementation of an increase in the minimum wage will not magically empower them to do a better job than the good job they have already done. Those management teams that have not effectively managed time and motion have not done so because they do not have the ability. The implementation of an increase in minimum wage will not somehow magically enable them to do what, in the past, they have been unable to do.

3. Employers might hire fewer workers in the entry level jobs needed to begin a career.

Employers will hire the number of workers they need to hire to get the job done. This will be determined by (as discussed in number two (2) above) their ability to manage time and motion. There may be a marginal area should wage compression, in fact, take place, an unlikely scenario, where an employer can hire an experienced person by paying only 5% more. If the employer perceives that the experience is worth paying 5% more, an experienced person will be hired in lieu of hiring an entry level person. This would be a rare occurrence. (How often has this happened where you work?)

4. Provides an incentive for employers to invest in automated processes, technology, and machinery to increase productivity rather than human resources.

While this may be true in some instances there are two things to be considered:

- Many minimum wage jobs, based upon current levels and affordability of technology, typically are not automatable, and

- The majority of automation projects undertaken, in today's world, do not produce the significant productivity results expected. The typically planned elimination of labor costs either does not materialize or offsetting costs pop up somewhere else in the production process. There were great improvements, related to automation, in both farming and manufacturing prior to 1990. Since that time the significant improvements have been in automation of administrative functions (word processing, production planning, transportation scheduling, etc.).

While there is constant discussion of productivity by economists, business leaders and members of government, the reality is, the time of significant jumps in improvement in output per labor hour realized at the current automation phase may be behind us. Automation in distribution and retailing (e.g. self-driving trucks and unattended convenience stores) may be on the verge of generating a new era of significant jumps in productivity, however, at this time, it is too early to tell. Additionally, vision systems should improve within the next five to ten years to the point that a lot of functions that are not now automated will, in fifteen years, be automated (there will be jobs for electrical engineers, systems analysts, and programmers – if American workers are employed to do the work).

For now, employers will hire the headcount needed to get the job done OR the job will not get done and the employer will suffer a loss of profit.

NOTE: There appears to be weakness in the reported measurement of US productivity assessment; whereby, the actual improvement is overstated. This relates primarily to the effect of importing parts and components, as well as, outsourcing of services to foreign countries on the apparent output per US applied labor hour. This subject will be addressed further in Discussion Guide 2.

5. Prices might be increased to offset higher labor costs.

Yes, this is true unless organizational hierarchy or grade wage compression is used to finance the increase in minimum wage. This has not been the case historically; therefore, price increases should be expected.

Initially, demand will fall as prices go up. However, to the degree that the Inverse Domino Effect is implemented (as historically has been the case) demand will come back (wage rate increases re-institute the level of demand). Therefore, initially, employers will cut headcount and then subsequently hire workers back.

If the minimum wage increase were to be financed through wage compression, there would not be any resulting drop overall in the economy nor would there be any drop overall in employment levels. However, there would be a change in the mix of demand. Some employers would need to lay people off and some employers would need to hire people.

6. For small companies, already stressed owner/operators might take on more responsibility.

This is in part true.

Some small business owners work very hard. The stress brought on by the need to reduce costs to offset the increase the minimum wage increase would be overburdening for these people.

This period would pass as other wages in the community adjusted upward and as market prices increased (inflation).

Most small businesses that employ workers that would be directly affected by the minimum wage increase would experience an initial drop in sales revenue due to passing through the wage as a price increase. This would not lead to a need for the owner to take on more responsibility, but it might lead to financial stress.

7. Wages for higher paid workers might be suppressed, and salary increases might be lower for those not impacted by a higher minimum wage.

It would be great if this were to happen. From a macroeconomic perspective, this is a Pro not a Con. This would be especially true with higher level civil service jobs and with the upper 10% of the jobs (by pay) in the private sector. It would be very desirable if the whole of the minimum wage increase could be financed by a reduction in CEO wages (again, not possible in reality – but, this would be an ideal solution from a macro-economic perspective).

8. There are better ways to address poverty, such as income tax credits for low-income workers or tax policies that encourage asset development and savings for low-income families.

In the section the issue of separating social programs from <u>Developing a Basis for Weighing Pros and Cons</u> the setting of a minimum wage was raised.

If you decided that, from your perspective, the minimum wage issue is about paying a fair day's pay for a fair day's work (a living wage), and not about addressing poverty then point number eight (8) is not up for discussion.

If you are operating in the intellectual mode of addressing poverty through any means, then you are justified in intertwining social program issues with the issue of minimum wage. In this case, point number eight (8) is up for discussion.

Tax credits might be a better way of addressing poverty. However, the credits would need to be paid for or other community programs would suffer. The way to pay for the tax credits is to raise taxes on other Americans. There are a select many in Congress who would not support the needed tax increase.

9. Increased labor costs result in lower profits for businesses. Lower profits mean that businesses have less money to put back into their enterprises for job creation and business expansion.

Increased labor costs historically have not resulted in lower profits for businesses. To verify this, you need simply to look at the profit history of US corporations. Why? Because price increases (inflation) offset labor cost increases. What does lower profits for many businesses is the reduction in real incomes (income adjusted for inflation) realized by 90% of the American citizenry over the last seventeen years. As real incomes are reduced people buy less from home builders, plumbers, hairdressers, automotive body shops, restaurants, dentists, veterinarians, etc., etc., etc.).

The concept that lower profits, resulting from minimum wage increases, means less money available to put back into businesses for job creation doesn't hold water. This is because the US businesses, as a whole, have never experienced lower profits because of labor cost increases (some individual businesses have had this experience; but from the perspective of the overall economy other businesses have experienced offsetting profit gains). Additionally, businesses now (2017) hold a humungous excess of funds (idle money). There is, therefore, plenty of money available for investment in job creation as is required to service demand.

This is contrary to what you might hear from Sally the owner of a beauty shop that employs six people or Jim, the owner of a machine shop that employs 200 people. What you are hearing are Sally's and Jim's stories. You are not hearing, from Sally and Jim, the story of business overall (again, review the profit history of American businesses). Additionally, most people are afraid of change. This is true for business people. What you are hearing, also from business people, is exasperation prompted by anxiety over the idea that there will be wage increases (change). Some of this is justified as there might be fallout (winners and losers) as some business owners adjust and others do not. This is capitalism at work. This is one of the benefits of capitalism and citizens should want this to happen. Further, this would be the case in either an unregulated capitalist system or a highly regulated capitalist system.

Discussion points: What thoughts, if any, do members of the discussion group have on the pros and cons discussed above? Include in your discussion of cons a comparison to your "basis for weighing pros and cons" (as you did above for pros). Do any members of the group have other pros or cons they think should be added to the lists?

More on What We Know

a. Per the University of California-Irvine economist, David Neumark, about half of the people working minimum-wage jobs come from households that are above the poverty line; 45 % of minimum wage earners lived in households earning $63,000 or more. **– see citations (Jacoby).**

These are working spouses (full and part-time), people holding second jobs, working children living at home, etc.

If you hold the opinion that working spouses, those who hold second jobs, children living at home, and other such workers should not be paid a fair day's pay (living wage) then, to you this is a very important point.

If you hold the opinion that all workers are entitled to a fair day's pay for a fair day's work, then this point may be a point of interest to you, but it holds no substantive meaning for you.

b. Per Martin Rafanan, co-chair of St Louis Workers' Rights – according to the Bureau of Labor Statistics, 48 percent of the jobs by the year 2020 will be low paying McDonald's type, low-wage jobs. **– see citations (Jacoby).**

I do not have a way to verify that this will or will not be the case. However, I can intuitively verify that this is a trend and that this trend, depending on your age, is economically unhealthy for you, your children and grandchildren.

It may become true that there will be far fewer jobs in our economy in the future that require a substantive level of skill to perform than there are today. This would logically mean much lower pay for many members of the community. Should this be the case, the <u>community must develop a way to pay workers for their time and effort that is</u> <u>different from the way workers are paid, today.</u> To say otherwise would be to say that lower paid workers (perhaps to be some of your children or grandchildren) are not entitled to marry and have children. This discussion, which I believe is necessary for US citizens to have, is beyond the scope of discussion on the subject of the current "minimum wage."

However, do not go down the road of thinking that a return of "manufacturing jobs" will turn the trend upward (prior to 1938 child labor in manufacturing was not uncommon – **how well do you think these children were paid**). Manufacturing jobs paid well because of the time in history in which the manufacturing sector in this country expanded. From the late 1800's through till the fall of the Soviet Union there was pressure on the extremely wealthy to treat American workers well. Two world wars took place during this time (America's wealthy needed American workers on their side); communism posed a threat to America's wealthy; and against both of these backdrops unionization of the workforce expanded. Additionally, the technology and the global economic cooperation did not exist as was needed to facilitate the move toward globalization of the US economy.

Had things been then as they are now, except for the highly skilled manufacturing jobs, manufacturing jobs would <u>not</u> have commanded a high wage. However, it would provide a more substantive economic base for the country if the manufacturing sector were to expand. There would, therefore, be a positive outcome should manufacturing jobs return.

NOTE: Some US states have begun rolling back restrictions related to child labor. What is your state doing?

    c. Dr. Joseph Sabia of San Diego State University found that over the past twenty years:
- Each 10% rise in the minimum wage has reduced employment for less educated young adults by 2.3%. **– see citations (Sabia).**

Dr. Sabia's numbers might be a little to the high side. Regardless the concept is logical. As real wages of high school degreed workers trend closer to the minimum wage, the probability that an employer will be able to hire a degreed worker for minimum wage or only for slightly more goes up.

Therefore, it is probable that jobs that would have previously gone to less educated workers will go to workers with a high school degree.

However, the problem is not a product of a raise in minimum wage but of:

- A national decline in those wages (real wages) that are above the minimum wage
- Possibly a decline in the job mix in that the relative number of those jobs, that in the old days, would have been paid a higher rate has decreased, and
- A regularly repetitive high level of unemployment.

d. Since it was established in 1938, the federal minimum wage has not kept pace with inflation. In real dollars, the peak value of the federal minimum wage was in 1968, when the wage was set at $1.60. That would be $10.56 in today's economy, well above the current $7.25. **- See citations (Majeur)**

This represents a 31% pay cut.

Adding to the difficulty for minimum wage earners is an upward trend in involuntary part-time work (workers take part-time work out of desperation because they are unable to find full-time work).

To get a good perspective on the substance of this situation each American voter should compile a personal budget assuming that working members of their household, who contribute to the household budget, are earning minimum wage. Make certain that the diet you assume (groceries you buy) provides adequate protein and vitamins as your body and brain will need to enable you to work effectively (not be fired) in your job or later in a better paying job should you land one. (See US Department of Agriculture Dietary Guidelines - **http://www.cnpp.usda.gov/DietaryGuidelines**.) Also, budget with and without food stamps.

Discussion points: What thoughts does your discussion group have on each of the points discussed in the section More on What We Know? *In particular, does the group have any ideas on how those in low paid jobs should be paid if the trend continues to be the creation of a proportionately high level of low paid jobs in the US economy? Without a change in the way these workers are paid – how will people manage to get married and have families? NOTE: if the current trend continues there will not be an adequate supply of higher paid jobs for low-wage workers to move up to.*

Recap of Key Points

What would be the key impacts on the US economy, based upon past experience, of the increase in minimum wage? The effect would be:

- Possibly incremental inflation. NOTE: As of December of 2014 it is possible that the country will experience deflation sometime in the near-long term. Deflation is considered by most economists and the Fed to be undesirable. An increase to minimum wage may provide an upward inflationary force that will to some degree diminish the degree of deflation, should deflation occur.

  Deflation is the economic situation in which prices of goods and services throughout the economy diminish. As a result, the citizenry waits longer to purchase a product than they would in an inflationary economy. This is because they know they will be able to buy the product cheaper later on. This delay in making purchases slows the economy and leads to recession or depression.

- An eventual near-long term adjustment to all wages and eventually a re-balancing of "real wages" (IDE) such that every worker was back in his/her original economic position; unless there is a COL (cost of living) adjustment provided for in the minimum wage guidelines. The minimum wage workers will experience some advantage in real income improvement if a COL adjustment is included in the guidelines.

- A near-long term minor loss of jobs directly tied to the wage increase. Since 2008 employers have been operating from the perspective of a recessionary economy (although the economy has turned) and jobs have been cut to the bone. Most employers would not have the option of eliminating jobs to offset the increase in wage for any minimum wage employees in their companies. However, some for-profit and non-profit employers who are unable to manage the adjustment (primarily through price or donation increases for the company's goods and services) will go out of business. Surviving business will eventually cover the loss of market supply and, as a result, hire the equivalent of the displaced workers. Additionally, local governments are typically funded to a significant degree on fixed income budgets (property taxes, license fees, etc.) that do not automatically reflect inflation (as do income taxes, sales taxes, etc.). To the extent that the wage increase causes a breach in these budgets, there will need to be a cut in public jobs, probably combined with a reduction in or slowing of public services, or a reduction in civil service wages. If taxes such as property taxes and license fees were adjusted for inflation, it would be possible for the governments to hire back most, possibly all, of those who were laid off.

- A lot of unhappy retirees on fixed income; this would cause some loss of jobs for workers who provide services to retirees.

- A lot of unhappy lenders who are tied into charges for loans (namely interest rates) that are not inflation adjusted. This would not result in job losses.

- Possibly an indirect loss of jobs as the Federal Reserve (Fed) makes adjustments to its targeted unemployment rate in an effort to maintain inflation at or near 2%. (The Federal Reserve, the community at large, and I need you and your friends to come up with a better way to control inflation.)

- Possibly restrained US Gross Domestic Product growth tied not directly to the minimum wage increase, but to the Federal Reserve's attempts to control inflation.

- A morally necessary adjustment to low wages that would improve the ability of low-income workers to take care of their families better than they now can. However, as inflation sets in they will end up back where they are now in real wages/purchasing power. This could be fixed by the introduction of a COL adjustment <u>after a significant base adjustment</u> is made.

One more point:

It is both possible and probable that the introduction of a valid cost of living adjustment would render increases to the minimum wage "inflation neutral." If the adjustment is tied to the prior year CPI (Consumer Price Index) or some other measure – the inflation adjustment would always be "playing catch-up," so-to-speak. This is a good subject for some sharp economists to study.

Questions:

Mark all you feel are reasonably correct.

1. What can be said regarding the practice of a community established minimum wage is:

    a. Possibly an indirect loss of jobs as the Federal Reserve (Fed) makes adjustments to its targeted unemployment rate in an effort to maintain inflation at or near 2%. (The Federal Reserve, the community at large, and

I need you and your friends to come up with a better way to control inflation.)

    b. Based on history, an increase in the minimum wage can be expected to help drive inflation.

    c. After the federal minimum wage setting practice was implemented in 1938, the result was:
- The US economy spiraled downward and has yet to recover
- Most American businesses filed bankruptcy, and
- The start-up of a fast food restaurant chain, McDonald's, that relied on workers paid at or near minimum wage, failed.

    d. A rising tide lifts all boats; likewise, a raise in the minimum wage has supported a rise in all wages. Unfortunately, as wages have gone up so has inflation. Therefore, real wages (the boats) do not go up. Also, in the US real wages are declining.

2. What is the effect of market forces on wages?

    a. Demand for labor will keep wages at or above that necessary to provide workers with a livable wage.

    b. The approximate average manufacturing wage (from various sources) in China is $2.67 - $3.50 per hour ($1.50 for garment workers) and in India $1.47 - $2.00 per hour. American workers do not wish to compete with this and should not compete with this.

    c. We now live in a global economy; it is, therefore, reasonable that business owners will bring immigrants from China and India to compete with Americans for low-wage jobs.

    d. The market should determine what an employee is paid; this includes the global market. If 25% of Americans need to work for only $2.00 per hour because of global competition – this is OK.

3. General statements related to the issue of a minimum wage increase:

    a. An advantage of "competition" is that it drives down consumer prices; a disadvantage is that it also drives down wages. The downward pressure could push wages to zero (technically speaking) unless the community establishes some level of control.

b.   Historically, the pay for non-minimum wage jobs over time increased in line with or to a greater degree than the increases dictated by established federal minimum wage standards.

c.   Inflation economically hurts people on fixed incomes (principally seniors) and lenders who have lent at fixed interest rates.

d.   Minimum wage workers who have a spouse who earns over $35,000 per year are not entitled to a fair day's pay (living wage) for a fair day's work.

e.   Those workers who, over their career due to personal limitations or circumstances, do not develop the ability to earn significantly more than the minimum wage should forego thoughts of marrying and having children. This is true even if at some time in the future 35% of the workforce falls into this category.

Discussion

Before reading more of the discussion guide, discuss with a friend, neighbor, fellow congregation member, civic club member, relative or someone you meet while waiting for a bus or train, the ramifications your answers to the question(s) might have on the US economy and society. Then write down your conclusions as formulated in answers to the above questions. Next, think about the ramifications that the answers will have on the quality of life for your family.

A whole list of questions could be compiled of the above type that you should be asking yourself based on the information covered in this chapter. You should be asking yourself these questions so that you can form substantive opinions before the next time you vote for a candidate who may or may not agree with the opinion(s) you have developed.

CHAPTER 10: CURRENT ISSUES - This Project Needs Your Support

Using the Keystone Pipeline project as an example of a project requiring public support or input (either direct vote or through representation) the chapter explores the process of analyzing the benefits and costs to be realized by the community.

Chapter 10 covers:

- General discussion
- Keystone XL Pipeline project
- Minimum voter analysis

General Discussion

Occasionally a project of some sort becomes a political issue. This ranges in character from local to national issues. Examples include the building of a new high school, prison, convention center, big box retail store, theme park, race track and many others. Often the proponents of said projects claim the projects will boost the economy and create jobs.

Does a project typically boost the economy (temporarily or permanently)? This depends on what economy you are speaking of. For instance, new federal prisons are needed to accommodate the growth of the US population. However, sometimes aging prisons are replaced, and the decision to replace the prison is related to the age of the prison and not to population growth. Let's pretend a new federal prison is to be built in Madison, Wisconsin.

What is the effect on the economy and jobs? If the prison is built to expand the prison system as needed to accommodate population growth, then the construction of the prison expands the economy and adds jobs. If, however, the prison is built to replace an old prison that is located in St. Paul, Minnesota the national economy expands temporarily, temporary construction jobs are added, but no permanent jobs are added. In fact, since new prisons are designed to be managerially more efficient than old prisons, it is probable that jobs are lost. Further, from the perspective of St. Paul, the local economy shrinks, and jobs are lost. From the perspective of Madison, the local economy expands and jobs are added.

NOTE: Although construction jobs typically are deemed to be temporary, they are better described as intermittent. This will be addressed further in Discussion Guide 2. However, in short, the conversion labor applied to a construction project provides an incremental rise for the economy, which in turn leads to the need for additional construction. (Think about all of the construction companies that have existed for fifty or more years – these have not been temporary in character. Construction projects are temporary, but the construction industry is permanent; although construction activity is highly variable and intermittent.)

Generally, if costs are reduced (product cost, transportation cost, or otherwise) competitive pressures eventually drive down product price. This enables the consumers to spend less on a given quantity of a product. They can then buy more of the same product than previously or buy more of other products.

For instance, if the cost of transporting strawberries was reduced and subsequently the price of strawberries was reduced, the consumer would have more pocket change. He/she could then afford to buy more strawberries or bananas. If the consumer spent all of this additional pocket change on bananas, as opposed to strawberries or placing it in a savings account, some workers employed in transporting strawberries would be laid off and additional workers would be hired for growing, picking, packing and transporting bananas. This would equate to approximately the same number of workers who lost their jobs transporting strawberries. Unfortunately, the vast majority of growing and picking jobs would be located outside of the US. The economy would not have expanded, and the net effect in the job market may be a slight loss of jobs (a growth in banana packing and transportation jobs; but the money for growing and picking would go out of the country to banana producing countries). However, the consumer would enjoy an improved standard of living; as he/she could still buy the same quantity of strawberries, but also he/she could buy more bananas than previously.

Under our strawberry and banana scenario, <u>the cost savings were passed through to the consumer</u>. This is an important aspect for consideration on any cost reduction project. It is important because it converts a situation from one that leads to a direct loss of jobs to one that possibly has minimal negative job impact, is job neutral, or if the reduced cost leads to an increase in exports, adds jobs. <u>Without this pass-through there is, more often than not, a loss of jobs</u>. This is true as long as the country has an excess of idle money.

This brings us to the project selected as an example, the Keystone XL Pipeline project.

Keystone XL Pipeline Project

The Keystone XL Pipeline (Phase 4) has been approved at the federal level. Few investment projects make the news as has this one. It is one of a few projects that US citizens overall have become aware of (maybe the only one for some citizens). Therefore, it is used herein as an example.

Is the Keystone XL Pipeline project good for the US economy and does it or does it not create jobs for Americans? To attempt to answer these questions, let's start at the beginning.

Why do companies invest? Primarily to improve profits.

The key means of improving profits are:

- Introducing new products
- Increasing demand for current products, and
- Reducing costs.

The first two categories may increase the number of jobs in the macroeconomy and the third may: (a) eliminate jobs from the economy, (b) be job neutral, or (c) add jobs.

Pipelines are built for the purpose of reducing transportation costs. They compete with truck, barge, and rail transportation options.

Some representative analytical considerations we need to look at are:

- Typically the more expensive an option the greater is the level of labor required to exercise the option. (Recall in Chapter 3, it took George more man hours to dig coal than to pump the oil needed to heat a house; therefore, it was more expensive to mine coal than oil.) A greater level of required labor equates to a higher level of jobs than does a lower level of required labor.

- Conversely, the less expensive (fewer man-hours worked / therefore, fewer jobs) an option the more competitive a country is in global markets. In some cases, an improved competitive global position increases international demand and leads to an increase in the number of jobs.

- As the discussion related to strawberries and bananas demonstrated, the combination of lower cost and competition often result in a lower price for a product. This makes consumers happy. Additionally, the lower price paid for product "A" leaves more money in consumers' pockets to spend on products "B,

C, K, L, etc." This results in a higher level of jobs related to providing the community with products "B, C, K, L, etc." If the lowered costs are passed through to lower consumer prices than a cost reduction project may become job neutral; or better yet add jobs to the economy via increased exports. <u>However, to what degree does a lower transportation cost for oil work its way through to lower prices for American consumers?</u>

Using the pipeline option versus the railroad option as an example (the railroad option is easier to analyze than the truck and barge options), in brief, there is labor required for:

- Manufacturing the steel and other materials that goes into making:

  a. Pipe, connectors, control equipment and other components in a pipeline system
  b. Train engines, tank cars, rails, railroad ties, signals and other components required for a railroad system.

- Manufacturing the product requires:

  a. Relatively little labor for the pipe and other components of a pipeline
  b. A significant level (much greater than that of a pipeline) for the combination of train engines, tank cars, rails, railroad ties, signals, and other components of a railway system.

- Installing the product:

  a. Laying a pipeline and building control stations requires a lot of labor
  b. Laying a railroad track, including all of the mechanics (train signals, fueling stations, crossing signals, etc.) requires a lot of labor. However, is there currently adequate track in place to handle the additional capacity requirements?

- Maintenance of the system:

  a. Maintaining a pipeline system is costly; therefore, the maintenance requirements create jobs
  b. Maintaining a railroad system is costly; therefore, the maintenance requirements create jobs.

The Keystone XL (Export Limited) Pipeline Phase 4 is the fifth phase of a five-phase project. Phases 1-3b are complete. Phase 4 is an inland project designed to facilitate moving increased quantities of Canadian oil and some US oil through the phases 2 and

3a pipelines that deliver from inland starting at Steele City, Nebraska to refineries in Houston, Texas (a port city) (Wikipedia).

The Keystone XL Pipeline is a project aimed at both increasing demand for Canadian oil and for reducing the cost of transporting any oil that is transported through the pipeline. The benefit of the increase in demand will be realized by Canadian companies while the cost reduction will be realized by both Canadian and American companies.

- From a US point of view, the Keystone XL (Export Limited) Pipeline project is primarily a cost reduction project – pitting the costs of transporting by railway (barge and truck, also) against the costs of transporting via pipeline. The pipeline will provide construction jobs, but <u>it will eliminate incremental capacity ramp up related jobs</u> for building railway tank cars, train engines, signals, etc. and long-term current and potential railway related jobs.

- There is a very large portion of the oil from this project slated for shipment overseas (primarily China). Additionally, oil is a commodity. The price of oil is to a large extent determined by world demand, not US demand. Therefore, there may or may not be a reduction in energy costs (prices that fall below that which they would have fallen anyway, or that increase less than they would have increased anyway) (probably not) here in the US as a result of completing the pipeline.

- The Enbridge Northern Gateway Project was approved in June of 2014 and then rejected in June of 2016 by the Federal Court of Appeal, to transport Canadian crude oil to Canada's west coast. The future of this pipeline is unclear; but, two other Canadian pipelines have been approved (I did not research these). The current plan is for this oil to be refined in China. How this will relate to shipments through Houston, Texas is unclear. However, for now, TransCanada is continuing to push the Keystone XL pipeline. Should the volume of oil planned to pass through Houston be reduced or eliminated, the result will be:

  a. An increase in Canadian pipeline-related jobs and a decrease in Canadian railway jobs, and
  b. A loss of both current and potential pipeline and/or railroad jobs, refining jobs, and shipping jobs in the US.

As of November 2017, the option of transporting the oil to and out of a port in western Canada has not been discussed to a significant extent in the US media. TransCanada, the company developing the Keystone XL extension, has been working on obtaining approval for the US segment of the Keystone XL Pipeline system since 2008, if a west coast option is viable for TransCanada's purposes – most likely – they would have taken it by now.

- Unlike the situation in the strawberry and banana discussion – there will not be additional handling or packing or processing or other types of jobs created. Why? <u>The crude oil will arrive at the Texas refineries either way; by pipeline or rail</u>. Therefore, to the degree that non-transportation (i.e., refining related jobs) jobs are added to the economy, most likely <u>they will be added with or without the pipeline</u>.

There are more obscure, but very real, economic concerns related to transportation safety. These concerns include the negative economic impact of oil spills. Keeping with the comparison of pipeline to railway tank car:

- Tank car derailments and fires have increased as the volume of oil transported has increased. The cost of one explosion/fire in Canada is estimated to be over a $1 billion.

- Pipeline leaks are decreasing due to improvements in design, but some portions of the Keystone XL pipeline flow through earthquake-prone areas of America. A major pipeline break would require significant costs for repair and cleanup. Additionally, there may be major negative economic effects on agriculture and water supplies.

It is very difficult, and I suspect impossible, to find direct macroeconomic justification for the pipeline as related to US jobs. It should, through land leases and service contracts, bring some economic benefit to the country. Whether or not direct job losses (barge, trucking and railway related) versus the economic benefits of land leases and service contracts produces a net economic benefit (if the land lease monies are spent, versus saved, then some indirect jobs will be provided by the project and the service contracts will provide direct jobs) is not possible to assess without completing a very large analysis. However, <u>it is not likely the case</u>.

This discussion does not provide adequate information upon which a citizen can base an economic decision. However, to the date of this discussion paper, no articles or abstracts presenting a substantive economic analysis assessing the project had been identified by this author.

Minimum Voter Analysis

This discussion does, however, provide the reader with information and boundaries as to what might and might not be the case. In doing so, it provides an example of the minimum review that any voter should make of any project that requires some type of public support or approval prior to implementation.

Should a project be proposed for your neighborhood, town, city, state or country that requires public support (new school, convention center, new city hall, big-box store, pipeline, railroad expansion, etc.) the minimum analysis you should complete should mirror that in the Keystone example above. You will probably find it beneficial to join up with others to undertake such an analysis.

If voter approval on a project is not required – but, there is a public hearing on the project, you need to be prepared to join the conversation with the right questions.

Discussion points: What project(s) has been completed in the last twenty-five years in your state or locale that required the voters to understand what was or was not the possible costs and outcomes of the project(s)? What was the employment outcome – for the local economy; the state economy; and the US economy? Are there any projects expected in the near future?

If your discussion group has any members who have worked in manufacturing – what is their opinion of which approach, pipeline or railroad, would create the greatest number of manufacturing jobs (pipeline, valves, controls, etc. vs. railroad ties and tracks, signals, engines, oil cars, etc.)?

If your group has any members who have worked in construction – what is their opinion of which approach, pipeline or railroad, would create the greatest number of construction jobs?

How many individuals in your group do you think completed at least a basic analysis on the Keystone XL Pipeline project?

Questions:

Mark all answers that are reasonably correct.

1. Some reasons business people invest in projects to:

    a. Increase operating costs

    b. Decrease operating costs

    c. Because the sun will shine on their project

    d. Just because.

2. Some non-economic considerations:

   a. If trucks are used to transport the oil from Canada to Texas, the highways in that corridor will become very traffic congested. I do not live in that corridor, therefore, I am ok with using trucks versus a pipeline.

   b. If trains are used to transport the oil from Canada to Texas, the people in that corridor will need to wait more frequently and longer at railroad track crossings than will be the case with the pipeline option. I do not live in that corridor, therefore, I am ok with the inconvenience that would be incurred at railroad crossings.

   c. A broken pipeline might pollute (underground oil spill like the BP spill in the Gulf of Mexico) the water supply for millions of people. I believe this to be a much greater risk both to health and to financial stability (peoples' home and property values would drop radically and not recover in value for many years) than that risk caused by train derailments (NOTE: the cost of a derailment in Canada was estimated to exceed $1 billion).

   d. Truck transportation is probably the safest in terms of ground pollution – but, the air pollution caused by the trucks versus railroad or pipeline would be significant.

CHAPTER 11: CURRENT ISSUES - National Debt

Chapter 11 covers:

- General discussion
- Key definitions of economic activity measurement
- Three scenarios reviewing federal deficits and surpluses:
  - The average tax rate collected is 20% of GDP and the government expenditures equal the government revenue
  - The average tax rate collected is 20% of GDP and the government spends at a rate that is equal to 25% of GDP
  - The average tax rate collected is 25% of GDP and the government spends at a rate that is equal to 20% of GDP. In other words, the government expenditures are less than revenue
- When does the US pay-down the national debt?
- Historically, the government has not paid down debt.

General Discussion

- Here's the budget math. Between 1946 and 1974, debt-to-GDP fell from 121 to 32 percent, even though the government only ran surpluses in eight of those years (and the surpluses were generally much smaller than the deficits). That's because nominal GDP -- just the cash size of the economy -- grew much faster than debt did. As **Greg Ip** of *The Economist* points out, fast nominal GDP growth, and the easy monetary policy that requires, is the only way governments have ever successfully reduced debt ratios in the past. Austerity alone will fail. (See Europe).
[http://www.theatlantic.com/business/archive/2013/02/why-the-us-government-never-ever-has-to-pay-back-all-its-debt/272747/; MATTHEW O'BRIEN, FEB 1, 2013.]

In this study guide, we will discuss in simple terms some basics of the character of the national debt. The chapter explores what will and what will not work as means to reduce the national debt.

To fully follow the detail of discussions in Congress or presented via the news media you will need an education in the various standards of measure used to track the wide variety of economic activities; including the national deficit, national debt, and the many other words and phrases, as well. There are quick study guides on economics that deal with these matters available at many bookstores and libraries. After you understand the basics as presented herein, it will be easier for you to follow the discussions in these guides. Based upon what is covered herein, however, you will have the understanding a voter needs to follow the general direction and meaning of discussions on the subject of national debt.

Key Definitions of Economic Activity Measurement

National Deficit -

The annual amount by which government expenditures (spending) exceed government revenue (primarily taxes collected) in a given fiscal year (12 months ending September). This almost always refers to the federal deficit only, but on rare occasions, it is used to mean the total of all government deficits: federal, state and local.

National Surplus –

The annual amount by which government revenue exceeds government expenditures in a given fiscal year. This almost always refers to the Federal Surplus only, but on rare occasions, it is used to mean the total of all government surpluses: federal, state and local.

National Debt-

The running total of all of the government's deficits and surpluses from the first day the government was formed if the net is a negative value. In even simpler terms, it is what the government owes in borrowed funds at any given moment. This can refer to the Federal National Debt only, but on rare occasions it is used to mean the total of all government debt: federal, state and local. **- See citations.**

Gross Domestic Product (GDP) –

The total value of the domestic output of all goods and services (products) for a period under discussion: usually a particular calendar year, the federal government's fiscal year, ending September 30th, or a 12 month period of a time other than a calendar year.

Gross Domestic Income (GDI) –

An infrequently quoted figure that is similar to GDP, but GDI is a closer approximation to that which people and businesses refer to as income than is GDP.

Scenarios – Federal Deficit and Surplus

Let's examine several scenarios that relate to the creation of a federal deficit or surplus in the economy. We will not examine the state and local aspects; however, to some degree, they are the same. Also for the purpose of simplicity, we will assume that the only source of federal government revenue is an income tax (no gas tax, import tariffs, communications license fees, etc.). NOTE: many local government activities are financed by fixed types of taxes such as license fees and property taxes.

Scenario A:

In this scenario, the average tax rate collected is 20% of GDP and the government expenditures equal the government revenue.

There is not a deficit or a surplus and there is no increase or decrease in the federal debt.

Scenario B:

In this scenario, the average tax rate collected is 20% of GDP and the government spends at a rate that is equal to 25% of GDP. In other words, the government expenditures exceed the government revenue.

There will be a deficit created.

If the total Gross Domestic Product were $10 trillion, in simplistic terms, the government would have collected approximately 20% or $2.0 trillion and would have spent approximately 25% or $2.5 trillion. The government revenues would have had an approximate shortfall of $500 billion (deficit), and the government would need to borrow this $500 billion. Historically, this borrowing has been accomplished through the selling of government bonds and borrowing from the Social Security Trust and Federal Employees Retirement System (federal employees' pension funds).

The net cumulative total of all government surpluses and deficits equals the national debt. Therefore, the national debt would have increased by $500 billion.

This approach can improve the economy if the community is not overloaded with debt. There is considerable disagreement amongst economists on the determination of when a community is overloaded with debt. In relative terms Japan has twice the national debt as the United States, yet its economy has relied for many years on constantly increasing debt.

Due to a reduction in income tax rates (primarily favoring those with potential excess idle money – thereby, leading to an increase in economically idle money at the expense of active money) combined with a recession magnified by financial corruption (that has not been adequately fixed by Congress, as of December 2017 and, therefore to some degree continues today and will resurface in full bloom. at a point in the future), a change in the demographic makeup, and offshore sourcing of products, the forecast for the US is a continuation of deficits and therefore increasing debt. At some point, the community will not be able to meet its debt obligations if a significant portion were to be called (cashed out). But perhaps more importantly, the ensuing high level of interest charges that go with a high level of debt will create an overly burdensome drag on the economy.

Scenario C:

The logic of the discussion for Scenario C is a little difficult to follow. However, it is necessary only that the reader grasps the general concepts. You can leave the details to economists to deal with. Further, the magnitude of the effect of slight changes in the level of active versus idle money in the economy may not seem worthy of mention. However, a slight change can generate a ½ percent change in GDP, which is worth billions of dollars to the economy and to paychecks.

In this scenario, the average tax rate collected is 25% of GDP and the government spends at a rate that is equal to 20% of GDP. In other words, the government expenditures are less than revenue.

If the total Gross Domestic Product were $10 trillion, the government would have collected 25% or $2.5 trillion and would have spent 20% or $2.0 trillion. The government would have collected approximately $500 billion over (surplus) what it needed for expenditures. This unneeded money could be used to pay down the national debt.

At first, this sounds good. Are we not all happy when we make our last car payment and even happier when we make our last house payment?

Remember that **macroeconomies do not work the same as household and individual business economies.** Additionally, the federal government budget and the US macroeconomy work in tandem. We should not be happy should this happen. In fact, we should be unhappy. Why, because a pay-down of the debt is more likely to divert active money to idle money versus maintaining a neutral status or increasing active money. Further, a relative increase in idle money will lead to a slowdown in the economy that will lead to an increase in unemployment.

What happens when you are finished paying off your car or house? The answer is you now have more money to spend on other things, pay-down other debts, or save. Most people spend this money and some save it. To the degree you spend the money you help bolster the economy. To the degree you save your new found money you may or may not help bolster the economy. Regardless, that which you place into savings will have less of a positive effect on the economy than that which you spend (active versus idle money).

So what does all of this mean?

NOTE: Keep in mind that the reader needs only to grasp the concepts; not dwell on the details – much the same as would be the case, for most readers, when reading a magazine article.

Most likely when you paid off your debt <u>your income remained the same</u>; therefore, you had more money available for spending or saving. What happens when a macro-economy's government pays down government debt? When a macroeconomy's government pays down debt <u>the government experiences a drop in potential income</u> (taxes collected) and the private sector experiences a drop in revenue. Why, because a pay-down of the debt diverts active money (the government's surplus) to idle money versus maintaining a neutral status or increasing active money. The money received by the debt holders will most likely be allocated to idle money type financial instruments (savings accounts, certificates of deposit, traded corporate bonds, traded corporate stocks, etc.). Basically, the money allocated to idle money type of financial instruments is, from a practical perspective, temporarily taken out of circulation.

The level of slowdown in the economy will depend upon the amount of idle money already in the economy before the pay-down of the government debt and the level of substantive demand in the private sector for borrowing money. Recall that idle money (savings) deposited with lending institutions, to a great degree, is lent out to others and put back into circulation – thereby, becoming active money (but this takes time and slows the rate of money circulation).

The debt pay-down to a debt holder is completed as a lump sum and the interest payments avoided would have been spread out over time. Therefore, in the long run, the debt pay-down results in a lower cumulative cash outlay for interest payments; the principal of the debt is paid under any option (either paid down from surplus or with new debt). Interest payments take away from the level of money to spend. Money spent is active money. Interest payments received by the holder tend to go, at least to some degree, into idle money types of alternatives. Therefore, it is preferable that the government spends money on goods and services versus on debt interest. Additionally, should interest rates seek high levels (7-8-9%) and the debt levels continue to grow the interest payments due will overwhelm the government and the taxpayers. Would it be wiser for the government to spend the surplus (thereby, increasing private sector revenue and profits) or pass the surplus through to the taxpayers as a refund (again, increasing private sector revenue and profits) as opposed to paying down debt? Either could be possible; it depends. This chapter, however, addresses debt not stimulating the economy. Additionally, the analysis required to make this determination is complex and the outcome of the analysis would be different at different periods in time. For instance, you might not want the government to pass the surplus through to the taxpayers during a period of high inflation.

Non-substantive borrowing demand may be accommodated (return to bad loans) if lenders accumulate too much in deposits as a result of the pay-down of government debt. In other words, lenders will be tempted to make bad loans. They were not only tempted prior to 2008; they did make bad loans. This practice contributed to the financial crises of 2008/2009. However, the practice did boost the economy temporarily prior to the crash; thereby, initially offsetting the slowdown in the economy that would have occurred due to the pay-down of the debt (end of Clinton's term). You bailed the lenders out and you did not send anyone to jail; therefore, they may not have learned anything from the crises (apparently, you did not learn anything either). Therefore, if excess idle money becomes too abundant it is reasonable to expect a repeat of the 2008/2009 crises.

To recap (it should be expected that) when the government pays down debt the economy slows down and unemployment goes up in the near term. But, the avoidance of interest payments over time accelerates the economy and lowers unemployment. These factors need to be weighed by the government in the process of deciding whether or not to apply any surpluses (a rare occurrence) to the debt.

There is, therefore, a very big difference between the outcomes of you paying down your debts and the government paying down its debts.

Discussion points: What is the difference between your payoff of the loan on your automobile and the government's payoff of debt it owes? If you pay off your debt do you have more money to either spend on other things or save? If the government pays off its debt does it have more money to spend on other things or save – short-term effect and long-term effect? If the government had a surplus during a period of high inflation would you prefer that the surplus be refunded to taxpayers or used to pay down debt?

When Does the US Pay-down the National Debt?

First of all, the government has not often paid down the debt. Paying down the debt requires that the government generates a surplus with which to pay-down the debt. The federal government has run a surplus only in twelve years since WWII, 1946.

It appears that the national debt is paid down only during periods of irrational exuberance. Not the stock market irrational exuberance addressed in 2001 by Greenspan, Fed Chairman 1987-2006; but a buyer (both personal and business) state of irrational buying exuberance. It appears that periods of irrational buying exuberance and irrational stock market exuberance are to a degree related. It is periods of irrational buying exuberance that generate annual government surpluses. I stated "appears" as I do not have the staff and other resources needed to properly research the subject and have not found anything that addresses the issue.

Think about this – is it reasonable for the price of having a house built, on a national basis, to spiral upwards by more than the rate of inflation. No! Yet, there have been many times in history when, on a national basis, this has happened. There can be significant geographical shifts in the population causing a run-up in prices (both the house and the lot it sits on[9]) in this area or that (Dallas, Atlanta); but there should be offsetting decreases in house and lot prices in the locations from which those relocating came (Detroit, Allentown). Of course, as in late 2008, there have been just as many times that the housing market has crashed. Yes, to a significant degree the rise in home prices just prior to 2008 was a product of financial corruption; but the run-up was in play before that corruption was in full swing. Additionally, the unsubstantiated rise and subsequent crash have happened several times before, during our country's history, when corruption was not a factor (note: from the early 1900's through to the Great Depression corruption was a factor).

There are periods in which the population simply buys at irrational rates and in irrational ways. This is greatly facilitated by the ability to run up loan balances – credit cards, second mortgages, etc. During these periods the supply side of the economy recognizes income from labor on the demand side which has not, yet, been worked.

From a macroeconomic standpoint, the economic benefits of future labor, to be worked, are realized today; in essence pulling these economic benefits away from future periods (one month, one year, five years, etc.) and realizing the trading power of these today. This causes a disproportionate run-up in incomes for many businesses and many

---

[9] On a national basis the growth in population through both births and immigration will lead to increases in lot prices different than normal inflation; but, tied to population increase.

individual citizens. Taxes are paid on this run up at a level that is disproportionate to that which would represent a healthy balance of demand and supply should irrational buyer exuberance not be a factor. The taxes paid on the run-up provide the monies needed to pay-down the national debt. However, guess what, eventually the bubble bursts and there is an economic recession, and the national debt grows again.

Yes, the general population is always buying on credit; but, during periods of irrational exuberance the degree of borrowing increases significantly.

Historically, Government Has Not Paid Down Debt

Since the end of WWII the federal government has had only 12 years of surpluses. These are the only years in which the debt has been paid down (reduced, not eliminated).

Spending exceeded revenues (taxes collected) in all of the other years.

Since the beginning of the country (George Washington till now), on an annual basis, the federal government has carried a debt except for 1835. President Jackson paid off the debt for one year – this facilitated the onset of a significant recession and resulted in a greater debt load today than would be the case otherwise.

Is this good or is this bad?

Let's pretend that you earn $30,000 per year and your total debt, excluding payments on your home (which is in lieu of rent) is $3,000. A $3,000 debt is not a great burden for you to carry. Now let's pretend that you owe a debt of $32,000. A $32,000 debt is a much greater burden for you to carry than a $3,000 debt. Why is $32,000 a greater burden? Because you are paying out 11 times the interest and principal payments on a $32,000 debt as you are paying on a $3,000. If the simple interest rate at which you borrow is 7%, on $3,000 your interest payment is approximately $210 per year, whereas on $32,000 it is approximately $2,240 per year. You could have bought a lot of groceries or provided a bigger retirement nest egg with the $2,240. However, since you did choose to incur the debt you need to pay interest instead of buying the extra groceries or providing a bigger retirement nest egg.

The government pays interest on its debt. If the government did not carry debt, it could use this money to buy more groceries (whereby US soldiers would no longer complain about the mess hall food), improve the country's education system, improve upon the country's highways, etc.

It does not matter if the money the government spends goes into the economy as expenditures for goods and services or as interest payments, it helps drive the economy. However, the money spent for goods and services creates more downstream active money than does the money spent on interest payments. Interest payments, in relative terms, create a drag on the economy. Therefore, no debt or little debt is preferable to a large debt. NOTE: US government debt plays a role in the management of the money system – this subject will be addressed in Discussion Guide 2.

What about the pay-down of the debt principal? The pay-down of the debt itself has infrequently happened and then only to an insignificant level. An advanced analysis comparing the national economic outcome of paying down the debt versus carrying the debt principal would be interesting to see, although it may be purely an academic exercise. However, the key way to reduce the interest payments on the debt is to reduce the principal. Therefore, a reduction in the principal owed may be a good thing if it were doable.

Historically, it has not been doable. **This is because it is not doable**. The reason for this is discussed in Chapter 2 (see the discussion on the tandem relationship between government expenditures and government revenues). However, holding the debt to a low level relative to the Gross Domestic Product has been doable and is, at times (possibly at all times), desirable.

President Jackson's temporary payoff of the debt was due to a short-lived timing variance that was easier to implement when tariffs versus income taxes were the government's major revenue source. Additionally, he sold off government lands (an absolute, not a relative, source of revenue). Today, a surtax on idle money would duplicate an absolute source of revenue and therefore allow for a partial pay-down of the debt.

The Gross Domestic Product increases as a result of population growth, improvements in productivity, and inflation. There is a possibility that increased specialization will create an increase in GDP. This is true, more so, in countries which lag in economic development than in countries with advanced economies.

Let's pretend that your household income jumped from $30,000 per year to $60,000 per year. The $32,000 debt you are carrying would now be less of a burden for you. If later in life your income grew to $90,000 the $32,000 of debt would be even less of a burden for you. But, when your income increased from $30,000 per year to $60,000 per year you increased your debt (you shouldn't have, but you did) to $40,000 and when your income increased further to $90,000 you increased your debt to $50,000.

At an income of $60,000 the debt burden of $40,000 is less of a burden for you than was a debt of $32,000 when your income was $30,000. At an income of $90,000 a debt burden of $50,000 is far less of a burden for you than was a debt of $32,000 when your income was $30,000.

Recalling that everything in economics is relative; let's see how this looks when viewed as the percentage of debt to income:

YOUR DEBT VERSUS
YOUR INCOME

	YOUR DEBT	YOUR INCOME	DEBT AS PERCENT OF INCOME
STARTING INCOME	$ 32,000	$ 30,000	107 %
1st INCREASE	$ 40,000	$ 60,000	67 %
2nd INCREASE	$ 50,000	$ 90,000	56 %

A $32,000 debt as compared to a $30,000 income is 107% of income; whereas, a $50,000 debt as compared to a $90,000 income is only 56% of income (still a large debt to carry – but much easier to carry than $32,000 on an income of $30,000).

Even if in real dollars your income had not increased – as in the total income increase was due only to inflation – the burden is less.

How much of an issue might inflation be? If in 1979 you were earning $10,000 and you stayed in the same job at the same grade and you received annual pay increases equal to inflation your pay in 2016 would have been $36,384. Your real income (purchasing power) would be the same in 2016 as it was in 1979; although in "nominal (inflated)" dollars your earnings had more than tripled. How does this relate to the assumed $30,000 of starting income above? Just as the $10,000 grew due only to inflation – your $30,000 would have grown to $109,153. If you held your debt at $32,000, your debt to income relationship would have improved significantly. Even though your debt increased from $32,000 to $50,000, your debt to income percentage relationship would, still, have improved significantly.

Discussion points: What would you do if your income doubled – A) pay cash for everything you purchased; B) borrow more money (bank, credit card, etc.) and then pay the interest and principal owed over time; C) pay-down any loan balances you have, then pay cash for all new purchases; D) increase your tithe to your religious organization; E) do something else with the money or F) a combination of _____ and _____ and _____? What are the advantages and disadvantages you would consider before making your decision as to which way to go? Why might your decisions for your household differ from those you might make if you were making decisions relative to the income, expenditures, and debts of the US government?

With this background, let's address the national debt.

The debt after WWII was **$271** billion and the 1946 Gross Domestic Product (GDP) (approximate national income) was **$222** billion. The debt equaled **121%** of the country's Gross Domestic Product. The debt as a percentage of GDP fell to a low of **32%** in 1974. In 1974 the debt was **$483** billion versus a GDP of $1,500 billion. As you can see the debt in 1974, **$483** billion, is greater as an absolute number than the debt in 1946, **$271** billion. But as a percentage of GDP, the debt in 1974 is much lower than the debt in 1946, **121%** versus **32%**. Following are some highlights of the federal debt and GDP:

FEDERAL DEBT AS A PERCENTAGE
OF GROSS DOMESTIC PRODUCT
(IN $billions)

	FEDERAL DEBT	GDP	DEBT AS PERCENT OF GDP
1946	$ 271	$ 222	121 %
1974	$ 483	$ 1,500	32 %
2000	$ 5,629	$ 9,952	56 %
2017 est	$ 20,245	$ 19,300	105 %

At the beginning of this chapter is an excerpt from an article written by Matthew O'Brien and published in *The Atlantic*. Matthew uses two phrases that require a little clarification:

a. "Just the cash size" – this refers to the increase in the GDP in the actual dollar value of the economy as measured <u>in the dollar value of the day</u>. This is the GDP as measured in 1950 and reported in 1950 dollars, as measured in 1999 and reported in 1999 dollars, as measured in 2015 and reported in 2015 dollars, etc. "Just the cash size" is determined by a combination of inflation (see "Nominal GDP" in "b" below), population growth, and, possibly, productivity improvement.

b. "Nominal GDP" – this refers to the GDP measure without adjustment for inflation, as in "just the cash size." It is the change in the dollar value of the GDP including the year to year inflation. This is as opposed to "real" dollars or "constant" dollars which represent an expression of purchasing power of a dollar as adjusted for inflation. Another term used for "nominal" is "current." The growth in GDP not attributable to inflation is primarily attributable to population growth and, possibly, productivity improvement. Technically speaking – the difference between Nominal GDP and real GDP is inflation. "Just the cash size" and Nominal GDP refer to the same thing.

Matthew makes the point that the growth in nominal GDP, in relative terms, was far greater than the growth in the federal debt. The debt grew in all years but eight, in which there were surpluses; yet, the debt dropped from a high of 121% of GDP in 1946 to a low of 32% in 1974. This is the same as the relative debt to income experience you had in the pretend exercise previously discussed. Your income increased from $30,000 to $90,000 and your debt increased from $32,000 to $50,000. However, as a percent of your income, your debt fell from 107% to 56%.

Matthew also makes the point, quoting Greg Ip, that "Austerity alone will fail." As you saw in Chapter 2, austerity (budget cuts) will not only fail, it will either have no effect or it will make the situation worse (retard GDP growth and increase unemployment – **the extreme opposite of what the community wants**). It is common for economists, politicians, and businesspeople to confuse the characteristics of household and business budgets with the characteristics of the budget for a government that works in tandem with and is mutually dependent with the budget/actual for the macroeconomy in which the government resides.

The federal government expenditures for the past 50 years have averaged 20.1% of GDP; the revenues have averaged 17.4% of GDP and the shortfall has averaged 2.7% of GDP. **- See citations.** With this continued shortfall in revenue versus expenditures, the federal debt will continue to grow. Any cut in government spending, as you saw in the Government Money Flow exercise in Chapter 2, will result in a reduction in revenue for both the government and the private sectors of the economy. If the private sector could make up the difference in government spending cuts, this would allow the implementation of a budget reduction as a means of reducing the debt. It is illogical that the private sector, within the framework of the current US economic system, could create a situation in which more than 8 out of 10 workers (80%) are required to support the demands of 10 out of 10 workers and their households (100%) plus other household providers and their households, as is now the case. The current structure of the US economic system appears unable to support a private sector solution. **This is a very important point.** You should review Chapter 2 again, if necessary, to shore up your understanding.

Recognizing the weaknesses in the US economic system, economists ranging from very conservative to very liberal are proposing ways to re-engineer the system. Proposals reviewed, by this author, put forth some good ideas, but overall do not hold promise. Possibly the current system with a few major adjustments will provide a better quality of life for the citizenry as a whole, plus their children and grandchildren, than that which is now the case.

Should reduction of the debt be deemed desirable, then **an increase in taxes is the only option under the current economic system**. The structure of the tax increase would need to be such that it <u>attaches to potential idle money and idle money</u> versus active and potential active money or the tax increase would be detrimental to the economy and possibly lead to an increase in the debt. The debt reduction would be limited to the available idle money that could be applied to reducing the debt.

Discussion points: Pretending that you are a member of Congress, how would you justify a budget in which the taxes collected are less than the money you plan to spend? Would you be able to reduce federal government expenditures as a means of reducing the federal national debt? What would be your position relative to <u>taxes</u>, <u>expenditures,</u> and <u>debt</u>? Is there an advantage to the citizens in general of converting idle money into active money? If so, how would you do it? What are the advantages and disadvantages you would consider before making your decision as to which way to go?

Questions:

Mark all answers which you feel are reasonably correct.

Question #1:

1. General statements about economic situations:

    a. Mark Jones is a residential home contractor. Mark typically earns $125,000 per year. During a period of irrational exuberance, marked by expanded mortgage credit and inflated appraisals, Mark's volume of homes built doubled. Mark's earnings were $350,000 per year for three years. Mark paid a lot more in taxes each of the three years than he normally paid. Additionally, government expenditures, excluding those for non-employment, remained at the same level as experienced before the onset of irrational exuberance. Therefore, the increase in taxes paid by Mark was applied to reducing (helped reduce) the national deficit.

b. Home prices have soared upward, many times, in the US's history and likewise crashed. Many home buyers who do not know not to buy at the top of a market surge have lost a lot of money.

c. The lowering of interest rates by the Federal Reserve will cause investors to divert money for certificates of deposit to the stock market in the belief that they will get a higher return. This flow of money into the stock market drives the stock market pricing up and as a result, those invested in the market feel they are wealthier than perhaps they are - the wealth effect. This leads to a loosening of spending control, by such individuals, which helps to stimulate the economy and thus helps lower the deficit or, at least, prevent it from growing to a height it would otherwise grow. At some point in time the economic growth related to the wealth effect stalls and the economy slows.

   Note, the low interest rates initiated in 2009 in response to the financial crises have supported growth for many years. The low interest rate policies possibly spurred investment (this is uncertain), consumer buying directly related to the lower cost of borrowing, and excessive consumer buying, for some, due to the wealth effect.

d. In order for banks to lend to small and middle market businesses at the same level as they did in the six-year period prior to the 2008 financial crash, they would need to follow the same irresponsible and sometimes corrupt practices they followed leading to the crash. This would be of benefit to you and your family as well as a means to reduce the deficit.

2. From your point of view, the federal government:

   a. Should continue to collect less in taxes than it spends.

   b. Should reduce payouts for Social Security to help reduce the debt.

   c. Should increase taxes in a manner that focuses on potential idle money and idle money.

   d. None of the above.

3. A major business employer in your areas lays off 50% (300) of its workforce; also, a federal government office, due to budget cutbacks (with tax reductions), lays off 50% (300) of its workforce –

a. The private sector business layoff will hurt your local economy and lead to other layoffs in your community and a reduction in profits for local businesses.

b. The government layoff will hurt your local economy and lead to other layoffs in your community and a reduction in profits for local businesses.

c. The government layoff and tax reduction will increase the "demand" for private sector goods in both your local community and the nation (e.g., Allen, an ex-government employee who earned $50,000 per year lands a job in the private sector at $50,000 per year – therefore, demand increases).

d. Because demand will increase due to the layoff and tax reduction, related to the government cut-back, the employment of Allen in the private sector will not displace any private sector workers.

e. Because demand will not increase due to the lay off and tax reduction, related to the government cut-back, the employment of Allen in the private sector will either displace a current private sector worker or cause an unemployed private sector worker, who would have landed the job, to remain unemployed (i.e., private sector unemployment will increase).

CHAPTER 12: CURRENT ISSUES - "Fix Social Security"

Chapter 12 covers:

- Background
- Current situation – what do you get, now?
- Fortified cultural fix
- Survival of the financially fittest
- Fixes to the current programs
- Pay-as-We-Go
- Raising or eliminating the Social Security wage cap
- Raising the Social Security taxes by 2% points
- Raising the SS retirement ages
- Expanding immigration
- Privatizing Social Security.

This chapter focuses on Social Security, not on both Social Security and Medicare. However, these two programs are facing financial challenges and in some instances are subject to the same problems and fixes. Additionally, Social Security and Medicare are interdependent from the perspective of the recipients. Where these overlaps exist, Medicare is mentioned in the text. Medicare will be addressed in more depth in Discussion Guide 2.

*Within the framework of Social Security are two major programs – Old Age and Survivors Insurance (**OASI**) and Disability Insurance (**DI**). This chapter focuses only on the old age provisions of OASI. SI and DI will be addressed in more depth in Discussion Guide 2.*

Background

This chapter explores several problematic issues related to the current Social Security System and options for improving the situation. The options range from the most basic to the somewhat complex in character. It was difficult to simplify the discussion where the subject matter is complex. Additionally, there is a selection of numerical data that is pertinent to the discussion that was also difficult to simplify. I have attempted to put across the essence of the discussion such that the reader does not need to spend a lot of time reviewing the complexities of the discussion. A once or twice read over should provide the reader with the understanding of the subject matter to that level needed to make decisions as a voter. There is no need to memorize the details. However, there is a need to recognize that the integrity of the Social Security program is a matter of very great importance to the majority of Americans.

The 2018 cap for Social Security withholding is $128,700 (workers and employers pay SS tax on the first $128,700 of wages) and there is not a cap on Medicare tax. The tax rate for employers and employees each is 6.2% for Social Security and 1.45% for Medicare. The workers' pay indirectly includes the value the employer pays as the employer's share, as does the cost of any benefit. Therefore, regardless of how the payments are classified, it is the employees who bear the taxes (15.3% in total) [6.2% + 6.2% + 1.45% + 1.45% = 15.3%]. The taxed monies for the Social Security portion of the taxes collected are deposited into the Social Security Trust Fund. This fund is a designated amount of money within the framework of the government's accounting records. It is not an account separate and independent in the same way as a trust parents might set up for their children, or a benefactor might set up for a charity.

Philosophically, we can say that both the employers and employees pay a share of the Social Security Tax. The employees contribute as the tax is deducted from their paychecks. The employers contribute as they put up the capital needed to develop the business and pay a social security tax on top of the wages they pay. However, the market determines the price of the product and the effect of this fact is to squeeze the tax out of the employee, as the tax cannot be passed through to product pricing. (NOTE: A business must maintain an adequate return on investment as needed to attract capital; therefore, there must be a profit. Only to a small degree, and only in situations where profit is marginal and the labor market is tight, might one argue that the tax burden is borne by the employer.) The employer's share is not an add-on to the cost of wages but a payment in lieu of wages. The burden of the tax, as stated previously, is carried by the employee.

Several times in this chapter, I refer to that portion of the Federal National Debt owed to the Social Security (SS) Trust Fund. Currently (2017), this balance is just under $2.8 trillion. The fund's balance grew as the revenue (Social Security taxes) collected exceeded the payouts required for supporting Social Security recipients. Soon the opposite will happen; the payouts will begin to exceed the revenues under the current tax structure (proportionately more people are retiring than previously due to the aging of baby boomers, those born post WWII, between 1946 and 1964).

The debt owed to the fund grew as Congress borrowed money from the trust fund to use for purposes such as defense, highway construction, and education. At some point in the near future (time estimates vary) the government will need to begin paying back the SS Trust fund so that the SS Administration can make payments to retirees and others. **Where will the money come from?**

The money will either come from: (1) the issuance of new public debt and, when that becomes too burdensome, an increase in taxes or (2) simply from an increase in taxes. Either way, the money will come from the earnings of working Americans. However, there is a major problem. Between 1961 and 1971 the US births per woman dropped dramatically from over 3.5 to less than 2.0 and remained at approximately 2.0. This resulted in a situation in which the number of workers available to support retired seniors will drop from 2.8 working Americans per retiree in 2017 to 2.1 workers per retiree by 2033.

Per the Social Security Administration's Trust Fund Trustees –

"adjustments to taxes or benefits that offset the effects of the lower birth rate may restore solvency for the Social Security program on a sustainable basis for the foreseeable future. Finally, as Treasury debt securities (trust fund assets) are redeemed in the future, they will just be replaced with public debt. If trust fund assets are exhausted without reform, benefits will necessarily be lowered with no effect on budget deficits". (Social Security Administration, The Future Financial Status of the Social Security Program, http://www.ssa.gov/policy/docs/ssb/v70n3/v70n3p111.html#mn1.)

The catchphrase "fix Social Security and Medicare" is being used by some in Congress as code meaning to reduce or eliminate Social Security and Medicare. No, it is not necessary to sacrifice for our children, nor is it necessary to burden our children with debt to keep Social Security and Medicare intact. **- See citations.** In 2018/19 a simple rebalancing of the tax system will contribute significantly to alleviating the problem (supplementing such a fix with an increased level of immigration may or may not be necessary – see section <u>Expanding Immigration</u> on page 182). There is plenty of wealth and income in the system as needed to keep every citizen in at least marginally good shape. However, ten years down the road it may be necessary to do more. If you wait until the last minute the financial stress on the community will be greater. Now, is the time for you to make well-grounded decisions.

In the meantime, those Americans that financially fall into the country's lower class are suffering a significant reduction in lifespan. **As net real household/personal incomes of Americans continue to drop** (net of the effects of the increase in female participation in the workforce, increased child care requirements, and increased contribution levels to employer-provided insurance), this situation will expand to include more Americans. I refer to this phenomenon as "death creep.**" - See citations.** To a significant extent, this degradation of lifespan appears to be attributable to the financial situation low-income citizens are in during their senior years (or before). For many Americans the problem of an early death is not twenty years from now – but today.

The fact is, the majority of Americans do not and will not have adequate funds to finance their senior years of life (yes, they did save for retirement – they put money into Social Security). **- See citations (SS Adm.).** Additionally, there is a large group of young Americans coming of working age during the 2008 recession and their lifetime earnings potential has been greatly reduced. They will, in real dollars, be earning significantly less than did those in my generation and <u>the possibility for many of</u>

adequately preparing for retirement is very slim at best. This is not a question of philosophy or one of work ethic – this is a question of simple math. Income minus money for a minimal healthy diet, minimal adequate shelter, minimal adequate health care, minimal adequate etc. equals little to no money left for savings. Keep in mind that God used mathematics in defining the universe; so you must look to the mathematics of a situation both when analyzing the situation and defining a proper solution.

There is the fact, also, that the Social Security funds will begin to draw down at some point in the future (there are various estimates as to when – the furthest out, I have seen, is 20 years). The difference between what will be needed and the funding that will be available, based on current funding methods (tax level and cap) is called the *Social Security gap*. Additionally, the Medicare fund is projected to dry up at some future point (the furthest out estimate, I have seen, is 12 years).

The next fact is that not only can many seniors not survive without Social Security and Medicare <u>at its current **real** income levels</u>, but, as the SS system is currently defined, that their children and grandchildren will be worse off than they. Exacerbating this situation, many corporations are phasing out defined benefit pension plans**. - See citations.** Additionally, the Fed has introduced ZIRP (zero interest rate policy) and is considering NIRP (negative interest rate policy). Although interest rates are being increased as of early 2017, future recessions will occur and the options of ZIRP and NIRP will, most likely, be re-visited. Income options for retirees are shrinking. This will lead to an additional shortening of lifespans for those Americans in the lower and middle classes.

So where does a real fix lie? That depends on what we mean by a "real fix":

- Should we drop back to survival of the financially fittest; or

- Should we implement a system that will give every American (citizens of a land of plenty) a decent and dignified retirement?

Current Situation – What do you get, now?

**Estimated Average Monthly Social Security Benefits
Payable January 2017**

All Retired Workers	$ 1,360
Aged Couple, Both Receiving Benefits	$ 2,260

https://www.ssa.gov/news/press/factsheets/colafacts2017.pdf

Social Security is supplemented by Medicare Part A and B, Food Stamps, Supplemental Security income for those in poverty, and some states offer supplements.

Most people get Medicare Part A at no additional cost (i.e., you paid for it, already, through your payroll deductions and your employer's payroll assessment).

In general, Medicare Part A covers services (like lab tests, surgeries, and doctor visits) and supplies (like wheelchairs and walkers) considered **medically necessary** to treat a disease or condition. [http://www.medicare.gov/what-medicare-covers/part-a/what-part-a-covers.html.] The categories of other key Part A coverage are:

- Hospital care
- Skilled nursing facility care
- Nursing home care **(as long as** custodial care **isn't the only care you need)**
- Hospice
- Home health services.

www.medicare.gov/your-medicare-costs/.../costs-at-glance.html

The standard Part B Medicare premium for 2018 is $134; part B is, in part, supported by the Social Security Administration. The deductible is $183 per year. Retirees need to take Part D which covers prescription drugs separately from part B. Part D insurance premiums vary by state and by provider (insurance company).

Part B covers things like:
- Clinical research
- Ambulance services
- Durable medical equipment
- Mental health
- Getting a second opinion before surgery
- Limited outpatient prescription drugs

[http://www.medicare.gov/what-medicare-covers/part-b/what-medicare-part-b-covers.html]

Many retirees will find it beneficial to purchase Medicare Supplemental Insurance. This can be very expensive for most Social Security Recipients (cost prohibitive for many). The premiums vary by state and provider.

In addition to Social Security checks and Medicare support, 55% of seniors are members of households that use food stamps. The degree of assistance provided through food stamps varies by state. **[http://www.ssa.gov/policy/docs/ssb/v67n4/67n4p71.html]**

Fortified Cultural Fix

First, let's consider a cultural fix that is accompanied by a little help from the government (community). This is to some degree a version of "survival of the fittest." Simply when mom and dad cannot any longer financially sustain themselves, they move in with their children. The eldest son takes on the responsibility, and if there are not any sons in the family the eldest daughter does so. The other siblings contribute financially each month to help offset the costs. Zoning restrictions may need to be changed in some neighbor-hoods, but this could be accomplished by a simple federal law dictating change.

This will be difficult in a country where net real personal incomes have been trending downward, as taking care of mom and dad will cost money. (Household incomes are up since 1967 but down since 1997; but, currently marginally trending upward. This, upward trend, is a reflection of an increase in two wage earner households. Household income as reported, unfortunately, does not deduct for child care, disclose the trend in after-tax real household income, or deduct for the increase in the employee's share of employer provided insurance.) However, this is the mode of operation in many third world countries where people live on a lot less than do Americans and, yet, they bring mom and dad into their home to live. (Husband and wife and mom and dad live in a two-room apartment.) Therefore, it is achievable.

I worked with a man, Bill, who was the youngest of seven children. All of Bill's siblings were doing well financially. Bill was earning around $85,000 a year in 2017 dollars.

Bill's mom and dad had seen to it that all of the kids had a good start in life. Most had a college degree. Mom and dad had prepared as appropriately for their final years as could be expected of a couple with a high middle-class income. But, mom and dad both became ill and medical bills ate up their savings (this was before Medicare and Medicare supplemental insurance implementation). Bill, his wife, and three kids took in mom and dad. Bill's siblings, who per Bill, were perhaps spoiled by mom and dad when they were children, responded only minimally to Bill's request for financial help. Helping Bill and his wife meet the expenses of looking after mom and dad would mean giving up leather seats in their cars and one less TV in the house (in today's world – it might mean the kids' need to give up their cell phones). Bill's kids, as a result, were shorted, to a significant degree, with financial help for college.

To add insult to injury, none of Bill's siblings would temporarily take in mom and dad so Bill and his wife could go away on vacation. Therefore, they did not go away on vacation.

Problems like those experienced by Bill and his wife could be tackled by federal law, supported by the option of a <u>wage and asset garnishment</u>, requiring siblings to help with their fair share financially. **- See citations.**

Such a law would need to be enforceable by the community and automatically kick in, such that the Bills of this world will not need to incur the time and expense taking legal action. They will have enough on their plate as it is. Of course, Bill and his wife still would not be able to go away on vacation – but the government (community) can't fix everything.

As for those seniors who face financial problems and who did not have children or whose children preceded them in death, the cultural fix would be they would finish their lives living with the homeless members of our society.

Survival of the Financially Fittest

Should we decide a fortified cultural fix is not the best solution; then what about straight-up "survival of the financially fittest?" This is simple. Mom and dad, as individuals, are responsible for taking care of themselves in their senior years. If they raised their kids right, the kids would help.

We operated for most of our country's history based upon survival of the financially fittest. This approach was tempered by the fact that sometimes the children took care of mom and dad when they were no longer able to provide for themselves. However, to this latter point, I have been unable to find information as to the degree this was in fact true. I did find that in England many elderly were committed to workhouses where conditions were extremely poor and unhealthy. If workhouses were necessary, then perhaps, many children were not helping mom and dad.

Implementation of (reversion to) a survival of the financially fittest approach is, of course, a moral question. It is an approach that is clearly unacceptable to men and women of religion – but, not all people in America are men and women of religion and this is a democracy. This being the case, the option is definitely on the table.

Additionally, historically, this approach didn't work; this is why Social Security was implemented. The problem was not only that those in poverty had not saved adequately for retirement (which they hadn't; it was not possible) but that many lawyers, doctors, accountants and others who could have saved had not. This fact was magnified by the Great Depression, as many citizens lost their savings due to job loss or the stock market fall.

Discussion points: What advantages and disadvantages does the discussion group see with the fortified cultural fix and the survival of the financially fittest approach? China has implemented laws of a cultural fix character guaranteeing grandparents visitation with grandchildren. Therefore, the concept of a fortified cultural fix is not unexplored territory. Survival of the financially fittest was practiced up until the time that Social Security was established (1935).

Fixes to the Current Programs

Several fixes have been proposed to <u>truly</u> "fix" Social Security, and perhaps provide the funding necessary to improve upon the program. All of these, except the option of increasing the retirement age, involve increasing the Social Security taxes. Versions of these, principally (there are mixtures of these and various time horizons offered), are:

- Eliminate the Social Security cap (top annual wage to which the tax is applied)
- Increase the tax by 1% point, and the SS Gap will be reduced by 54%, and
- Increase the tax by 2% points, and the SS Gap will be reduced by 76%.
  http://money.usnews.com/money/blogs/planning-to-retire/2014/11/14/5-potential-social-security-fixes 5 Potential Social Security Fixes, Emily

  Brandon, Nov. 14, 2014, Money, US News.

NOTE: As a reference point, in China the employer's assessment for social security (which includes pension; medical insurance throughout life, not only for senior years; work-related disability; maternity and unemployment) is over 30% of wages and the employee's assessment is over 10% of wages (ratios vary by state and locale).

I do not have the resources to evaluate these approaches, but I can consider the general economic effect of each. What is important to recognize, however, is that none of these represent a huge undertaking – they are all fairly simple to implement. Additionally, somewhere in the midst of these proposals is a place for the application of sound mathematics. Therefore, there is in the midst of these, if we are to maintain the programs as is, at least a partially true and necessary solution.

During the peak of the 2008 economic crisis, the President implemented a Social Security tax holiday. This took the form of a reduction in the tax rate. The logic behind the reduction was that leaving more money in peoples' pockets would enable people to spend more money and thus help boost the economy. It is, therefore, logical that taking additional money out of peoples' pockets will slow the economy. Taking money out of peoples' pockets is not a good idea when many Americans still are experiencing recessionary induced pain. Additionally, the effects of the 2008 recession will probably continue to create an employment problem for another ten to fifteen years (irrespective of the August 2017 4.4% reported unemployment level). It is, therefore, <u>best that any solution as much as possible targets **idle** and **potentially idle** versus **active** and **potentially active** money in the system</u>. (Recall from Chapter 2 that money is either "active" or "idle" by degrees – it is not absolutely active or absolutely idle.)

If the average employee works 45 years and is retired for 12 years, then, his/her retirement years equal 26% of his/her working years. 21% of the money earned by the retiree in his or her working years will be needed if we assume the retiree is able to live on approximately 80% of that expended per year during his/her working years (financial planners typically propose that retirees need 80% of their working income to maintain their lifestyle during retirement). How will this work out if the retiree does not have adequate savings available to supplement Social Security? Only a maximum of 12.4% (employer's plus employee's share) was put aside through Social Security deductions, and this is less than 21%. **Further, the 12.4% covers both OASI and DI. Further, the OASI covers Survivors Insurance (SI).** The answer is simple – it doesn't work out.

Disability Insurance payouts run around 14.5% of the total of OASI and DI (12.4% of wages). Therefore, approximately 1.8% points of the 12.4% collected are applied to covering DI. Survivors Insurance payouts run around 10% of the total of OASI and DI. Therefore, approximately 1.2% points of the 12.4% points collected are applied to covering survivors of deceased workers. This leaves 9.4% to cover payouts to retirees, retiree's spouses and retiree's dependent children (12.4% [employee's plus employer's tax] - 2.1% - 1.8% = 9.4%).

To make the situation worse, the total tax rate (employee plus employer) was lower than the current rate, 12.4%, for much of the employee's career. If Americans, on the average, are going to insist on living longer lives (at least for the moment) then either the tax rate has to be increased or the workers have to work longer (NOTE: My previous comment on death creep; as US citizens of lower economic classes are experiencing; the longevity problem is somewhat being alleviated (see Chapter 6). Further, as these people expire and others move into their economic position they too will expire early – see Chapter 2, section <u>Shifting Composition of Household Economic Classes</u>).

Let's examine the effect on the economy of three choices:

- Raising or eliminating the Social Security tax ceiling
- Raising the tax rate by 2% points on both the employer and employee, and
- Moving out the Social Security sign-up ages for retirees.

Pertinent to the effect on the economy of any of these actions is what will happen to the money <u>if a choice is not exercised</u> and what will happen to the money <u>if a choice is exercised</u>. **Will the economic activities related to the money redirected, via changes to the tax structure or rate, <u>increase active money</u> or <u>increase idle money</u>, or simply maintain the level of overall economic activity by having no effect on either active or idle money?**

Before launching the discussion of options, let's review a non-option. We do this only for a point of reference.

Pay-as-We-Go

Some have suggested implementing a pay-as-we-go solution. Under a pay-as-we-go approach workers today support retirees today. Money goes straight from the workers' paychecks into the SS system and then immediately to the SS retirees (money remains active). For the most part, this is the way the system is operating now. The Trust Fund is off to the side and still growing; but money is not, in essence, extracted from the fund and paid to retirees. The money paid to the retirees is simply money that is not put into the fund. [Harvey, John T. **Why Social Security Cannot Go Bankrupt**, April 8, 2011, Forbes, **http://www.forbes.com/sites/johntharvey/2011/04/08/why-social-security-cannot-go-bankrupt/**.] <u>This has historically worked because the ratio of workers to retirees made it workable</u> – but shortly this will not be the case. Using this approach alone will lead to a larger tax burden on workers than most workers will consider manageable.

I address it here, simply, so you have some information under your hat should some politician lay the proposal in front of you. As has been the case with several other sections of this discussion guide the reader needs only to focus on the concept and not the detail. Read the information in much the same manner as you would read an article in a magazine.

(1) Financial planners typically propose that retirees need 80% of their working income to maintain their lifestyle during retirement; (2) the US government calculates incomes representing poverty levels; (3) SS recipients currently receive payouts from the system, and (4) The Social Security Administration projects that the number of working Americans per SS Recipient will decrease from 2.8 to 2.1. These factors have been incorporated into the schedules below.

2017 USA ESTIMATED MEDIAN WAGE (Est)	2017 USA POVERTY LEVEL		80 % OF MEDIAN WAGE	2017 PER SSA SS RETIREE AVG PAY-OUT
	1 PERSON HOUSEHOLD	2 PERSON HOUSEHOLD		
$ 30,000	$ 12,060	$ 16,240	$ 24,000	$ 16,320

Est - 2017 data will be available in September of 2018; therefore 2017 is estimated.

The above numbers are comprised of a mix of retirees, including those who retired at the earliest retirement age to those retiring at the standard age or later. Some numbers are reported by the Department of Labor and the SS Administration as medians and some as averages. There would be slight differences in the numbers depicted above and discussed below, if the calculations were based solely on medians for all data. Therefore, the schedule above and the discussion are based on approximate numbers. NOTE: The estimation basis for "Current Median Wage" are found at:
--- http://www.ssa.gov/oact/cola/central.html, and
--- https://aspe.hhs.gov/poverty-guidelines

Key points related to the above schedule (assuming SS retirement recipients were earning the median income of **$30,000** and are to receive the average payout of **$16,320**):

(NOTE: Median pay is that pay at which 50% of Americans earn above the pay level and 50% earn below the pay level. In other words, it is that pay level that is smack in the middle.)

- The **current average payout** per year by Social Security in 2017 is $16,320 per retiree. This is $4,260 above the poverty level of a one-person household and $7,680 below what the working man or woman earning a median wage will need, $24,000, to maintain his/her standard of living should he/she retire next year.

  (80% of $30,000, median wage of American worker, as needed to maintain lifestyle = $24,000)

- The average two-person household, <u>if both persons were earning near the median wage ($30,000 in 2017) during their qualifying working years,</u> near the end of 2017 ($60,000 total) will receive approximately $32.640 ($16,320 each (X's) 2 people = $32,640).

  o This is approximately $16,400 above the poverty level for a 2 person household.

o It is $15,360 below that needed for a 2 person household, in which each was earning near the median wage, to maintain the couple's current lifestyle (80% of $60,000 = $48,000).

PAY-AS-WE-GO ANNUAL ASSESSMENT PER WORKER AND % OF MEDIAN WAGE

CURRENT 2017 > 2.8 WORKERS/SS RETIREE			PROJECTED 2033 > 2.1 WORKERS/SS RETIREE		
1 PERSON POVERTY LEVEL	80% OF MEDIAN WAGE	CURRENT AVERAGE PAYOUT	1 PERSON POVERTY LEVEL	80% OF MEDIAN WAGE	CURRENT AVERAGE PAYOUT
$ 4,307	$ 8,571	$ 5,829	$ 5,743	$ 11,429	$ 7,771
14.4%	28.6%	19.4%	19.1%	38.1%	25.9%

Highlights related to the schedule:

- The current, 2017, total annual SS direct cost for supporting retirees is approximately $16,320 per retiree annually (see the previous schedule). (NOTE: Here and elsewhere, there are administrative costs on top of the direct payout to the retirees.)

- The current level of SS payout per retiree would require an assessment of <u>19.4% of the median pay</u> for working Americans in 2017 and 25.9% of median pay in 2033. (NOTE: Median pay is that pay at which 50% of Americans earn above the pay level and 50% earn below the pay level. In other words, it is that pay level that is smack in the middle.)

   a. On a pay-as-we-go system these amounts 19.4% of median wage ($30,000) and 25.9% of median wage, respectively, based on 2017 and 2033 ratios would need to be paid into the SS Administration by the employees and employers in total (not each) to support mom and dad at the current **real** income level of SS retiree average payout ($16,320 per SS recipient). <u>An additional tax assessment would be required to cover Disability Insurance (DI) and Survivors Insurance (SI). Plus there will be an assessment to cover administration costs.</u>

   b. The % of Median Wage of the SS contribution assessment based on the 2033 ratio of workers to SS retirees (2.1 workers per retiree) of 25.9% is considerably higher than the current <u>total</u> employee/employer's contribution. This current total of 12.4% is now spread over retirement (9.4%),

Survivor Insurance (1.2%), and Disability Insurance (1.8%). At the current median wage, this is a difference on SS retirement alone of $2,357 more per worker per year. Survivor Insurance, Disability Insurance, and administrative cost assessments must be added on top of this.

    c. At the projected 2033 <u>worker to SS retiree ratio of 2.1</u> the contribution to the SS Administration per worker will need to be 19.1% of the median wage to provide a single mom or dad <u>with a retirement income equal to the **poverty level**</u>. Added to this, also, will be assessments for DI, SI and administration costs. This too (poverty level assessment/payout) is above the current contribution level of 12.4% with approximately 9.4% going to support retirement.

As the reader can see, the cost of pay-as-we-go becomes overburdening. Possibly, the best approach is (and would have been) some modification to what we now have that spreads the cost of living for a citizen's retirement years over his/her career.

<u>However</u>, not enough was set aside under previous, and for that matter current, guidelines. Therefore, working citizens will need to supplement those of us who have gone before them via a partial pay-as-we-go system. This will be somewhat difficult because you did not have enough children to help support the system. Although difficult, it will be manageable. **Converting <u>idle and potentially idle money</u> in the community into <u>active money</u> would help considerably**. Additionally, immigration could help alleviate the problem; however, today immigration is managed based on the needs of business not on the needs of the general citizenry. This could be changed. It could be managed for both business needs and general citizenry needs.[10]

---

[10] Contrary to what many Americans think, immigrants do not to a highly significant degree take American jobs. The immigrants <u>create additional domestic economic demand</u> that must be serviced by someone as the American workers are already busy servicing those who were/are here. This additional demand is serviced by immigrants - immigrant "A" works to service the economic demands of immigrant "B" and vice versa. If the immigrants did not come – the demand would not exist; therefore Americans would not be working to satisfy the non-existent demand. Some immigrants do send money back to family in the country they came from. This money leaving the country does not contribute to increased demand in the US. Thereby, the number of jobs that would have been available to both natural born citizens and immigrants is reduced. Based upon what I could find – immigrants send an average of 10% of their income back home. This practice does reduce demand in the USA that in turn **may** result in a reduction in jobs roughly equal to 10% of the immigrant workforce. Immigrants do take jobs that might have gone to Americans during economic recessions. I have not been able to find any substantive studies that quantify the situation; <u>but I suspect, due to the multiplier factor</u> (to be covered in Discussion Guide 2), <u>that there is a net increase in jobs for Americans.</u> This scenario applies to both legal and illegal immigrants.

The Pay-As-We-Go annual assessment schedule presented above and recalculated using an estimated 2017 "average" income ($49,000) **http://www.ssa.gov/oact/cola/central.html** and **http://www.bls.gov/oes/current/oes_nat.htm#00-0000** adjusted for guesstimated inflation] instead of "median" income is provided in Appendix "C." Using the average income results in a lower percentage of wage assessment for both providing "poverty level" and "current real income level" retirement checks for seniors. However, for "average" to be effectively used there would need to be a complete elimination of the Social Security cap.

Discussion point: How does the group feel the pay-as-we-go approach compares to the fortified cultural fix approach?

Raising or Eliminating the Social Security Wage Cap

People who earn wages above the Social Security cap are inclined to save money. The money they save typically will go into savings accounts, CDs, traded stocks and bonds, etc. These uses of money are, in today's economy, forms of incremental <u>idle money</u>.

An incremental tax on those earning above the cap will lower the amount this group places into savings and other forms of idle money. This incremental tax money collected will go into the Social Security Trust Fund. Initially, as it has in the past, the SS Trust Fund will continue to grow. Further, as has been the case in the past, the government will continue to borrow from the fund to spend on other government activities (highway construction, defense, education, etc.). The money would, therefore, move from idle status to active status boosting the economy, creating more profits, and creating more jobs.

The process of government spending, as is the current practice, takes the form of other government programs (highway construction, defense, education, etc.) <u>borrowing</u> from the Social Security fund and then <u>spending</u> the money. This approach is used in lieu of increasing other taxes or issuing bonds. The action will fortify the economy in the near-long term. However, at some point the other government programs (highway construction, education, research, etc.) will need to pay back the Social Security Trust Fund as the need for money to pay retirees will require the use by the SSA of the claims for money in the fund. This will require an increase in income tax rates. Therefore, many of those taxed will slow their buying activity which will slow the economy. This will be more true or less true depending on the degree the <u>money taxed would have become active or idle money</u>.

Most likely the pay-down of the debt, owed to the Social Security Trust, will take place concurrently with the need for money for payouts to retirees (money paid back to the Social Security Trust fund will quickly go out the door as payments to retirees). The retirees will not get more money than previously, but they will get the same amount (if the fund is appropriately repaid). Therefore, the purchasing level of retirees will remain constant. The net effect, short and long term, will be to increase the level of velocity (rate of spending) of active money and more potential idle money taxed will become active.

Raising the Social Security Taxes by 2% Points

The maximum of all of the solutions proposed, as found by this author, requires the implementation of a 2% point increase <u>to both the employee's and employer's share</u> of the Social Security tax. Let's take a look at what would happen to the economy if this were implemented.

First, 2% is a lot of money to a family of four with a household earned income under the median for the country (approximately $57,000 in 2017 [est. – data for 2016 from Census Bureau for 2016 will be available in September of 2017 – therefore, had to estimate]) and it is a huge hardship on a household with a household income of $25,000. There will be a question of the ability of many Americans to adjust their spending patterns. Definitely, some could give up cable television and rely solely on an antenna (in most areas of the country) and limit their household to one phone. Some in the lower income quartile may also need to reduce <u>the level of protein</u> in their diets to an unhealthy level. Many, without food stamps, are or would be at this level now.

Typically wages make up 50% of an employer's costs in manufacturing and a higher percentage in many service industries. Therefore, corporate profits, which run around 9% of revenue on the average, would be reduced to the 7% to 8% range; or wages would be pushed down to accommodate the increase in tax. Therefore, a combination of lowering profits and wages could result from an increase in the tax.

In the near term, as noted in the previous section, the additional Social Security taxes collected would be lent by the Social Security Trust Fund to other government programs (if the tax rates are increased within the next year or so the trust fund balance will grow before the start of drawdown (reserves are projected to peak around 2020 - http://www.ssa.gov/policy/docs/ssb/v75n1/v75n1p1.html). These programs would, in turn, quickly spend the money (putting it back into the economy as active money). This would, in the worst case, make the increase in social security taxes macroeconomically neutral in the near term. To the degree the increase in SS tax tapped potential idle money (i.e., implementation of a graduated SS tax) the economy would experience upward pressure (more jobs).

An increase in the Social Security tax rate will create more of a negative effect on the economy than the lifting of the cap. This is true as it would tap more active money versus potential idle money than would lifting the cap. Without the necessary staff to complete an analysis, I cannot guesstimate as to how significant this effect might be. I can only say that from a macroeconomic point of view – raising the cap is the better alternative. However, this alone will not be the answer. A combination of both options or several options is necessary. I suspect that a combination of several options is necessary – including moving out the retirement age and increasing immigration. (NOTE: Various political organizations, think tanks and government agencies, with staffs of more than just one person, have been challenged when attempting to determine the impact of raising the cap, increasing the tax or assessing other options.)

Discussion points: What are the group's thoughts on raising the cap and/or raising the tax?

Raising the SS Retirement Ages

Note, the numbers used in this section are rough approximations.

There is, also, the option of moving out the retirement age for Social Security purposes to the ages of 69 and 72 (69 for early retirement and 72 for normal retirement). The key issue with this option is that mom and dad must be able to land work at a living wage until they reach the Social Security retirement age. (Mom and dad must have a way to stay alive until they reach retirement age.)

69 and 72 are further out than most options proposed by economists and members of Congress. But most options proposed do not completely close the Social Security gap, and many options only marginally address Medicare. Increasing the early retirement age to 69 and the standard age to 72 would bring the nation closer to solving the Social Security gap problem; it would, also, have a significant positive impact on the financial shortfall in Medicare.

Employers will not employ senior citizens in lieu of younger workers (the children and grandchildren of senior citizens) without a push from the community. There are several ways a "push" could be implemented. As a basis for discussion, I have followed through a train of thought for one of these.

As an option, this problem could be fixed by requiring businesses with 200 or more employees to hire a select percentage of people within each five-year age band above the age of 40.

Using this option as a basis for discussion, there are others, the related issues are examined below. However, although there are other options, **all options must address the points addressed in this example, or the required results will not be realized.**

The key issues are mom and dad's physical fitness and the mix of jobs available in the economy. As will be discussed below, **an incremental economy over and above the current economy can be created for mom and dad** – but the job mix in that economy will be approximately the same as it is in the current economy (same relative number of construction jobs, accounting jobs, beautician jobs, etc.). How does this cause a problem?

- Pretend dad is a carpenter who at the age of 58 developed spinal problems. Dad will not be able to do carpenter work at the age of 59 – so what can dad do? Dad can paint houses, sell cars, coach college football, serve in Congress, etc., but there are a lot of people in the same spot dad is in and there will not be enough jobs available in the job market of the types of things dad and these others can do. Dad is in a jam. There are jobs dad can do regardless of his bad back. Therefore, he is not disabled; there is an oversupply of job seekers for those jobs (both young and old), something dad cannot control; and dad can't do anything about his back.

- Pretend mom is an accountant for a regional retail clothing chain. At the age of 61, mom suffered several mini-strokes. Mom can no longer handle the complexities of accounting work, but she could easily work as a retail sales clerk, mom still drives so she could work as a real estate agent; like dad above, mom can work in lots of jobs, so she is not disabled. Mom, however, has the same problem as dad - too many senior people, because of their physical condition, want the types of jobs mom is now restricted to doing.

As a community, we will have very significant problems to deal with in providing employment for mom and dad. There will be millions of senior Americans who are in the gray area between being disabled and being able to carry on with their lifetime work. Today at the age of 66, or as early as the age of 62, there are millions of such people, but they have the option of taking Social Security before the age of 69. Therefore, <u>any proposal for moving out the Social Security retirement age must include an aspect dealing with the people in the gray area.</u>

As real incomes come down for the majority of Americans, the issue of moving the Social Security qualification age out becomes more serious. Many senior moms and dads today who led economically lower upper class, upper middle class, or middle class lives were able to save adequately to help bridge the gap between the point in time they fell into the gray area (those that did) and the point at which they could sign up for Social Security (an early point at age 62 and a normal point at age 65). It will be far more of a challenge for their children, now in their late forties to save adequately. In fact, for many it will not be possible. Therefore, the community's solution to dealing with those in the gray area needs to recognize that the problem will expand significantly in the near-long-term future.

What happens if mom and dad remain in the workforce? **Will that not result in the displacement of many younger workers who need jobs to feed themselves and their children?**

The answer is **"Yes."** As the economic system is currently designed and managed, younger workers will be displaced by mom and dad. The question to answer is: "how can senior moms and dads be employed without displacing younger workers?"

The answer as to "how" is the community needs to build a bigger pail; a pail that can hold six gallons of water, versus only five gallons of water.

Keep in mind that:

Demand = Number of Jobs in the Economy (the size of the pail)

=

_____   Number of Workers Employed (the water to fit into the pail)

Following is some data you will need to follow the discussion (based on 2016 data):

SOCIAL SECURITY DATA

APPROXIMATE TOTALS AS OF DECEMBER 2016

| (In Millions) | | AVERAGE MONTHLY RECEIPT PER RECIPIENT |
NUMBER OF RECIPIENTS	ANNUAL PAYOUT	
44	$ 722,421	$ 1,360

How to read numbers stated in Millions:

44 = 44 million

$722,421 = $722.421 billion

APPROXIMATE CURRENT RECIPIENTS
UNDER AGE 70

| (In Millions) | | ESTIMATED AVERAGE MONTHLY RECEIPT |
NUMBER OF RECIPIENTS	ANNUAL PAYOUT	
19	$ 284,898	$ 1,265

IF UNDER AGE 70 RETURNED TO WORKFORCE

(In Millions) NUMBER OF RECIPIENTS	EST ANNUAL MEDIAN EARNINGS @ $30,000/YR (a)	EST ANNUAL SOCIAL SECURITY /MEDICARE CONTRIBUTION (b)
19	$ 563,040	$ 86,145

(a) This would provide a $563 billion boost to the economy; if the current payout to those in this age group were maintained (approx. $285 billion) through other forms of government expenditures.

(b) 15.3% of earned income.

Approximately 44 million, in total, of moms and dads now (as of the end of 2016) receive roughly $722 billion ($1,360 per month) in Social Security retirement payments. Most of this money is worked back into the economy (i.e., spent by senior moms and dads) quickly. Based on a combination of this level of spending by mom and dad and the level of spending of workers not receiving Social Security (primarily younger workers under the age of 65) a certain number of non-Social Security recipients (primarily younger workers) are employed in a job. To enable the economy to accommodate employing the senior moms and dads, as the Social Security retirement age is moved out, without un-employing younger workers this $722 billion (adjusted for inflation) of government spending <u>must be maintained or increased. Additionally, it must be **incremental**, to what mom and dad will earn if we put them to work and, in relative terms, to the overall economy.</u> (Or, from an opposite perspective – what mom and dad earn must be incremental to the $722 billion.) This means the $722 billion is not a fixed number. As pointed out in Chapter 1 to this guide everything in economics is relative. The $722 billion is relative to the Gross Domestic Product (GDP) and the number of seniors as a percentage of the working age population. To keep relative employment steady the $722 billion will need to be adjusted upward as GDP increases. Additionally, as the over 60 crowd becomes an increasingly greater portion of the population (as it is forecasted to do) the makeup of the $722 billion of expenditures will need to be adjusted to accommodate the demographic change. Plus the aggregate of all other government spending must remain at a <u>relatively constant level</u> (to GDP) or increase (federal, state, local – does not matter economically if financial responsibility is transferred between federal and state or vice versa, as long as the relative total remains the same or increases) except for that which is variable with need (e.g., unemployment payments).

When the country had 100 million workers the targeted unemployment <u>based on today's Fed practices</u> would have been approximately 6% (i.e., assumed to be 6% per our discussion). At 150 million workers the targeted percentage would be the same (6%), and at 200 million workers the target would be the same (6%). To hold inflation in check the Federal Reserve must maintain a relative number of able-bodied could be/would be workers within the non-employment (unemployment plus other) category. If fourteen million jobs were added to the economy to accommodate mom and dad, <u>long-term</u> inflation would remain in check, practically speaking, as long as overall non-employment remained in line with the Fed's target for unemployment as a percentage (recall there are other influences).

How can keeping mom and dad in the workforce be accomplished? It can be accomplished through the implementation of a senior workers transition stimulus package (SWTSP). If all seniors currently under the age of 70 were to be transferred off of Social Security **today** and into waiting jobs, there would be approximately 18.7 million seniors rejoining the workforce (rounded to 19 million in the schedule). If they earned the current median income of $30,000 the package required would be $563 billion. By the end of the first year, the increase in personal expenditures enabled by the increase in senior income would provide the increased demand for goods and services needed (a six gallon pail) to employ the seniors. Except for leakage, an additional stimulus would not be necessary. Further, the increase in wages and expenditures would work its way back through the tax system such that the resulting increase in tax collections would recover most of the $563 billion of stimulus monies (See Appendix B - Penny Money Flow exercise).

What leakage would occur? The two types of leakage of greatest concern, as discussed previously, are that related to a negative balance of trade (more product value is imported into the US than exported from the US) and the transfer of money from active to idle status. These are both problems for the overall US economy related not just to the retention of seniors in the workforce. However, they will detract from the effectiveness of the senior transition project just as they detract from the effectiveness of the overall economy and will need to be compensated for as part of the transition package. A more exacting discussion of leakage and what is needed to accommodate it is beyond the scope of this text (of interest; see Appendix F for an example of an exercise that incorporates leakage).

As the seniors (under age 70) are transitioned from would-be retirees to remaining in the workforce, the $722 billion of Social Security payments mentioned above will be reduced by roughly $285 billion. This translates into an overall loss of jobs for both seniors and non-seniors. As mentioned above, for the transition to be successful the $722 billion of expenditures must be maintained. Therefore, the community must replace the $285 billion of Social Security expenditures (that would have been paid to seniors now remaining in the workforce) with an equivalent level of expenditure for other programs. This may include an increase in the time span for and amount of unemployment benefits, a significant improvement in benefits for survivors of soldiers who lost their lives in action, a significant pay increase for soldiers of lower rank, etc. Not only must the $722 billion remain in place it must be increased to accommodate inflation. Additionally, the $722 billion as adjusted over time must remain in place until the end of time on earth.

The transition program **would not be implemented "today" as discussed above – it would be phased in.** Therefore, there will not be a need for a $563 billion stimulus package on day one of the transition. For example, if the transition is implemented in every other year step-ups (phased in) over an 11 year period there will be a need for a $113 billion stimulus package in each year of step-up. As would be the case with an immediate transition (implemented in one day "today") and the needed $563 billion transition stimulus package, the increase in seniors' wages and expenditures would work its way back through the tax system. As such, the resulting increase in tax collections would recover most of the transition stimulus monies initiating a cycle of private expenditure/tax collection/government expenditure; private expenditure/tax collection/ government expenditure; private expenditure/etc. as depicted in Appendix B (Penny Money Flow exercise).

Just what is a "step-up" anyway? If the target was established to move the average SS retirement age out five years and this was to be accomplished by advancing the age by one year every other year, each advance would be a step-up. If done every two years over 11 years, as discussed above, there would be a step-up at the beginning of years 1, 3, 5, 7, and 9. 11 years = 10 years plus 1 year for lag in implementation (all moms and dads will not find a job day one of each step-up / plus there will be bugs to work out). The stimulus would not be re-established at the end of year 11.

SWTSP REQUIREMENT
IMPLEMENTED IN FIVE STEPS
OVER AN 11 YEAR PROGRAM
(IN MILLIONS)

TOTAL REQUIRED CREATION OF ADDITIONAL DEMAND	STEP-UP MAINTAINED FOR 11 YEARS
$563,040	$112,608

We could review another five or six pages on this subject, but by now you should have the idea of the subject. Most importantly for a transition to succeed the total of other government expenditures could not be <u>reduced except in response to a reduction in need</u> (as the number of unemployed reduces the need for expenditures for unemployment support reduces; conversely should it increase the expenditures must increase).

There appears to exist a phenomenon that may naturally (in economic terms) provide for the employment of relatively more seniors. As the ratio of working Americans to senior could be/would be retired Americans changes from 2.8 to 2.1, a need for businesses to employ more seniors will develop. To the degree this happens, it will offset some of the required stimulus program investment as discussed above. The effect of this possibility on the economy's ability to employ seniors without displacing younger workers will <u>depend on such factors as the level of consistency of spending by domestic governments, overall spending by retired seniors, and immigration</u>. Should this phenomenon come about as expected, it **might** provide jobs for over 20% of the seniors needing to continue in or return to the workforce. - **See citations.**

In the above discussion, I have attempted to demonstrate that in any program developed to raise the SS retirement age all of the bases must be covered and all of the dots must be connected. I have not, however, covered all of the bases as this would require an additional 30 to 50 pages and this guide would then begin to approximate a textbook.

What types of issues have I not discussed? Below are a few examples.

- Construction companies have, in relative terms, fewer jobs that seniors can do versus insurance companies. Hiring quotas by age bands would need to take this fact into consideration

- Today when a 63-year-old tells a potential employer that he plans to work until he is 70, the potential employer is somewhat inclined to believe this. However, if the retirement age is moved out, it is far less likely that a potential employer will believe a 67-year-old who states he plans to work until he is 74. Perhaps the age hiring bands for people over 63 would need to be by one year versus by five-year increments. Also, special unemployment provisions would be needed for people over the age of 66.

- To lighten the cost burden on private industry employers, should civil service employers (federal, state, county, city, military-related civil service) be required to hire a disproportionate portion of the senior workforce than should private industry employers?

- If mom and dad cannot go onto Social Security, if they become disabled at the age of 63, they will need to go onto disability. Therefore, disability programs will need to be expanded to support mom and dad.

Recap of Key Issues Relative to Raising the Social Security Retirement Ages:

- Mom and dad's physical fitness relative to the mix of jobs available in the economy.

- How to employ senior moms and dads without displacing younger workers?

- The $722 billion of government payout for Social Security must be:

a. Maintained or increased in some form of government spending. Therefore, the approximate drop of $285 billion in SS payouts that will occur as senior moms and dads are retained in the workforce must be replaced with other spending (e.g., better pay and benefits for lower rank military personnel)

b. A senior employment stimulus package must be incremental to the overall economy

c. The aggregate level of all other government spending must remain at a relatively constant level or increase (federal, state, local – does not matter economically if financial responsibility is transferred between federal and state or vice versa, as long as the relative total remains the same or increases) except for that which is variable with need (e.g., unemployment payments).

- To hold inflation in check the Federal Reserve must maintain a relative number of able-bodied could be/would be workers within the unemployment category (i.e., assumed to be 6% per our discussion and influenced by all forms of non-employment /workforce participation). A special unemployment program will be needed for senior moms and dads continuing in or returning to the workforce.

- Disability Insurance programs (DI) will need to be expanded and modified to serve those senior moms and dads who under the current programs would elect to go onto Social Security at an earlier age.

- Raising the Social Security retirement ages can be accomplished through the implementation of a senior workers transition stimulus package (SWTSP).

- To lighten the administrative burden on private industry employers, should civil service employers (federal, state, county, local, military-related civil service) be required to hire a disproportionate portion of the senior workforce than should private industry employers?

Discussion points: Does the group feel that it is realistic to expect Congress to maintain some type of senior SWTSP program? How many in the group have or have had a parent who could not work past the age of 65?

Expanding Immigration

If we accept that the level of payout to retirees for Social Security is OK, then the primary problem with Social Security is the drop in the ratio of workers to retirees (2.8 to 1 versus 2.1 to 1; FYI, earlier in our history the ratio was 6.0 to 1). If we do not accept that the level of payout is Ok, then issues besides the ratio issue may become the primary issue(s). Regardless, the ratio will remain a key issue if not the primary issue. Therefore, we should be able to fix a significant portion of the Social Security shortfall by increasing the number of workers per retiree.

It is too late for Americans to have the number of children needed to support the Social Security system. We had our opportunity, and we blew it.

There is the option of increasing the number of immigrants assimilated into the country.

Historically, immigration policy has been focused on serving the needs of big business and wealthy landowners. There is no reason it could not be focused on serving the needs of all Americans.

To do this, Congress will need to develop a master demographic plan that covers a 50 to 75-year time frame. This would provide a framework to use as a basis for determining the right number of immigrants needed and the format of the immigrants' personal households (i.e. single, married, married with children, etc.) Most likely, some form of married with children is desirable as we do not want our children and grandchildren to face the same imbalance problem now facing retirees and workers.

The plan would need to provide protection for native-born American workers as the level of immigration is increased. I have listed a small sampling of protections below. You and your friends can add others to the list. Remember, when developing your list, all of the bases must be covered and all of the dots must be connected.

Here are a few ideas:

- The increased level of immigrants should be admitted only during economic recovery periods – not during recessions

- A "hire Americans first" program should be implemented

- A national rent control program combined with a government program to expand the number of housing units available should be established. The expansion program can be in the form of direct government projects or subsidized private sector projects

- Controls need to be implemented to protect landlords not operating within the framework of the expansion program. That is, Jack and Jill, who own a duplex and live in one side and rent out the other, as well as, Mary, Sue, and Bob, who formed a corporation to build 400 apartment units, must be economically protected from the effects of the expansion program

- Controls to keep dishonest developers, contractors, landlords, bond issuers, etc. from ripping off the taxpayers and tenants must be implemented as a prerequisite to the initiation of a housing expansion program

- A cap on population should be defined; based upon a sound demographic analysis. The US, based upon the supply of readily available natural resources, can easily support a population which is double the current population. However, there is a point at which the country will become overburdened.

What about the fact that automation may someday eliminate jobs and there will no longer be enough work for all of us? Everything in economics is relative. Therefore, should this happen (it has been forecasted several times in history - as farm work was automated and then, again when factories were first automated, and again when computers were developed) then we will all work only 30 hours a week. This will be equally true (i.e. it will not be any different because we brought in zero additional immigrants or 100 million additional immigrants) if the population is 300 million, 600 million, or 900 million.

A study of this option requires a lot more manpower than I can muster and is best left to the government. I will not tackle it any further here.

However, note that an increase in immigration would significantly reduce the burden on your children and grandchildren. This is good for your children, your grandchildren, and you; and good for the immigrants.

Privatizing Social Security

What about privatizing Social Security? There are pros and cons to the idea.

Historically, the government has relied heavily on its ability to borrow from the Social Security trust fund. Under privatization, money would be directed to the private equity and bond markets and would no longer be as readily available to other government functions (government bonds would still be purchased – but, the volume would drop significantly). The loss of this ability would lead to a needed significant increase in general taxes. This is, of course, going to happen as the Social Security Trust Fund monies are withdrawn to pay retirees, but not as quickly (if managed properly by you and Congress) as would be the case with privatization. The government could raise taxes immediately, or it could issue public bonds and not have to raise taxes until some later date (this writer holds the opinion that the country would soon reach a financial breaking point if bonds were issued). If the latter approach were followed the necessary tax increase would be much larger than it would be if it were done up front. Additionally, the vast amount of monies would most likely be invested in the traded stock (equities) market. This money would become idle, resulting in a negative impact on the economy. This would be somewhat offset by the creation of the "wealth effect" for holders of traded stock not held by the Social Security trust.[11]

The addition to the stock market of excess money would drive the market to even higher levels of irrational exuberance, whereas the market is generally overpriced in large part because there are too many dollars (excess money) chasing too few (limited supply of) investment opportunities. At some point, probably after 2030, there would be a major and permanent, as measured in real dollars, market crash. This crash could be delayed by significantly increasing the proportionate annual number of immigrants accepted into the country (This is needed because you did not have enough children as needed to support the Social Security/Medicare programs). This would provide additional citizens to pay into the SS program and, therefore, further exert upward pressure on the stock market. At some point, maybe fifty years from now, the country would become overcrowded. At that time the stock market crash would happen (when your grandchildren are ready to retire and become dependent on the SS Trust Fund balance which will, as a result of a market crash, become insufficient).

What about traded corporate bonds? Should the Social Security fund invest in these? The Social Security fund would need to depend on the advice of the same people (or their genetic offspring) who magnified the 2008 recession by committing fraud, mainly in the area of home mortgages; but also, to a large extent in the form of stock market manipulation. As recently as July 2014, it was reported that Wells Fargo and several other major lenders were repeating the same practices but this time with subprime automobile loans. **- See citations.** If you want to trust these people with your money go ahead; but count me out. Before you decide everything might now be ok read the biblical verse by Matthew regarding "the eye of the needle."

There are other pros and cons that the reader can find online or in periodicals, so I will not go into these. From this writer's perspective the cons far outweigh the pros; however, you may have a different take.

Discussion point: Share your observations on this subject with your discussion group.

---

[11] The **wealth effect** is the change in spending that accompanies a change in perceived **wealth**.[1] Usually the wealth effect is positive: spending changes in the same direction as perceived wealth. http://en.wikipedia.org/wiki/Wealth_effect

Summation

What is important to you as a voter is that you elect congresspeople and presidents who are capable of seeing the big picture, covering all of the bases and connecting all of the dots. Such candidates would at a minimum place in the upper quartile (1 out of 4 people) for both mathematical skills and mathematical comprehension. (These are two different intellectual functions, the first involving memorization of relationships and the second the exercise of natural intelligence; an individual can score high in math skills and average in math comprehension and vice versa. However, someone who scores high only in comprehension can learn math skills, and this is not necessarily vice versa.) While probably over 90% of the general citizenry can understand this guide and after reviewing this guide follow and assess the options that politicians will present; one (the politicians) must place in the <u>upper quartile to be able to develop substantive options</u>.

How can you, the voter, assess a candidate's level of ability? While there are certain groups of people who can, on the group average, be expected to possess these abilities (physicists, tool and die makers, air controllers, neurologists, engineers, professional pool players, etc.) there is no way to tell other than through psychometric testing and brain scans. You as a voter cannot test the candidates; therefore, you need to keep your ears open and listen to the candidates. Then determine, to the best of your ability, whether they possess the mathematical comprehension ability needed for helping to put the country on the right track or if they will instead be an obstacle.

This math issue, by the way, applies not only to the development of a "Social Security fix" but to all aspects of all economic issues. Additionally, in the modern world, it applies to many other categories of political concern; including, but not limited to, defense, climate change, education, and the development of energy alternatives.

Questions:

Mark all answers that are reasonably correct.

1. If the community opts to go the direction of a fortified cultural fix or to some mixture of cultural fix and a significant reduction in the level of benefit each recipient will receive - this will result in a change in the lives of many citizens:

   a. I have the financial ability to support my mom and dad should they live in my home.

b. I have the financial ability to support mom and dad if they continue to live in their own home or an assisted living home.

c. Mom and dad have long-term care insurance, which will adequately provide for them in their old age should social security be reduced significantly. A prerequisite here is that mom and dad, in their old age, will be able to afford to make the insurance premiums so as not to lose their policy.

d. People in some other countries share two-room apartments with their senior mom and dad; if they can do it so can I.

e. We (my spouse and I) have the financial ability to support both my spouse's mom and dad and my mom and dad should it become necessary.

2. Eliminating the Social Security cap is:

a. Unfair to people of higher incomes as they will contribute significantly more to the Social Security Program than they will receive in benefits.

b. All working citizens contribute to the high incomes (provided the necessary conversion labor) enjoyed by those with incomes in the upper 1% bracket; therefore, it is reasonable for the community to require a disproportionate share from those who would be affected by a lifting of the cap.

c. We must do unto others as we would have them do unto us; this is true whether we are a "we" or an "other." Therefore, it is reasonable to require all citizens to give based upon what they can afford, even if some such citizens do not accept this Christian position.

d. The community as a whole must provide for the community as a whole; whether one is religious or not - this is a basic inalienable responsibility of the community.

e. I own the economic system; the system does not own me.

3. Should the Social Security retirement benefits age be moved out by five years:

a. The current laws designed to prevent discrimination against job applicants who are over the age of forty are adequate to prevent discrimination against job applicants who are over the age of sixty-four.

b. There will be no need for the community to incorporate specified hiring bands for seniors into the employment discrimination laws.

c. The community should not provide any type of senior workers transition stimulus package (SWTSP) designed to prevent the displacement of younger workers by senior workers returning to or remaining in the workforce.

d. A senior workers transition stimulus package, if properly designed by Congress, will produce an increase in the gross domestic product (GDP). Thereby, increasing cumulative profits and cumulative wages; thereby, increasing the taxes collected because of the increased tax base; and will result, via taxes on the increase, in a recovery of the stimulus package monies – except for leakage – in the years after the initial implementation.

e. A senior workers transition stimulus package would be, to a significant extent, self-funding.

4. "A disadvantage of this option [raising retirement age], like any proposal to reduce retirement benefits but not disability benefits, is that it would increase the incentive for older workers nearing retirement to apply for disability benefits. Under current law, workers who retire at age 62 in 2038 will receive 70 percent of their primary insurance amount (what they would have received if they had claimed benefits at their full retirement age); if they qualify for disability benefits, however, they will receive 100 percent of that amount. Under this option, workers who retired at 62 in 2038 would receive only 55 percent of their primary insurance amount; they would still receive 100 percent if they qualified for disability benefits." (Congressional Budget Office, November 13, 2013, *Raise the Full Retirement Age for Social Security*)

a. Raising the retirement ages will be a very complicated task. Although many of us are living longer than originally planned (excluding those in lower income brackets), many of us are not necessarily physically suited for many jobs that are and will be available.

b. The state governments currently process disability claims, and in some states this is done ineffectively. This must be improved significantly. Especially, since some seniors will suffer early dementia and will not have the mental where-with-all to deal with state departments and systems that operate ineffectively. If necessary, the federal government should be empowered to audit the operations of the state claims processing functions for effectiveness and fairness, and to take over such functions where they do not appear adequate.

c. My children will be able to retire on 70% of the average current Social Security payment of $16,320, or $11,424. My grandchildren will be able to retire on 55% of the average current Social Security payment, or $8,976.

d. For the country to have a retirement program that works effectively and is affordable to the citizenry, it is necessary that the increase in obesity and smoking be successfully addressed. Additionally, it is necessary that the increases in diabetes and thyroid disorders be successfully addressed.

CHAPTER 13: OPINION – Why are there Different Economic Theories?

Chapter 13 covers:

- Because there are differences in people
- The influence of native intelligence
- Maturity.

Because There are Differences in People

Why are there different economic theories? Because there are differences in people. All those who hold a Ph.D. in economics were not created the same. All possess a high level of academic intelligence (ability to memorize information and relationships); but, not all possess a high level of native intelligence (critical thinking skills, objective reasoning skills, ability to deal with time and spatial relationships, mathematical comprehension, etc.). Some possess a high level of personal maturity; some possess a low level of personal maturity, and most are in between.

Both of these classes of psychological profile characteristics, native intelligence, and maturity, heavily influence what a person thinks within the boundaries of understanding on a given subject matter.

What is meant by "boundaries of understanding"?

In the construction field a support beam that is to hold a 5,000 pound load, at a minimum, must be able to hold a load of 5,000 pounds. If the beam cannot hold the load, the beam will break – there is no room for opinion on this matter. All contractors, therefore, must agree that this is the case. There is a very definite lower boundary regarding the lower limit when defining what support beam is necessary to support a 5,000 load. However, for reasons of providing a safety margin, some contractors may argue that a beam capable of supporting a 10,000 pound load should be used to support a 5,000 pound load. This line of reasoning provides assurances that in an earthquake or hurricane less damage or no damage will be incurred to the structure of which the beam is a part. Some contractors may argue that even a 10,000 pound load rated beam is inadequate – that a 14,000 pound load rated beam should be used to support a 5,000 pound load. At some point the load rating of the support beam drives the cost of the beam up to a point that it becomes cost prohibitive. This point provides the top limit of the boundary of understanding.

Contractors can argue amongst themselves all day long as to whether a load rating of 6,000 pounds, 10,000 pounds, 13,000 pounds, etc. is necessary – but their arguments must stay within the upper and lower boundaries of understanding.

The field of economics is far more complex than the field of contracting. The "boundaries of understanding" are very wide and very fuzzy. As the level of global trade has increased, the ability of even the brightest economist to comprehend the big picture and identify the "boundaries of understanding" has been tasked. It appears that some economists become so overwhelmed that they lose sight of the basics; such as those discussed in this book.

From your perspective, as a guy or gal who needs to vote, the complexities are not overly important. An economist who is an advisor to an investment house needs to be very exacting in his/her economic predictions. A variance of 1/10th of a percent can mean a gain or a loss of millions of dollars. An economist employed as a professor needs to publish, publish, publish. He or she must reach into the farthest corners of complexity to develop subject matter to write about. However, the typical voter only needs to consider the basics. As stated in the section <u>ARITHMETIC AND RELATIVE POSITION</u> of Chapter 1, at the beginning of this book, 95% of what there is to know about economics can be understood through understanding basic arithmetical relationships. Expanding upon this theme, 5% of what there is to know is extremely complex. This 5%, however, is only of use to those who require very refined information regarding the economic aspects of this or that. You and I are not concerned with refined information regarding this or that – we are concerned with the general structure of the economic system. We can understand what we need to understand by focusing only on the basics.

We will now examine how the psychological profile of an economist might control his or her economic perspective.

The Influence of Native Intelligence

Psychologist, Psychiatrist, and academics use various terms when describing human intelligence. Terms used include, but are not limited to, general intelligence, natural intelligence, native intelligence, academic intelligence, memory, fluid intelligence, crystallized intelligence and many more. Sometimes the same terms are used to mean different things. There is a lack of consistency. Therefore, I have listed some of the intellectual properties that are included under the umbrella of my favorite term – "native intelligence." All of these can be and frequently are measured by psychologists.

An individual must be capable of scoring high in these areas if he or she is going to effectively develop and/or absorb complex economic theories. They include (plus others):

- Critical thinking skills
- Objective reasoning skills
- Mathematical comprehension
- Abstract reasoning, and
- The ability to deal with time and spatial relationships.

The most important member of the native intelligence family is "critical thinking." There is an old adage that "human intelligence cannot be improved upon." This adage is referring to one's critical thinking abilities. Critical thinking abilities can be diminished or destroyed by alcohol, cocaine, marijuana, automobile accident, sports injury, and many other means – but otherwise, it appears, that which an individual is born with is what an individual lives with.

This leads us to my economic theory, which is a theory, not about economics, but economists.

All economists, who score 90 or above on a 100 point scale, in the above listed intellectual properties, subscribe to the same economic theories. Those that score 51 to 90 subscribe to various economic theories based on reasons other than substantive economic logic. This may include the same theories as those subscribed to by those in the upper group, or it may include theories rejected by economists in the upper group.

However, focusing on the upper group – it will be true with the majority of such individuals that they preach the same theories, but a minority, for various reasons, will preach different theories.

This brings us to discussing the effect that personal maturity has on the expression of this or that economic theory.

Maturity

That's mine, that's mine, that's ours, that's ours

As there are many aspects of human intellect, there are, also, many aspects of human maturity. Here we are concerned with possession maturity.

When we are infants, through our eyes, the world is about us. As we begin to move about and interface with others through play, we perceive that the toys are "mine, mine." Some of us begin sharing our toys very early in our development – the toys are at that point, but often to a limited degree, perceived as "ours." Most of us, in varying degrees and at various points in life, move up the ladder from "that's mine, that's mine" to "that's ours." Some of us never leave the stage of "that's mine, that's mine."

The progression through stages does not happen on a dime. Those that progress, progress over time through various stages. Psychologists have sophisticated terms and definitions for these stages, but I have kept it simple and delineated the stages as:

- That's mine, that's mine
- That's mine
- That's ours, and
- That's ours, that's ours.

I believe these stages as listed are adequate for discussion purposes with one caveat. Perhaps the only one to display the stage of "THAT'S OURS, THAT'S OURS (all in capital letters)" has been Jesus of Nazareth.

Of those who progress beyond the first stage, some get stuck in the second stage and some advance to the third. Those who progress to the fourth stage, must stay at this stage as it is the last stage I have provided.

If an economist is personally:
- Stuck at one of the first two stages of possession maturity and
- Places in the upper 10% of native intelligence as discussed above,
he or she may express economic theories that are contrary to that he or she knows to be more correct - if there is a personal economic or psychological benefit to doing so.

Many of us, when faced with temptation, give in to temptation. Economists, including those who possess superior native intelligence, are no different from the rest of us.

On the Wrong Page

Within the context of the prior discussion, there is a simple misunderstanding of economics subscribed to by some economists.

It is not uncommon to find an economist that believes economics is a function of philosophy and ideology. It is not. Economics is a function of the sciences of mathematics and psychology.

This means that there are no liberal or conservative economists. Anyone who describes themselves as a liberal or conservative economist is not an economist.

If the economy could talk, it would explain to these people that it just doesn't care about their philosophy or ideology.

Questions

1. People, in general (not only economists), who are stuck at one of the first two levels of possession maturity are more likely to:

    a. Want more back from the community than they substantively contribute to the community.

    b. Form bonds with others that will enable them to lay claim to that which is substantively more than their fair share of the economic benefits of the community's economic output (birds of a feather stick together).

    c. If able, attempt to manipulate the economic perspective of members of the general population to create patterns in voting that will lead to personal benefits for themselves that are contrary to the good of the community.

    d. Attempt to get most members of the community to vote against such members' personal interests and the interests of their families.

    e. None of the above.

2. Most people in the general population are:

    a. Easily manipulated UNLESS they make a meaningful effort to analyze, at a basic level, those economic options that are laid out before them.

    b. More likely to vote for options that best benefit their families and community if they apply basic arithmetic to assessing economic options.

    c. More likely to vote for options that best benefit their families and community if they lay aside preconceived notions before analyzing the pros and cons of an economic option.

    d. Of the opinion that they own the economic system – the system does not own them.

e. None of the above.

Discussion point: With a friend, neighbor, relative, member of your congregation or club, or someone you meet while waiting for a bus or train, discuss the ramifications that the answers to the questions might have on the economy and society.

General Overall Review Questions

Mark all you believe to be reasonably correct.

1. An economic system manages:

    a. The allocation of various natural resources available to an economy.

    b. The application of conversion labor to natural resources available to an economy.

    c. The application of "thought" to a potential good or service desired by the people of an economy.

    d. The title to readily available natural resources.

    e. The means of trading the output derived from the application of conversion labor to readily available natural resources.

    f. The dilemma experienced by Tiny Tim in the novel A Christmas Carol was a result of the way in which the economic system managed the distribution of the output of the economy.

2. Things we know about various key classes within economic units/economies:

    a. Households can save money.

    b. Countries cannot save money.

    c. Businesses can shed people (i.e., employees).

    d. Countries that use a "relative" tax assessment means cannot reduce the national debt by reducing community (government) operating costs.

3. An economy develops as a result of:

    a. Application of conversion labor to a readily available natural resource.

    b. Wind passing through a windmill to grind grain.

    c. The discovery of a copper deposit.

d. The planting of crops.

e. The singing of a song in return for a trade.

4. Money:

    a. Is a record of the value of title to the value of conversion labor applied to produce something of economic value.

    b. Is used as a means of expression to attach value to natural resources.

    c. Can be used in exchanging all or portions of a particular resource or labor for all or portions of another and probably different particular resource or labor.

    d. Allows the holder of the value of conversion labor to delay exchanging his/her labor value for that of others until some later date (saved).

    e. Facilitates the desire of the holder of the value of conversion labor to pass this value on, to beneficiaries designated in a will.

5. Key aspects of an economic system that affect the quality of life for you and your children are:

    a. The method of determining title to natural resources and the means of production and distribution.

    b. The level of allocation of the benefit of your conversion labor to the "job creators" (whether it is inadequate or excessive).

    c. The degree to which the community taxes and spends the value of your conversion labor (whether it is inadequate or excessive).

    d. The degree of alignment with the needs of the greater citizenry for a good quality of life.

    e. The degree of compatibility with a democratic political system.

    f. Whether you own the economic system or the system owns you.

6. General statements about economics:

    a. The economy does not differentiate (doesn't care) whether a dollar is spent by an individual (for a car, TV, computer) or the community (highway, school, disability payment); the economy reacts the same either way.

    b. A community (government) expenditure provides additional macroeconomic "demand" in the form of different types of goods and services than the demand of persons and businesses. This "demand" might shift to demand for additional goods and services, as those demanded and provided by the private sector, <u>if government spending were reduced</u>. But, total demand would not increase; therefore, <u>no economic growth would be realized and no new jobs would be added.</u>

    c. The reduction of the inheritance tax for large estates (those exceeding 1,000 times the average household income) has not created a threat to American democracy.

    d. If Social Security payments are reduced (in real dollars) and Medicare is reduced or eliminated, I will have enough money to take care of my spouse plus my mother and dad should they live into their late 80's.

    e. I own the economic system; it does not own me.

7. If the economy improves following a reduction in US corporate income tax rates as depicted in Chapter 2, Section A (readers should also look at the discussion logic related to the Obama Social Security tax reduction found in the section "Fixes to the Current Programs" in the Chapter "Fix Social Security"):

    a. The economy works in cycles – there are periods of both expansion and contraction. If the economy improves, it will be a matter of coincidence, unrelated to the tax reduction.

    b. The economy will improve short term as more "active money" is added to the system. However, if the reduction is financed by an increase in federal debt – eventually there will occur an offsetting slowing of the economy.

    c. The economy will improve short term as more "active money" is added to the system. However, if the reduction is financed by a reduction in government spending – almost immediately after the tax reduction there will occur an offsetting slowing of the economy. The near-immediate effect will be a zero outcome for the US economy.

d. There will be a permanent improvement in the US economy due to the increase in money available for investment in America (a country that, in practical terms, has never experienced a shortfall in money available for substantive investment).

e. All of the above.

f. None of the above.

APPENDIX A - PERCENTAGES

Many people, most of the time – but, not all of the time, have difficulty working with percentages.

When do people **not** have difficulty? When buying chewing gum.

The sales clerk asks you for 53 cents (50 cents for the gum and 3 cents for sales tax) and you give the clerk 53 percent of a dollar. You have just used percentages to define a monetary (money based) relationship.

The word "cent" is slang for the word "percent." 53 cents means 53 percent of a dollar. You have been an expert in using percentages most of your life, and you didn't even know it.

Every time you buy or sell something for a value that is not an even dollar value you are using percentages.

The mathematical symbol for percent is - %.

For instance, if a salesperson tells you that you need to pay $8,700.67 for a used car. The 67 cents tacked onto the end of the price is equal to 67% of a dollar.

Governments use percentages when raising revenue to pay for operating the government.

When collecting income tax a government body (normally federal and state governments) applies a percentage figure to the income of a person or business. For instance, a state income tax might be expressed as 5% of income. This means the citizens must pay the government 5 cents out of every dollar earned to enable the state to facilitate building schools, highways, etc. and providing law enforcement, social services, etc.

The use of percentages is not limited to money. Percentages can be applied to non-monetary economic assessments as well.

Economists use percentages when analyzing aspects of an economy. For instance, an economist might say that 32% of American households do not have adequate earnings as needed to purchase adequate health care services. If there are 100 million households in America, then this statement means that 32 million American households do not have adequate earnings to pay for adequate health care.

APPENDIX B - PENNY MONEY FLOW EXERCISE

ASSUMPTIONS & INSTRUCTIONS:

1. **The exercise goal is to understand the flow of money through the economy. You will need six rolls of pennies (300 pennies) to complete this exercise.**
2. The idea is to use the pennies to represent the transactions of a pretend economy; the **transactions for a Monday and Tuesday are pre-scheduled.**
3. You will need eight participants and a facilitator to complete this exercise - each participant will be assigned to play an individual as scheduled below.
4. Six vendors make up a pretend private sector economy: **doctor, lawyer, software expert, gardener, house cleaner, and a masseuse.**
5. Each provides a service and none has any business expenses (done to simplify exercise); therefore their whole revenue is taxable income. In the exercise each vendor will receive income and pay taxes. Each pretend vendor should keep track of his/her pre-tax and after tax income received.
6. Total the receipts for the day for the Tax Man and for Net After Tax Earnings provided to the private sector economy; do likewise for cumulative amounts.
7. Total the net earnings per vendor; at the end of the exercise ask each vendor to tell the group how much they had earned.
8. On **Monday Sue and Jane,** Welfare Recipients, each receive 150 pennies from the government and spend it with the **doctor ($100) and the lawyer ($50).**
9. **Tuesday the doctor and lawyer** pay 20% to the Tax Man and spend their **net after tax earnings** as received from Sue and Jane (see schedule below): The doctor spends $160 ($200 income minus $40 tax) and the lawyer spends $80 ($100 income minus $20 tax). Respectively, each of five of the vendors receives: lawyer $80, software expert $40, Gardener $30, House Cleaner $50, and Masseuse $40.
10. **Wednesday the gardener, house cleaner, and masseuse** spend all their money **with each other** - YOU DECIDE HOW MUCH WITH EACH & FILL IN THE BOXES.
11. NOTE: As the amounts of the transactions become smaller (fewer pennies) it will be necessary to **round up or down to whole pennies for paying the Tax Man.** Calculate for each vendor the amount paid to the **Tax Man** and that kept by the vendor as After Tax Earnings *(see calculations for Monday and Tuesday).*
12. Calculate for each vendor the amount paid to the **Tax Man** and that kept by the vendor as After Tax Earnings.
13. **Thursday the software expert, house cleaner, and masseuse** spend all their money with the **doctor, lawyer and house cleaner** - YOU DECIDE HOW MUCH WITH EACH. Recall that the **software expert has 32 pennies** in his pocket he earned on Tuesday and has not yet spent.
14. Calculate for each vendor the amount paid to the Tax Man and that kept by the vendor as After Tax Earnings.
15. Total the receipts for the day for the Tax Man and for Net After Tax Earnings provided to the private sector economy; then do likewise for cumulative amounts.
16. By the end of Thursday, how much of the 300 pennies paid to Sue and Jane, by the government, will have been recovered by the tax man?
17. By the end of Thursday, how much after tax earnings will have been generated in the private sector economy - for each vendor & total?

ASSUMED SINGLE GOVERNMENT INCOME TAX RATE = 20% OF INCOME PAID TO TAX MAN / THE FACILITATOR

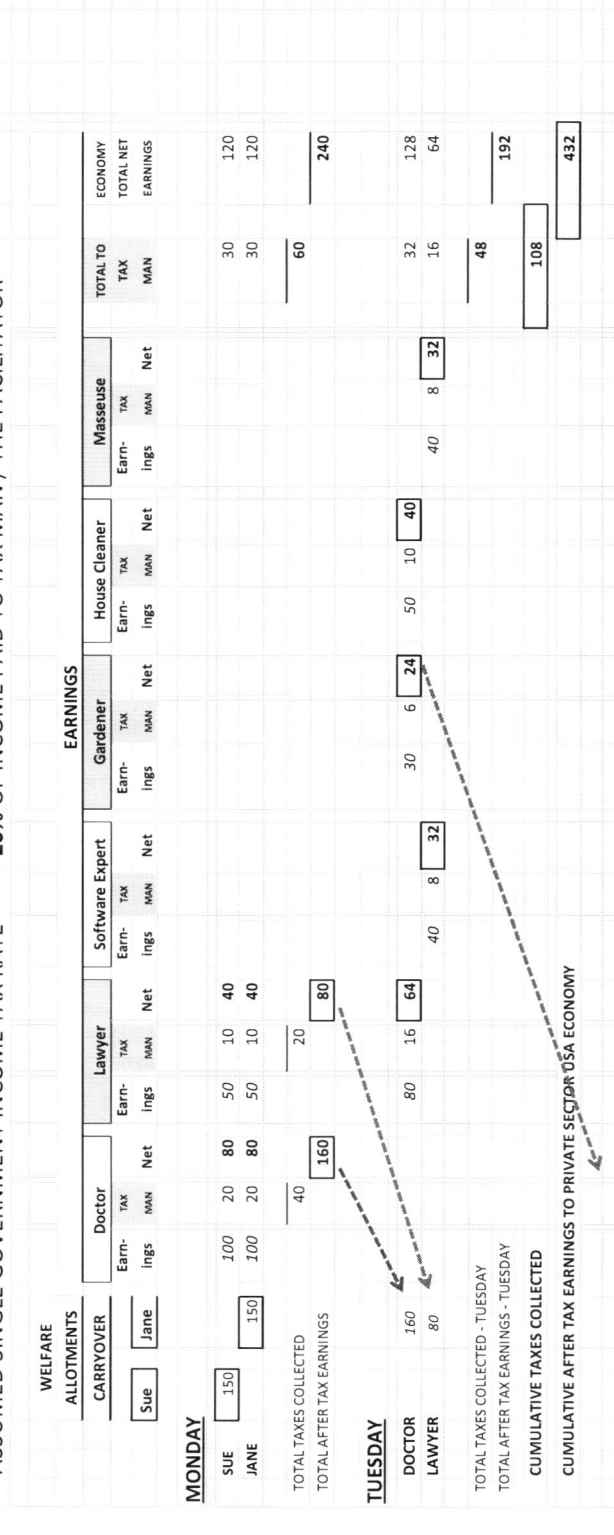

WELFARE ALLOTMENTS

CARRYOVER	
Sue	Jane
150	150

MONDAY

	Doctor			Lawyer			Software Expert			Gardener			House Cleaner			Masseuse			TOTAL TO	ECONOMY
	Earn-ings	TAX MAN	Net	Earn-ings	TAX MAN	Net	Earn-ings	TAX MAN	Net	Earn-ings	TAX MAN	Net	Earn-ings	TAX MAN	Net	Earn-ings	TAX MAN	Net	TAX MAN	TOTAL NET EARNINGS
SUE	100	20	80	50	10	40													30	120
JANE	100	20	80	50	10	40													30	120
TOTAL TAXES COLLECTED		40			20														60	
TOTAL AFTER TAX EARNINGS			160			80														240

TUESDAY

	Doctor			Lawyer			Software Expert			Gardener			House Cleaner			Masseuse			TOTAL TO	ECONOMY
	Earn-ings	TAX MAN	Net	Earn-ings	TAX MAN	Net	Earn-ings	TAX MAN	Net	Earn-ings	TAX MAN	Net	Earn-ings	TAX MAN	Net	Earn-ings	TAX MAN	Net	TAX MAN	TOTAL NET EARNINGS
DOCTOR	160			80	16	64	40	8	32	30	6	24	50	10	40	40	8	32	32	128
LAWYER	80																		16	64
TOTAL TAXES COLLECTED - TUESDAY																			48	
TOTAL AFTER TAX EARNINGS - TUESDAY																				192
CUMULATIVE TAXES COLLECTED																			108	
CUMULATIVE AFTER TAX EARNINGS TO PRIVATE SECTOR USA ECONOMY																				432

BLANK TO BE COMPLETED BY GROUP PARTICIPANTS

p 2

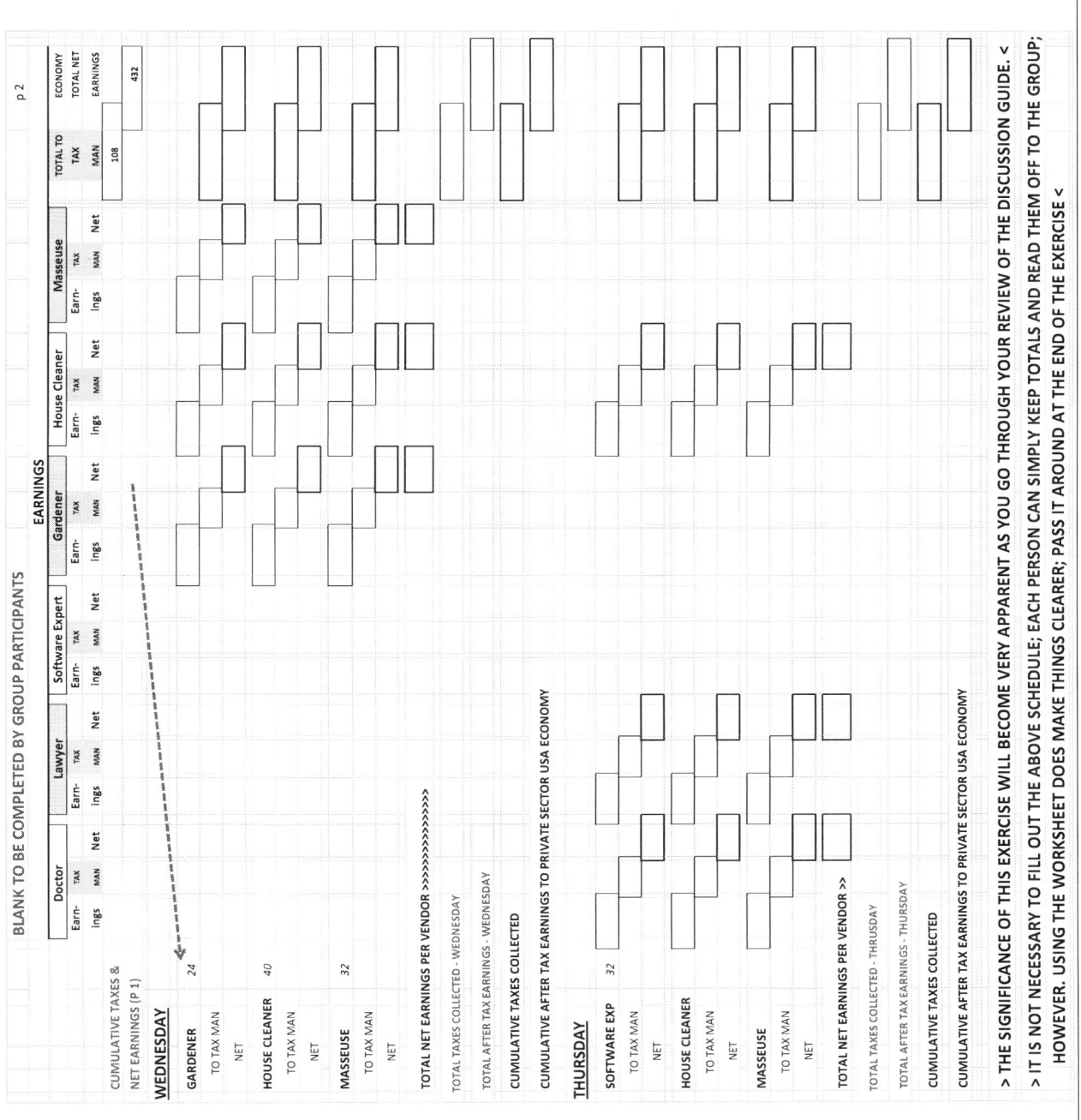

EARNINGS

	Doctor			Lawyer			Software Expert			Gardener			House Cleaner			Masseuse			TOTAL TO TAX MAN	ECONOMY TOTAL NET EARNINGS
	Earn-ings	TAX MAN	Net	Earn-ings	TAX MAN	Net	Earn-ings	TAX MAN	Net	Earn-ings	TAX MAN	Net	Earn-ings	TAX MAN	Net	Earn-ings	TAX MAN	Net		
CUMULATIVE TAXES & NET EARNINGS (P 1)																			108	432

WEDNESDAY

GARDENER 24
 TO TAX MAN
 NET

HOUSE CLEANER 40
 TO TAX MAN
 NET

MASSEUSE 32
 TO TAX MAN
 NET

TOTAL NET EARNINGS PER VENDOR >>>>>>>>>>>>>

TOTAL TAXES COLLECTED - WEDNESDAY

TOTAL AFTER TAX EARNINGS - WEDNESDAY

CUMULATIVE TAXES COLLECTED

CUMULATIVE AFTER TAX EARNINGS TO PRIVATE SECTOR USA ECONOMY

THURSDAY

SOFTWARE EXP 32
 TO TAX MAN
 NET

HOUSE CLEANER
 TO TAX MAN
 NET

MASSEUSE
 TO TAX MAN
 NET

TOTAL NET EARNINGS PER VENDOR >>

TOTAL TAXES COLLECTED - THURSDAY

TOTAL AFTER TAX EARNINGS - THURSDAY

CUMULATIVE TAXES COLLECTED

CUMULATIVE AFTER TAX EARNINGS TO PRIVATE SECTOR USA ECONOMY

> THE SIGNIFICANCE OF THIS EXERCISE WILL BECOME VERY APPARENT AS YOU GO THROUGH YOUR REVIEW OF THE DISCUSSION GUIDE. <

> IT IS NOT NECESSARY TO FILL OUT THE ABOVE SCHEDULE; EACH PERSON CAN SIMPLY KEEP TOTALS AND READ THEM OFF TO THE GROUP; HOWEVER, USING THE WORKSHEET DOES MAKE THINGS CLEARER; PASS IT AROUND AT THE END OF THE EXERCISE <

APPENDIX C - SOCIAL SECURITY % PAY DEDUCTION REQUIRED BASED ON USING AVERAGE WAGE

2017 USA ESTIMATED AVERAGE WAGE	2017 USA POVERTY LEVEL		80 % OF AVERAGE WAGE	2017 PER SSA: SS RETIREE AVG PAY-OUT
	1 PERSON HOUSEHOLD	2 PERSON HOUSEHOLD		
$ 49,000	$ 12,060	$ 16,240	$ 39,200	$ 16,320

PAY-AS-WE-GO ANNUAL ASSESSMENT PER WORKER AND % OF AVERAGE WAGE

CURRENT 2017 > 2.8 WORKERS/SS RETIREE			PROJECTED 2033 > 2.1 WORKERS/SS RETIREE		
1 PERSON POVERTY LEVEL	80% OF AVERAGE WAGE	CURRENT AVERAGE PAYOUT	1 PERSON POVERTY LEVEL	80% OF AVERAGE WAGE	CURRENT AVERAGE PAYOUT
$ 4,307	$ 14,000	$ 5,829	$ 5,743	$ 18,667	$ 7,771
8.8%	28.6%	11.9%	11.7%	38.1%	15.9%

APPENDIX D

1) The schedule below begins with the data as presented in the discussion text in Chapter 2, Section E, Schedule 1 and follows the flow of money until it becomes diminutive.

2) For simplicity, the example is structured such that the only people involved in doing business after the first Wednesday are George and Mary. George works for Mary and Mary works for George.

3) The final private sector after tax income for the example is $996.66. If we continued with the calculations it would become $1,000. This would require several sheets of paper.

DAY	VENDOR	Pay $	Tax $	NET PAY After Tax $	Pay $	Tax $	NET PAY After Tax $	Pay $	Tax $	NET PAY After Tax $	Pay $	Tax $	NET PAY After Tax $
Fri	Bob	100.000	20.000	80.000									
Fri	Sue	100.000	20.000	80.000									
Mon	Jim	80.000	16.000	64.000	20.000	4.000	16.000						
Mon	Jane	80.000	16.000	64.000	20.000	4.000	16.000						
Tues	Jane	64.000	12.800	51.200	16.000	3.200	12.800	4.000	0.800	3.200			
Tues	Mary	64.000	12.800	51.200	16.000	3.200	12.800	4.000	0.800	3.200			
Weds	Mary	51.200	10.240	40.960	12.800	2.560	10.240	3.200	0.640	2.560	0.800	0.160	0.640
Weds	Jim	51.200	10.240	40.960	12.800	2.560	10.240	3.200	0.640	2.560	0.800	0.160	0.640
Weds	George	40.960	8.192	32.768	10.240	2.048	8.192	2.560	0.512	2.048	0.640	0.128	0.512
Thrs	GEORGE WORKS FOR MARY	40.960	8.192	32.768	10.240	2.048	8.192	2.560	0.512	2.048	0.640	0.128	0.512
Thrs	Mary works for George	32.768	6.554	26.214	8.192	1.638	6.554	2.048	0.410	1.638	0.512	0.102	0.410
Fri	GEORGE WORKS FOR MARY	32.768	6.554	26.214	8.192	1.638	6.554	2.048	0.410	1.638	0.512	0.102	0.410
Fri	Mary works for George	26.214	5.243	20.972	6.554	1.311	5.243	1.638	0.328	1.311	0.410	0.082	0.328
Mon	GEORGE WORKS FOR MARY	26.214	5.243	20.972	6.554	1.311	5.243	1.638	0.328	1.311	0.410	0.082	0.328
Mon	Mary works for George	20.972	4.194	16.777	5.243	1.049	4.194	1.311	0.262	1.049	0.328	0.066	0.262
Tues	GEORGE WORKS FOR MARY	20.972	4.194	16.777	5.243	1.049	4.194	1.311	0.262	1.049	0.328	0.066	0.262
Tues	Mary works for George	16.777	3.355	13.422	4.194	0.839	3.355	1.049	0.210	0.839	0.262	0.052	0.210
Weds	GEORGE WORKS FOR MARY	16.777	3.355	13.422	4.194	0.839	3.355	1.049	0.210	0.839	0.262	0.052	0.210
Weds	Mary works for George	13.422	2.684	10.737	3.355	0.671	2.684	0.839	0.168	0.671	0.210	0.042	0.168
Thrs	GEORGE WORKS FOR MARY	13.422	2.684	10.737	3.355	0.671	2.684	0.839	0.168	0.671	0.210	0.042	0.168
Thrs	Mary works for George	10.737	2.147	8.590	2.684	0.537	2.147	0.671	0.134	0.537	0.168	0.034	0.134
Fri	GEORGE WORKS FOR MARY	10.737	2.147	8.590	2.684	0.537	2.147	0.671	0.134	0.537	0.168	0.034	0.134
Fri	Mary works for George	8.590	1.718	6.872	2.147	0.429	1.718	0.537	0.107	0.429	0.134	0.027	0.107
Mon	GEORGE WORKS FOR MARY	8.590	1.718	6.872	2.147	0.429	1.718	0.537	0.107	0.429	0.134	0.027	0.107
Mon	Mary works for George	6.872	1.374	5.498	1.718	0.344	1.374	0.429	0.086	0.344	0.107	0.021	0.086
Tues	GEORGE WORKS FOR MARY	6.872	1.374	5.498	1.718	0.344	1.374	0.429	0.086	0.344	0.107	0.021	0.086
Tues	Mary works for George	5.498	1.100	4.398	1.374	0.275	1.100	0.344	0.069	0.275	0.086	0.017	0.069
Weds	GEORGE WORKS FOR MARY	5.498	1.100	4.398	1.374	0.275	1.100	0.344	0.069	0.275	0.086	0.017	0.069
Weds	Mary works for George	4.398	0.880	3.518	1.100	0.220	0.880	0.275	0.055	0.220	0.069	0.014	0.055
Thrs	GEORGE WORKS FOR MARY	4.398	0.880	3.518	1.100	0.220	0.880	0.275	0.055	0.220	0.069	0.014	0.055
Thrs	Mary works for George	3.518	0.704	2.815	0.880	0.176	0.704	0.220	0.044	0.176	0.055	0.011	0.044
Fri	GEORGE WORKS FOR MARY	3.518	0.704	2.815	0.880	0.176	0.704	0.220	0.044	0.176	0.055	0.011	0.044
Fri	Mary works for George	2.815	0.563	2.252	0.704	0.141	0.563	0.176	0.035	0.141	0.044	0.009	0.035
Mon	GEORGE WORKS FOR MARY	2.815	0.563	2.252	0.704	0.141	0.563	0.176	0.035	0.141	0.044	0.009	0.035
Mon	Mary works for George	2.252	0.450	1.801	0.563	0.113	0.450	0.141	0.028	0.113	0.035	0.007	0.028
Tues	GEORGE WORKS FOR MARY	2.252	0.450	1.801	0.563	0.113	0.450	0.141	0.028	0.113	0.035	0.007	0.028
Tues	Mary works for George	1.801	0.360	1.441	0.450	0.090	0.360	0.113	0.023	0.090	0.028	0.006	0.023
Weds	GEORGE WORKS FOR MARY	1.801	0.360	1.441	0.450	0.090	0.360	0.113	0.023	0.090	0.028	0.006	0.023
Weds	Mary works for George	1.441	0.288	1.153	0.360	0.072	0.288	0.090	0.018	0.072	0.023	0.005	0.018
Thrs	GEORGE WORKS FOR MARY	1.441	0.288	1.153	0.360	0.072	0.288	0.090	0.018	0.072	0.023	0.005	0.018
Thrs	Mary works for George	1.153	0.231	0.922	0.288	0.058	0.231	0.072	0.014	0.058	0.018	0.004	0.014
Fri	GEORGE WORKS FOR MARY	1.153	0.231	0.922	0.288	0.058	0.231	0.072	0.014	0.058	0.018	0.004	0.014
Fri	Mary works for George	0.922	0.184	0.738	0.231	0.046	0.184	0.058	0.012	0.046	0.014	0.003	0.012
Mon	GEORGE WORKS FOR MARY	0.922	0.184	0.738	0.231	0.046	0.184	0.058	0.012	0.046	0.014	0.003	0.012
Mon	Mary works for George	0.738	0.148	0.590	0.184	0.037	0.148	0.046	0.009	0.037	0.012	0.002	0.009
Tues	GEORGE WORKS FOR MARY	0.738	0.148	0.590	0.184	0.037	0.148	0.046	0.009	0.037	0.012	0.002	0.009
Tues	Mary works for George	0.590	0.118	0.472	0.148	0.030	0.118	0.037	0.007	0.030	0.009	0.002	0.007
Weds	GEORGE WORKS FOR MARY	0.590	0.118	0.472	0.148	0.030	0.118	0.037	0.007	0.030	0.009	0.002	0.007
Weds	Mary works for George	0.472	0.094	0.378	0.118	0.024	0.094	0.030	0.006	0.024	0.007	0.001	0.006
Thrs	GEORGE WORKS FOR MARY	0.472	0.094	0.378	0.118	0.024	0.094	0.030	0.006	0.024	0.007	0.001	0.006
Thrs	Mary works for George	0.378	0.076	0.302	0.094	0.019	0.076	0.024	0.005	0.019	0.006	0.001	0.005
Fri	GEORGE WORKS FOR MARY	0.378	0.076	0.302	0.094	0.019	0.076	0.024	0.005	0.019	0.006	0.001	0.005
Fri	Mary works for George	0.302	0.060	0.242	0.076	0.015	0.060	0.019	0.004	0.015	0.005	0.001	0.004
Mon	GEORGE WORKS FOR MARY	0.302	0.060	0.242	0.076	0.015	0.060	0.019	0.004	0.015	0.005	0.001	0.004
Mon	Mary works for George	0.242	0.048	0.193	0.060	0.012	0.048	0.015	0.003	0.012	0.004	0.001	0.003
Tues	GEORGE WORKS FOR MARY	0.242	0.048	0.193	0.060	0.012	0.048	0.015	0.003	0.012	0.004	0.001	0.003
Tues	Mary works for George	0.193	0.039	0.155	0.048	0.010	0.039	0.012	0.002	0.010	0.003	0.001	0.002
Weds	GEORGE WORKS FOR MARY				0.048	0.010	0.039	0.012	0.002	0.010	0.003	0.001	0.002
Weds	Mary works for George				0.039	0.008	0.031	0.010	0.002	0.008	0.002	0.000	0.002
Thrs	GEORGE WORKS FOR MARY							0.010	0.002	0.008	0.002	0.000	0.002
Thrs	Mary works for George							0.008	0.002	0.006	0.002	0.000	0.002
Fri	GEORGE WORKS FOR MARY										0.002	0.000	0.002
Fri	Mary works for George										0.002	0.000	0.001
	Column Totals			**798.607**			**159.721**			**31.944**			**6.389**
	GRAND TOTAL THRU EXAMPLE CUT-OFF >>>>												**996.662**

APPENDIX E – EXAMPLE OF MONEY FLOW FOR A NON-SERVICE BUSINESSES

The examples in the discussion text, for simplicity, assumed all of the workers were in a service type of business and they had no costs for supplies or inventory. Many workers do not work in service businesses that have no costs of materials or supplies. Following is a more realistic, short example (leakage is ignored for simplicity):

- Peter receives a Social Security check for $500. Peter does not pay taxes on the $500.

- Peter spends $100 of his check at Vicki's Corner Grocery.

- Vicki realizes $10 of profit on the $100. Vicki's tax rate is 20%. – Vicki pays the government (community) $2 in income taxes.

- Vicki pays her supplier $50 to replenish her shelves with the groceries Peter bought. Her supplier earns $10 on her $50 purchase.

- The supplier's tax rate is 20%. The supplier pays the government $2 in income taxes.

- Vicki pays her employee $10 in wages out of the $100. The employee's tax rate is 20%. The employee pays the government $2 in income taxes.

- The employee is left with $8 after taxes are paid. He hires Linda to wash his windows for $8.

- Linda has no cost of sales as did Vicki and Vicki's supplier; therefore, the whole $8 is income to Linda. Linda, therefore, pays the government $1.60 in income taxes on her $8 in earnings.

- At this point the government (community) has spent $500 on Peter and recovered, due to the money cycling through the economy and the taxes collected as it cycled:

$2.00	from Vicki
$2.00	from Vicki's supplier
$2.00	from Vicki's employee
$1.60	from Linda

  For a total of $7.60 of the $500 expenditure on Peter.

- The money (Peter's $500 SS check) will continue to flow through the economy and, ignoring leakage, eventually, create $2,500 in after-tax private sector income.

APPENDIX F - DISCUSSION OF MONEY FLOW FOR A GOVERNMENT EXPANSIONARY ACTIVITY

Appendix F is more difficult to understand than is the content of the rest of the book. As stated in Chapter 1 – "there is no simple way to say some things." Therefore, do not be disappointed if you find it challenging to understand the content of this appendix.

The money system will be addressed in Discussion Guide 2. However, here a brief overview is provided to assist in your understanding of Government Expansionary Activity.

All transactions in an economy that employs a monetary (versus barter) system generate a multiplying effect. A $1 bill passes from hand to hand, minus taxes paid, supporting more transactions than that supported by the original $1 bill. However, this happens in different ways.

There are those ways that:

- Support everyday spending - we will call these "everyday activities"
- Provide for the accommodation of the demand increase related to population growth, "expansion activities"
- Provide for the accommodation of changes in demand patterns, "accommodation activities"
- Provide for an <u>increase in real dollar demand</u> other than those related to normal population growth and changes in demand patterns, "expansionary activities." This increase in demand does not typically relate to increases in demand during normal economic times. It could – but, the resulting growth may drive a high increase in inflation. Typically, expansionary activities are employed to offset dips in the economy (i.e. recessions and depressions).

Expansionary activities occur primarily in three ways: when the Federal Government engages in expansionary activities (i.e. stimulus programs), when the Fed engages in expansionary activities (encourages investment by lowering the cost of borrowing and increasing the availability of money for borrowing), and when exports increase relative to imports. The most effective of these activities is the expansionary activities engaged in by the Federal Government.

This appendix reviews various aspects of Federal Government expansionary activates. It is noted that expansion activities do incorporate, to a minor degree, an expansionary component. This is significant to the degree that such activities increase or decrease (negative expansionary activity) relative to that which is the normal level of activity at any given time and subject to actions by the Fed to control inflation.

Expansionary activities initiated by the Federal Government are magnified by the actions, of businesses and individuals to deposit excess money, which is then lent out by banks or other lenders.

In the Penney Money Flow exercises and Section E – <u>Money Flow Government</u>, of Chapter 1, we reviewed the effect of reductions in government spending, without regards to leakage, on the private sector economy and unemployment. In this appendix, we look at a **simplified example** of what happens when the Federal Government's spending is increased; **expansionary activity** (i.e. leading toward the expansion of demand). The effect of leakage (money leaving the active US economy) in relation to an expansionary activity is incorporated in the example. Additionally, the magnifying effect of monies deposited and then lent is incorporated into the example.

Examples of expansionary activities are:
- Increases to current defense spending (without offsetting decreases elsewhere)
- Increases in or extensions of unemployment insurance, and
- As discussed in this book, a Senior Worker's Transition Stimulus Package.

Leakage types addressed herein, as a percentage of dollars spent, are:
- The Trade Deficit relative to the period at which an expansionary expenditure is made (assumed to be 1 ½%)
- The Savings rate for the same period (assumed to be 5 ½%), and
- Other (assumed to be ½%).

Examples of "Other" leakage include:
- The net of unaccounted American tourist dollars spent overseas and unaccounted foreign tourist monies spent in the USA
- The net of profits extracted by foreign corporations doing business in the USA and that extracted by USA corporations doing business outside of the USA without repatriation.

In completing the Penny Money Flow exercise, we saw how a $100 reduction in government expenditures (budget cut) results in a $500 reduction in private sector revenue, income, and jobs. This relationship between the government expenditure and private sector revenue and is referred to as the **multiplier effect**. As reductions in expenditures are made a greater reduction (a multiple) in private sector revenue and income is realized, as well as, a reduction in the number of jobs supported by the economy. For the most part, the relationship will be the inverse of the effective income tax rate and subject to an adjustment for leakage.

What happens when the government increases expenditures? The same thing happens – in reverse. A $100 increase in expenditures results in a $500 increase in private sector revenue and income (at a 20% effective income tax rate) as adjusted for leakage; as well as, an increase in the number of jobs in the economy. However, the increase must be funded. This is done by increasing taxes or selling bonds. Bonds must be paid off at maturity; therefore, at some point in the future tax revenues must be increased or shifted from some other government use. This current or future tax increase has a negative impact on the economy (a negative multiplier) that, to a degree, offsets the effect of the positive multiplier. However, the net effect is positive. (NOTE: The negative multiplier effect [as related to taxes] is already in place when Federal Government expenditures are reduced. If the expenditure reduction is accompanied by a tax reduction – all that happens is a shift from public to private sector spending. Unfortunately, this shift causes an increase in unemployment as discussed previously in Government Money Flow Exercise and will be explained further in Discussion Guide 2.)

What about private sector expenditures – do they not result, also, in a multiplier effect? The answer is "yes." If we think of "profit" as a form of private sector tax, it is possible a portion of the inverse of this private tax will be realized in economic growth or contraction if the private sector increases or decreases its expenditures financed by profits. (We can think, also, of the whole price of the product as a private tax – this would apply in certain discussions unrelated to this discussion) I use the words "possible" and "portion" because business profits are allocated to paying taxes, dividends, investment, repaying loans, lending out unneeded cash, etc. That used for investment and lending which is related to "expansion activity" may provide upward pressure on the economy; that is, have a multiplier effect. The degree of realization of the multiplier effect as related to the other categories depends on what those receiving the money do with the money. For example, to what degree does this money re-enter the economy as active or idle money?

However, the business sector expands in response to increases in demand and anticipated demand; the sector does not engage in expansionary initiatives. Expansion and expansionary activities are not one in the same (private sector versus public sector [i.e. government/community] initiated growth is covered below). The expansion undertaken by the business sector acts to cement the realization of economic growth; thereby, fortifying the forces of the multiplier effect. The seed for growth (**root cause**) comes from "demand."

If, mathematically, both the public and private sectors of the economy can grow the economy by simply spending more money, why is not economic growth unlimited? This is not the case as the availability of readily available natural resources mined and the availability and the pace of work of conversion labor is limited in any period in time. The primary limitation, over time, in the USA is the availability of labor hours; as resources are abundant. The pace at which labor can work limits the pace at which the economy can grow. The pace at which labor can work is primarily determined by the natural limits of human endurance and speed, desire for personal time, and level of enablization (primarily investment in productive assets [machinery, equipment, software, etc.] and training).

If the pace of labor is a limitation – does this pace govern the speed at which transactions (someone sells some thing and someone else buys this thing) are completed? The answer is "to a large part, yes." The level and timing of demand sets the actual speed at which transactions take place. Since all demand fulfillment depends on labor worked or to be worked – the quantity and pace of labor worked is the major determinant. However, the level and pace of demand are also influenced by the availability of credit, by psychological factors such as the consumers' confidence in the economy, and by other economic factors interrelating within both the domestic and external economies.

Additionally, for relatively short periods of time, demand rises and falls (cyclical). This relates primarily to the durability of products procured both by consumers and the business supply chain and to the ability of the consumer to buy on credit. The propensity of consumers to procure products either directly or on credit is limited, too, by the wage levels of those in the workforce with a high propensity to consume (versus save; keeping money active as opposed to rendering money idle). Periodically, due to the issues of product durability and credit limitations, in layman terms, the demand dries up. Government spending provides a steady stream of income and jobs that act as a cushion for the economy when demand dries up. This factor helps set a bottom on recessionary periods and, thereby, facilitates faster recovery.

Wage levels are determined, in the aggregate, primarily by the markets (demand and price determinants) for the particular products produced by workers and the supply of labor of the type needed to produce the products. Within the framework of the market for a particular product, the market provides a sum to be allocated to profit and each of the costs for selling, materials, supplies, overhead, labor, and taxes. Each business then allocates the sum provided for labor amongst the workers at the business – from Board Chairman to Grounds Keeper. This allocation is, in part, determined by the supply of each type of labor required by the business. In some cases the supply is restricted to domestic labor and in other cases it includes overseas labor. The overseas option directly pushes down job type per job type wages; but, also, it pushes down unrelated job type wages as it increases the domestic competition for the jobs that remain in the USA.

Due to pace limitations the effects of a multiplier effect are spread out over a period of time. The period of spread is a topic of discussion amongst economists. This includes an assessment of the first year effect. There is a wide assortment of opinions of how much of the multiplier effect is realized in the first year following the introduction of an expansionary expenditure by the Federal Government.

Whatever the spread of the effect, a question to ask is "to what degree does the public and private sectors initiate expansion." The public sector has an ability, <u>which does exist in the private sector</u>, to initiate economic growth. This fact is limited by the restriction that the public sector, to exist, needs the private sector; therefore the public sector cannot enter into a zone of operation in which it is competing with the private sector for resources (capital/investment) and labor. It is unlikely that this would ever happen with regards to resources. The limit on labor could be defined as that point at which the Fed can no longer control inflation by managing the unemployment level.

Why does the public sector have a greater propensity to initiate growth than does the public sector? The public sector can:

- Capitalize on excess idle money (that money held by businesses and individuals that is not needed for consumption, savings, or substantive investment in productive assets), and
- Employ an economic practice akin to that popularly known as "supply-side economics." (**Supply-side economics** is a **macroeconomic** theory that argues **economic growth** can be most effectively created by investing in **capital** and by lowering barriers on the production of goods and services. **https://en.wikipedia.org/wiki/Supply-side_economics**,)

Within the boundary of the business sphere, excess idle money exists because businesses have no practical place to put it. Therefore, the option of capitalizing excess money is not available to businesses as a whole. At some given window of time, some businesses may have a lot of idle money while others have little or none. There, more often than not, exists a resistance within the public (potential stockholders) or other businesses (e.g. banks, venture capital firms, and potential stockholders) to invest in or lend to those businesses that are short on money and equity. In those situations which attract investment (either as equity or loans), idle money is converted into active money; but this may or may not help grow the economy.

- If a town has 20 restaurants and investment is made in a 21st restaurant it is unlikely that the economy will grow. Most likely, the only thing that will happen is that some business from the first 20 restaurants will shift to the 21st restaurant resulting in near zero economic growth. Note, the economic inefficiency of another source of supply to a market that is not short of supply will result in very minor economic growth. This will happen because of the associated redistribution of income – lowering the savings and consumption levels of some to provide for the savings and consumption of the employees and owners of the new restaurant.

- If a business brings a previously non-provided product to the market (e.g. the introduction of cell phones), and <u>the unemployment level is above the Fed's target,</u> and <u>the public is willing to reduce its saving rate,</u> growth will be realized. This growth, however, may be mitigated during periods of strong economic activity as the Fed takes actions to cool the economy. The growth benefit may, however, resurface, as the economy later reignites. This is the case as a new type of demand has been defined (e.g. cell phone demand) and it remains part of the economy.

Businesses make investments designed to provide a return based on forecasted demand (current real and anticipated). All such investment justifications start with a demand forecast. Therefore, contrary to what some economists and politicians think, in the non-theoretical world, businesses practice demand-side economics, not supply-side economics. Businesses have the practical ability to respond to (e.g. growth due primarily to population growth and demographic changes; and increased demand due to floods, hurricanes, war, etc.) and enable demand growth (provide wages) and recover growth (i.e. capacity is already in place) but not to initiate growth.

The <u>root cause</u> of business expansion is <u>demand expansion</u>. The popular concept that businesses initiate growth is a myth. Businesses, as a group, would need to practice supply-side economics to initiate growth.

What would need to happen to enable the business community to practice supply-side economics? All of the CEO's in the country would need to share their company's strategies and investment plans with all other CEO's in the country including their competitors. That's not going to happen.

On the other hand the community – by way of the government – can put excess idle money to work (convert idle money to active money) through taxing and/or borrowing such monies and then spending such monies. Additionally, the government can spend and invest with the objective of increasing demand for the total business sector or a segment of the business sector without regard to who is and who is not a competitor of this company or that. Here is a new label for folks to toss around – "**supply-side demand**." The Federal Government has the ability, when needed, to provide, that is supply, the increase in demand that will drive private sector investment in productive assets. At this point in the process, the private sector investment will fortify the demand (i.e. provide wages and increase the level of capacity). If the government decides to engage in such activity, this decision is referred to as fiscal policy. The resulting multiplier effect is called the <u>fiscal multiplier</u>.

There exists a second multiplier that is called the money (or monetary) multiplier. This is a multiplier that comes about as banks lend money that depositors have deposited and the debtor subsequently deposits the money in his/her bank account (i.e. at the same bank or a second bank). The second bank in a series of banks can lend money based upon the amount of lent money deposited; as can a third bank, a fourth, etc. It would require several pages to discuss the workings of the money multiplier; but only a simplified example demonstrating how it works is required (see Schedules A and B).

The example provided in schedule form demonstrates both the positive expansionary effect and negative tax effects of both fiscal and money multipliers. Additionally, the example accommodates an allowance for leakage. The first schedule depicts a five-year recap of detailed calculations for a $500 expenditure increase spread over five years. The second schedule is an abbreviated version of the full detailed schedule.

The example schedules are not attempted simulations of the real economy. They are a two-part presentation of a simple exercise designed to help the reader understand the multiplier effect and relationships.

The reader should realize while going through the example that to a large extent federal expansionary programs are self-funding. This is due to the relationship of the continuing stream of private sector spending that takes place, after the initial government expenditures, and the recovery of the expenditures through taxation of the spending stream.

Additionally, financing (taxation or borrowing) is required only for the shortfall between initial expenditures and that recovered through taxation.

Following the examples is an additional discussion that will make more sense if covered after the reader reviews the schedules.

EXAMPLES - BACKGROUND:

- At what pace does the fiscal multiplier move through the economy? This depends on the size and frequency of transactions (I sell some thing to you and you buy that thing from me). Economists' opinions vary significantly on this subject – from less than full recovery of the fiscal expenditure to 1.5 times the recovery in the first year following the expenditure. For example, a $100 government expansionary expenditure will generate $70 of private sector first-year benefit at a realization of .7 or $150 a realization of 1.5. Estimates for a complete realization of the multiplier benefit (i.e. ~$500, ignoring leakage) range from 3 to 5 years.

- How fast do the banks lend out the new money generated and saved? All of it is not lent out – but, typically banks lend out the newly deposited money in two to sixteen weeks.

- The expenditure by the government constitutes the first cycle of the multiplier and it generates a direct stream of transactions.

- Each transaction in the direct stream generates some savings which, when deposited then lent, starts a second cycle of transactions. The second cycle stream of transactions generates a third cycle, etc. At some point the benefits from the multiplier effect become diminutive and the schedule is concluded, although the full benefit has not yet covered.

- Note, the schedules presented are depicting a $100 expenditure – the benefits become diminutive much quicker in these schedules than would be the case if the expenditure were $10 billion.

EXAMPLES - SELECT SCHEDULE HEADINGS - DESCRIPTIONS:

"Consumption in Private Sector and Other Gov's" – Money spent in/by the private sector and state and local governments (Gov's) as a result of the $100 expansionary fiscal expenditure. "Spending" and "Consumption," economically speaking have the same meaning. "Spending" is used, here, when addressing money spent by the federal government and "Consumption" is used for spending by others.

"Federal Income Tax Recovered" – Each transaction generates some income on which federal income tax is paid. In this manner, the Federal Government (i.e. US Treasury) recovers some of the money taxed and spent, $100 (note: without leakage the government would recover the full $100 within a few years).

EXAMPLES – SCHEDULE ASSUMPTIONS:

- For simplicity, it is assumed that the complete multiplier effect is realized in the first year of expenditure and that the banks lend out savings instantaneously. A schedule that tracked a realistic depiction would be large and difficult to follow and would provide little to facilitate the reader's understanding.

- The example follows five (5) $100 fiscal expenditures made at the beginning of each of the five years. Both the positive and negative (tax increase) multiplier effect are scheduled, as well as the monetary multiplier effect.

- The tax rate is 15% and leakage is 7 ½ %.

"Leakage (7.5%) Detail" – Leakage occurring in the first cycle related to the government's direct expenditure of $100.

"Savings Conversion to Active $$ - 80% Lent" – It is assumed, for the example, that 80% of the savings deposits made are lent to borrowers

"Consumption in Private Sector & Other Gov's" under "Savings Conversion (Cycle 2 of Year)" – Money lent to borrowers is spent, thereby, initiating a second stream of consumption (spending transactions).

"Program/Project Funding"
"Private Sector & Other Gov's Negative Multiplier" – Expansionary programs and projects will be funded by either a direct tax increase or by incurring debt that will eventually be paid off by a tax increase.

"Financed by Direct Tax" – This section shows the negative multiplier effect resulting from the direct increase in tax (versus government borrowing) on the private sector as is needed to fund the $100 expenditure.

The annual tax revenue required to cover the $100 expenditure increase is $100. However, as the $100 moves through the economy $72.69 of the tax will be recovered. Therefore, the federal government's expenditure will, in part, pay for itself. The net tax increase for a year will be $27.31.

"Economic Effect" – The transfer of money via a tax increase from the private sector to the federal public sector will result in a reduction of private sector consumption. This has a negative multiplier effect that will, in part, offset the positive multiplier effect generated by the government's expansionary spending. An explanation of this calculation can be found on the training website for the CFA (Certified Financial Analyst) exam. http://financialtrain.com/fiscal-multiplier-and-balanced-budget-multiplier/. You will need to search on "Fiscal Multiplier and Balanced Budget Multiplier."

"Financed by Debt/Paid Off by Tax" – To simplify: assumed a bond is issued at the beginning of Yr.1 for the original expenditure of $100. Thereafter, a bond is issued at the beginning of each year for the difference between $100 and the taxes recovered - $27.31 ($100 - $72.69 [tax recovered] = $27.31), plus interest estimated for each upcoming year. Interest is calculated as a flat 6% in years 1-3 and as a flat 8% in years 4 & 5. ALL BONDS ARE DUE AT THE END OF YEAR 5. A bond payoff fund is set up at the beginning of Yr. 1 representing the total of the initial $100, plus the annual additional $27.31 for each of the years. A contribution is made to the bond payoff fund each year for the interest. At the end of the 5 years, the payoff fund is used to pay off the bond and interest due. Taxes are increased to accommodate the deposits to the bond payoff fund.

- Economic Effect of Expansionary Federal Government Spending of $100 Per Year: 5 YEAR PROGRAM / PROJECT - See Assumptions
- Financing Options: 1) by Federal Income Tax Increase - Across the Board, and 2) by Federal Bond / Repaid by Tax Increase
- With Private Sector & Other Governments' 5 Year Net Economic Advantage

TRANSACTION ACTIVITY OF AFTER-TAX DEMAND FOR EACH OF FIVE YEARS OF EXPANSIONARY PROGRAM

YR.	Incremental Fed Gov Spending	FACTORS Fed Taxes = 15.0% Leakage = 7.5% Consumption = 92.5%	CYCLE 1 OF YEAR Consumption in Private Sector & Other Gov's	Federal Income Tax Recovered	Federal Income Tax NOT Recovered	LEAKAGE (7.5%) DETAIL Trade Deficit 1.5%	Net Other 0.5%	Cycle 1 Savings 5.5%	SAVINGS CONVERSION CYCLE 2 OF YEAR Savings Conversion to Active $$ 80% Lent	Consumption in Private Sector & Other Gov's	Federal Income Tax Recovered	Cycle 2 New Savings	SAVINGS CONV. CYCLE 3 OF YEAR - LATER CYCLES ARE DIMINUTIVE AND NOT SHOWN Savings Conversion to Active $$ 80% Lent	Consumption in Private Sector & Other Gov's	Federal Income Tax Recovered	Cycle 3 New Savings
Yr. 1	$ 100.00	15.0%/92.5%	$ 467.75	$ 70.16	$ 29.84	$ 5.96	$ 1.99	$ 21.87	$ 17.49	$ 16.18	$ 2.43	$ 0.96	$ 0.77	$ 0.71	$ 0.11	$ 0.04
Yr. 2	100.00	15.0%/92.5%	467.75	70.16	29.84	5.96	1.99	21.87	17.49	16.18	2.43	0.96	0.77	0.71	0.11	0.04
Yr. 3	100.00	15.0%/92.5%	467.75	70.16	29.84	5.96	1.99	21.87	17.49	16.18	2.43	0.96	0.77	0.71	0.11	0.04
Yr. 4	100.00	15.0%/92.5%	467.75	70.16	29.84	5.96	1.99	21.87	17.49	16.18	2.43	0.96	0.77	0.71	0.11	0.04
Yr. 5	100.00	15.0%/92.5%	467.75	70.16	29.84	5.96	1.99	21.87	17.49	16.18	2.43	0.96	0.77	0.71	0.11	0.04
TOTAL			$ 2,338.77	$ 350.80	$ 149.20	$ 29.82	$ 9.94	$ 109.33	$ 87.47	$ 80.91	$ 12.14	$ 4.81	$ 3.85	$ 3.56	$ 0.53	$ 0.21

TRANSACTION ACTIVITY - CONTINUED

TOTAL: CYCLES 1 - 3 *

YR.	Consumption in Private Sector & Other Gov's	Federal Income Tax Recovered	Savings
Yr. 1	$ 484.65	$ 72.69	$ 22.87
Yr. 2	484.65	72.69	22.87
Yr. 3	484.65	72.69	22.87
Yr. 4	484.65	72.69	22.87
Yr. 5	484.65	72.69	22.87
TOTAL	$ 2,423.24	$ 363.47	$ 114.35

PROGRAM / PROJECT FUNDING

PRIVATE SECTOR & OTHER GOV'S NEGATIVE MULTIPLIER

YR.	FINANCED BY DIRECT TAX Annual Net Tax	Economic Effect **	FINANCED BY DEBT / PAID OFF BY TAX Debt Service Tax	Economic Effect **
Yr. 1	$ 27.31	$ (122.41)	$ 44.36	$ (198.85)
Yr. 2	27.31	(122.41)	47.02	(210.78)
Yr. 3	27.31	(122.41)	49.84	(223.42)
Yr. 4	27.31	(122.41)	56.49	(253.24)
Yr. 5	27.31	(122.41)	61.01	(273.50)
Yr. 6			(72.69)	325.89
TOTAL	$ 136.53	$ (612.07)	$ 186.01	$ (833.90)

NET ECONOMIC GROWTH BENEFIT FINANCED BY

DIRECT TAX	DEBT
$ 1,811.18	$ 1,589.34

* Cycles subsequent to Cycle 3 are diminutive and not shown.

** See "Balanced Budget Multiplier" at http://financialtrain.com/fiscal-multiplier-and-balanced-budget-multiplier/.

SCHEDULE B
- Transaction Cycles for a Year

FACTORS
Fed Taxes = 15.0%
Leakage = 7.5%
Consumption = 92.5%

CYCLE 1 OF YEAR

TRANSACTION	Incremental Fed Gov Spending	FACTORS	Pre-tax Avail	After-tax Avail	Consump-tion %	Net Consumed	Federal Income Tax Recovered	Trade Deficit 1.5%	Net Other 0.5%	Cycle 1 Savings 5.5%
	$ 100.00							LEAKAGE (7.5%) DETAIL		
1			$ 100.00	$ 100.00	100.0%	$ 100.00	$ -	$ -	$ -	$ -
2		15.0%/92.5%	100.00	85.00	92.5%	78.63	15.00	1.28	0.43	4.68
3		15.0%/92.5%	78.63	66.83	92.5%	61.82	11.79	1.00	0.33	3.68
4		15.0%/92.5%	61.82	52.55	92.5%	48.61	9.27	0.79	0.26	2.89
5		15.0%/92.5%	48.61	41.31	92.5%	38.22	7.29	0.62	0.21	2.27
6		15.0%/92.5%	38.22	32.48	92.5%	30.05	5.73	0.49	0.16	1.79
7		15.0%/92.5%	30.05	25.54	92.5%	23.62	4.51	0.38	0.13	1.40
8		15.0%/92.5%	23.62	20.08	92.5%	18.57	3.54	0.30	0.10	1.10
9		15.0%/92.5%	18.57	15.79	92.5%	14.60	2.79	0.24	0.08	0.87
10		15.0%/92.5%	14.60	12.41	92.5%	11.48	2.19	0.19	0.06	0.68
11 to 36		15.0%/92.5%	53.62	45.57	92.5%	42.16	8.04	0.68	0.23	2.51
TOTAL	$ 100.00		$ 567.73	$ 497.57		$ 467.75	$ 70.16	$ 5.96	$ 1.99	$ 21.87

SAVINGS CONVERSION CYCLE 2 OF YEAR

TRANSACTION	Savings Conversion to Active $$ 80% Lent	Consump-tion %	Consumption in Private Sector & Other Gov's	Federal Income Tax Recovered	Cycle 2 New Savings
1					
2	$ 3.74	92.5%	$ 3.46	$ 0.52	$ 0.21
3	2.94	92.5%	2.72	0.41	0.16
4	2.31	92.5%	2.14	0.32	0.13
5	1.82	92.5%	1.68	0.25	0.10
6	1.43	92.5%	1.32	0.20	0.08
7	1.12	92.5%	1.04	0.16	0.06
8	0.88	92.5%	0.82	0.12	0.05
9	0.69	92.5%	0.64	0.10	0.04
10	0.55	92.5%	0.51	0.08	0.03
11 to 36	2.01	92.5%	1.85	0.28	0.11
TOTAL	$ 17.49		$ 16.18	$ 2.43	$ 0.96

SAVINGS CONVERSION CYCLE 3 OF YEAR - LATER CYCLES ARE DIMINUTIVE AND NOT SHOWN

TRANSACTION	Savings Conversion to Active $$ 80% Lent	Consump-tion %	Consumption in Private Sector & Other Gov's	Federal Income Tax Recovered	Cycle 3 New Savings
1					
2	$ 0.16	92.5%	$ 0.15	$ 0.02	$ 0.01
3	0.13	92.5%	0.12	0.02	0.01
4	0.10	92.5%	0.09	0.01	0.01
5	0.08	92.5%	0.07	0.01	0.00
6	0.06	92.5%	0.06	0.01	0.00
7	0.05	92.5%	0.05	0.01	0.00
8	0.04	92.5%	0.04	0.01	0.00
9	0.03	92.5%	0.03	0.00	0.00
10	0.02	92.5%	0.02	0.00	0.00
11 to 36	0.09	92.5%	0.08	0.01	0.00
TOTAL	$ 0.77		$ 0.71	$ 0.11	$ 0.04

TOTAL

TRANSACTION	Consumption in Private Sector & Other Gov's	Federal Income Tax Recovered	Cycles 1-3 Savings
1	$ 100.00		
2	82.24	$ 15.54	$ 4.89
3	64.66	12.22	3.84
4	50.84	9.61	3.02
5	39.97	7.55	2.38
6	31.43	5.94	1.87
7	24.71	4.67	1.47
8	19.43	3.67	1.16
9	15.28	2.89	0.91
10	12.01	2.27	0.71
11 to 36	44.09	8.33	2.61
TOTAL	$ 484.65	$ 72.69	$ 22.87

In the real world versus the examples, the whole multiplier effect for each of the five years covers a period of three to five years. This is important to understand as:

- In a period of expansionary fiscal spending the timing of the benefit to be realized will lag the timing of the expenditures (patience s is required), and

- In a period of fiscal spending reduction – <u>mathematically</u> – the economic contraction will lag the timing of the reduction.

However, in a period of fiscal spending reduction if private sector expansion does not offset the reduction (highly unlikely) there will be a dip in the economy. This could trigger economic panic in the private sector and lead to an accelerated pace of contraction that will outstrip the available potential private sector expansion and lead to a recession.

To add insult to injury, if a fiscal spending reduction triggers a contraction of the economy, should the government then engage in offsetting expansionary activities the timing of the benefit to be realized will occur at a slower rate than the pace of contraction. In simple summary – it is harder to turn the economy upwards than downwards due to the impact of both psychological effects and the normal pace of expansionary multipliers.

As you can see from the example, the fiscal multiplier effect and the money multiplier effect work hand in hand. Because of the money multiplier, good lending decisions enhance the effect of the fiscal multiplier. Because of the money multiplier, bad lending decisions have a magnified negative effect on the economy (think 2008 financial crash). Bank management has historically proven that it cannot be trusted to manage responsibly. Therefore, as a voter, you need to determine your tolerance level for unnecessary economic instability. Based upon this determination, you need to encourage your politicians to regulate or not regulate banking practices. Although banks are privately owned – I encourage you to think they are owned by you and insist that things be done your way. There are economic factors we, as citizens, cannot control – but, banking practices is not one of these.

With this in mind, the balancing of expansionary and contractionary Federal Government fiscal activities and the regulation of banks must be done based upon sound analysis and with care. It is very important that congresspeople and presidents have the necessary level of native intelligence (critical thinking skills, objective reasoning skills, ability to deal with time and spatial relationships, mathematical comprehension, etc.). Politicians without these skills can hold a title, but cannot do the job.

It is your job as a responsible citizen and voter to see that the right people are elected.

DISCUSSION GUIDE No. 2 – Select Subjects

Below is a list of a few of the subjects to be discussed in the next discussion guide. There will be a section devoted to discussing structural issues of the economy and a section devoted to discussing current economic issues.

Structural Issues:

The relationship between the national debt and inflation. If the Fed succeeds in holding inflation to 2%, how will this impact the reduction in the national debt?

The character of the natural resource "implied value" and the provision of "money" to accommodate the implied value.

The gap between monetary economy and natural economy. What is different between a monetized economy (one in which money is used) and a natural economy (one based on direct trading – barter - of conversion labor and readily available natural resources)? Although monetization contributes significantly to enabling the economy and, thereby, the creation of jobs; are there aspects of monetization that contribute to less than full employment and cause other negative economic issues? Are there modifications possible that would better align the monetary system with the natural system?

Can the Federal Reserve's Dual Mandate be changed? If so, will a change in mandate result in a change in practice OR is the mandate a formal statement of a natural law of capitalism which cannot be changed within the framework of a capitalist system?

How do the basic industries relate to an economy overall and other industries? Economists have long held that the industries of farming, mining, and manufacturing are pertinent to the existence of a healthy economy. Yet, mining and manufacturing have suffered a serious relative decline in the last 30 years. What part does this play in the strength of the current economy and American jobs?

How does productivity improvement impact the economy and jobs? Has real productivity improved or is productivity improvement an apparent phenomenon representative of fallacies in the Bureau of Labor Statistics' productivity calculation? How does the importing of parts and components by manufacturers affect the government's productivity calculation? Has productivity improvement worked for the benefit of the community or only for the benefit of a few?

What is or would be the economic effect of redefining various wage levels? What would be the effect of lowering the wage level currently paid to many civil servants? What would be the effect of federal wage controls on CEOs and board members of publicly traded corporations (NOTE: the concept of fiduciary responsibility of corporate boards of directors appears not to be working)? More on the effect of a minimum wage increase; does it boost or slow the economy? (This subject is both a structural and current issue.)

How does the money flow of the private sector work? The money flow for the aggregate of all businesses and that of the government money flow discussed in this guide are in many ways similar but are also dissimilar. I know this sounds like a line from Alice in Wonderland. However, what will be both needed and provided is an exercise that demonstrates how the system works. A few key points related to the similarities and dissimilarities will be discussed.

Community's potential control over the private sector. There are limited direct means of control available to the citizenry, as a community (government), for keeping the revenue and costs of the collective business community in balance and at a desirable level. There, also, is limited direct means of control available to the private sector for keeping the revenue and costs of the collective business community in balance and at a desirable level. Additionally, it is possible that those means of control desired by big business stand in contradiction to those means of control that would be desired by small business.

How does the development of Third World economies impact the structure of US economy and jobs for Americans? Can Third World economies develop just a well without American companies transferring American jobs to these countries? What system, if any, could be used to help these countries without having a negative effect on the US economy and US jobs? Beyond satisfying religious values, what benefit is there to helping Third World economies develop?

Where does the Federal National Debt come from? Typically, economist measure government revenue and expenditures as a percentage of GDP. We will examine this relationship. Additionally, we will examine the concept of timing variance as it relates to several factors, including but not limited to population growth, population mix, and interest rates.

Current Issues:

Is the relative spending level for USA defense higher or lower than that of other countries? It is less costly, because wages are lower, to build an airstrip or a ship in many other countries than it is in the US. When comparing country to country defense expenditures, is it necessary to first adjust for differences in costs so that apples are compared to apples, not oranges?

What are the sources of increasing healthcare costs? What, if any, has been the effect of converting non-profit hospitals to for-profit hospitals? Do mini-surgery centers (out of hospital) help lower medical costs or raise medical costs? What are the five or six key differences between the US system and the systems used in countries with both better medical systems (as measured by results) and lower medical costs?

Disability Insurance (DI) and Survivors Insurance (SI) - Discussion as provided, herein, in Discussion Guide 1 for Social Security retirement.

Medicare - Discussion as provided, herein, in Discussion Guide 1 for Social Security retirement.

Does illegal immigration hurt or help the US economy? Who are those who benefit from illegal immigration? (Is it some of the same people who claim to oppose it?) Who are those who are hurt? Why is it not controlled through hiring screening (e-verify)?

How is technology affecting the US economy and the availability of jobs? Technological advances have enabled the overseas outsourcing of many would be American jobs. This outsourcing ranges from call centers to design engineering to medical billing to software development. Is there any reason US companies cannot outsource the CEO's job to countries with lower executive wages?

What does the future hold? Per the No Labels Policy Playbook "4% of US bachelor's degrees were awarded in engineering, compared to 31% in China". What does this mean to the future of outsourcing engineering jobs? Are there other potential areas of concern?

A review of QE, quantitative easing, ZIRP, zero interest rate policy, and NIRP, negative interest rate policy. What do these Federal Reserve initiatives mean to you, your children and grandchildren? Have they been effective as measured by the generation of improvements in the economy (did the economy improve by more than it would have without these practices?).

CITATIONS

Chapter 2- Developing a Sound Foundation

<u>What is the real number of non-employed?</u>

...objective of the Fed is to control unemployment and inflation as a package

Federal Reserve Bank of Chicago. Last Updated: 06/23/15, **The Federal Reserve's Dual Mandate, What Is the Dual Mandate?** https://www.chicagofed.org/publications/speeches/our-dual-mandate.

> In 1977, Congress amended The Federal Reserve Act, stating the monetary policy objectives of the Federal Reserve as:

> "The Board of Governors of the Federal Reserve System and the Federal Open Market Committee shall maintain long run growth of the monetary and credit aggregates commensurate with the economy's long run potential to increase production, so as to promote effectively the goals of maximum employment, stable prices and moderate long-term interest rates." THIS SITE PROVIDES GRAPHS PROJECTING BOTH INFLATION AND EMPLOYMENT LEVELS ANTICIPATED AS WELL AS THE TARGETS FOR EACH.

Davidson, Paul. **Fed minutes show debate on rate hike timing,** August 20, 2014, USA Today, http://www.usatoday.com/story/money/business/2014/08/20/fed-meeting-minutes/14338927/. THIS SITE PROVIDES SOME INSIGHT INTO THE THOUGHT PROCESS OF DETERMINING THE FED ACTIONS FOR MANAGING THE INFLATION AND UNEMPLOYMENT RATES.

Wikipedia. **Unemployment,** as of 07/15/2015, https://en.wikipedia.org/wiki/Unemployment. THIS SITE PROVIDES DEFINITIONS OF UNEMPLOYMENT MEASURES. <u>IN DEPTH</u>, BUT, WILL HELP THE READER FOLLOW DISCUSSIONS WHEN HEARING PHRASES SUCH AS "FULL EMPLOYMENT," "CYCLICAL UNEMPLOYMENT," "STRUCTURAL UNEMPLOYMENT," AND OTHER SUCH PHRASES. WHAT IS IMPORTANT IS THAT THE READER REALIZES THAT THE TERMS SUCH AS "MAXIMUM EMPLOYMENT" AND "FULL EMPLOYMENT" TYPICALLY DO NOT MEAN FULL EMPLOYMENT AS THOUGHT OF BY MOST CITIZENS.

Wikipedia. **Full Employment,** as of 07/15/2015, https://en.wikipedia.org/wiki/Full_employment. THIS SITE PROVIDES DEFINITIONS OF UNEMPLOYMENT MEASURES. <u>IN DEPTH</u>. SHOWS RELATIONSHIP OF EMPLOYMENT TO OTHER ASPECTS OF THE ECONOMY. WHAT IS IMPORTANT IS THAT SOME ECONOMIST FEEL THAT THE "FULL EMPLOYMENT," RATE (THAT UNEMPLOYMENT RATE NECESSARY TO CONTROL INFLATION), MAY BE, AS HIGH AS, 13%.

...an article by Jeff Kearns and published by Bloomber.com, January 2015

Kearns, Jeff. **Fed Raises Assessment of Economy While Staying Patient on Rates,** January 28, 2015, Bloomberg, http://www.bloomberg.com/news/articles/2015-01-28/fed-raises-assessment-of-economy-while-staying-patient-on-rates. THIS ARTICLE SITES THE 2% INFLATION TARGET OF THE FED; ALSO, AS DEPICTED IN THE CITATION ABOVE, REFERENCES THE DUAL MANDATE STATEMENT PUBLISHED BY THE FEDERAL RESERVE BANK OF CHICAGO.

...business cycles and demographic patterns

Owens, Brett. **Harry Dent's Outlook on Demographics, Debt, and Deflation,** Sep. 5, 2010, Seeking Alpha, http://seekingalpha.com/article/223886-harry-dents-outlook-on-demographics-debt-and-deflation. THIS ARTICLE REVIEWS WORK BY HARRY DENT, AN ECONOMIST WHO FOCUSES ON DEMOGRAPHIC TRENDS. THE ARTICLE CONTAINS SOME VERY UNDERSTANDABLE CHARTS

Chapter 2 continued...

THAT WILL HELP THE READER UNDERSTAND THE INTERPLAY BETWEEN DEMOGRAPHIC PATTERNS AND PERFORMANCE OF THE ECONOMY. IT IS AN EASY READ. HOWEVER, MUCH INFORMATION IS PROVIDED THAT IS UNRELATED TO THE TEXT OF THIS DISCUSSION GUIDE. ADDITIONALLY, THERE IS SOME SLANT TOWARD GETTING THE READER TO UTILIZE THE AUTHOR'S INVESTMENT ADVICE. REGARDLESS THE ARTICLE REPRESENTS A GOOD READ.

US Department of Labor, Office of the Secretary. **Futurework , Trends and Challenges for Work in the 21st Century,** Compiled by Robert I. Lerman and Stefanie R. Schmidt, The Urban Institute, Washington, D.C., Final Report August 1999. **http://www.dol.gov/oasam/programs/history/herman/reports/futurework/conference/trends/Trendsintro. htm** IN DEPTH. AN OVERVIEW OF ECONOMIC, SOCIAL, AND DEMOGRAPHIC TRENDS AFFECTING THE US LABOR MARKET. WHILE DATED (1999) THIS PRESENTATION APPLIES TO THE CURRENT ECONOMIC PERIOD.

Boston Federal Reserve Bank. **The Impact of Demographic Change on U.S. Labor Markets,** Undated (probably just after 2001), Compiled by Jane Sneddon Little and Robert K. Tries, **http://www.bostonfed.org/economic/conf/conf46/conf46e1.pdf.** IN DEPTH. COVERS A PERIOD OF APPROXIMATELY 100 YEARS. THE FOCUS IS ON DEMOGRAPHIC TRENDS, WORK AND FAMILY ISSUES, HEALTH AND PENSION PATTERNS, TECHNICAL CHANGE, ADJUSTMENT TO LOW UNEMPLOYMENT, GLOBALIZATION, AND THE PLIGHT OF LOW-SKILLED WORKERS.

What are Key Classes of Economic Units?

...to spend more than they previously were able to spend

Vague, Richard. **Government Debt Isn't the Problem—Private Debt Is,** Sep 9, 2014, **http://www.theatlantic.com/business/archive/2014/09/government-debt-isnt-the-problemprivate-debt-is/379865/.** THIS ARTICLE FOCUSES ON THE FINANCIAL/ ECONOMIC CRASH OF 2008. HOWEVER, ALTHOUGH NOT THE FOCUS – THE ARTICLE DEMONSTRATES THE RELATIONSHIP BETWEEN THE INCREASE IN PRIVATE BORROWING (PERSONAL, BOTH LOANS AND CREDIT CARDS, AND COMMERCIAL) AND THE UNWARRANTED GROWTH PRIOR TO THE CRISES MADE POSSIBLE BY THE EASY CREDIT OF THE TIME PRIOR TO THE 2008 CRASH.

Bishop, Meghan. **Credit Spending And Its Implications for Recent U.S. Economic Growth,** Undated (probably just after 2000), Mary Washington College, **http://org.elon.edu/ipe/bishop.pdf.** IN DEPTH. ALTHOUGH HISTORICALLY DATED (PROBABLY, 2001) THE PAPER IS THE BEST I FOUND IN TERMS OF UNDERSTANDABILITY BY NON-ECONOMISTS, WHICH ADDRESSES CREDIT GROWTH AND GDP (US GROSS DOMESTIC PRODUCT) GROWTH.

CHAPTER 3 - Basic Economic Relationships

Supply, Demand and Cultural Views

...some investment bankers do enjoy extremely high incomes

Wofford, Taylor. **Eric Cantor Lands $3.4 Million Investment Banking Job**, 09/02/2014, Newsweek, **http://www.newsweek.com/eric-cantor-lands-34-million-investment-banking-job-267924.** ERIC CANTOR IS THE EX-HOUSE MAJORITY LEADER AND A VIRGINIA POLITICIAN.

CHAPTER 4 – Applied Wealth

Land Grants

Harness, Charles. **This Land is My Land! All 5 Million Acres of It..,** May 2013 update.
http://chasreader.home.comcast.net/~chasreader/Lord_Fairfax.html. 5 MILLION ACRES OF WHAT IS
NOW TWO COUNTIES IN NORTHERN VIRGINIA.

Wikipedia. **James Bowie,** Undated, https://en.wikipedia.org/wiki/James_Bowie
James "Jim" Bowie (pronounced /ˈbuːi/ *BOO-ee*[1] or /ˈboʊi/ *BO-ee*;[2][3] c. 1796 – March 6, 1836) was a
nineteenth-century American **pioneer, soldier, smuggler, slave trader, and land speculator,** who played a
prominent role in the Texas Revolution, culminating in his death at the Battle of the Alamo. PAY
PARTICULAR ATTENTION TO THE PART ON LAND GRANTS.

Bamman. Gale Williams CG, CGL. **THIS LAND IS OUR LAND! TENNESSEE'S DISPUTES WITH NORTH
CAROLINA,** March 23, 1998, © 1996, 1997. All rights reserved, From Genealogical Journal, Vol. 24, Number
3, 1996, By Permission, **http://www.tngenweb.org/tnland/bamman.htm.** <u>IN DEPTH</u>

Wikipedia. **Land patent,** as of 07/15/2015, **https://en.wikipedia.org/wiki/Land_patent.** <u>IN DEPTH</u>.
EXPLAINS THE LAND GRANTING PROCESS AND HISTORY.

Nolo. **Who Owns the Minerals Under Your Property,** http://www.nolo.com/legal-encyclopedia/who-owns-
the-minerals-under-your-property.html? DEALS WITH MINERAL RIGHTS. WHO HAS A RIGHT TO
THE GOLD DEPOSITS ON YOUR PROPERTY?

Cultural momentum

...grandeur within a subgroup of a society

BBC, Brain Surgeon - **That Mitchell & Webb Look , Series 3 - BBC Two**
https://www.youtube.com/watch?v=THNPmhBl-8I, FUN VIDEO. VIDEO MAKES THE POINT ON
CULTURAL MOMENTUM. YOU DECIDE IF ROCKET SCIENTISTS HAVE NEGATIVE MOMENTUM OR
IF BRAIN SURGEONS HAVE OVERLY POSITIVE MOMENTUM. PER THE US BUREAU OF LABOR
STATISTICS - THE MEDIAN PAY IN 2015 FOR AEROSPACE ENGINEERS IS $105,000 AND THE TOP
10% EARN $155,000. THE MEDIAN PAY FOR A NUCLEAR PHYSICIST WITH A MASTERS DEGREE OR
Ph.D. IS $106,000. PER CNN MONEY – THE MEDIAN PAY FOR A NEUROSURGEON IS $368,000 AND
THOSE AT THE TOP EARN $691,000. **http://money.cnn.com/pf/best-jobs/2012/snapshots/63.html.** *(NOTE:
NEUROSURGEONS MUST BE COMPENSATED FOR ADDITIONAL TIME IN SCHOOL AND TIME AS AN
INTERN.)* FURTHER, PER THE BLS, THE AVERAGE EARNINGS OF LAWYERS IS $133,000 AND THE
AVERAGE PAY FOR LAWYERS IN THE UPPER QUARTILE IS $172,000.

...of medical doctor earnings will be re-enforced

Commins, John. **Will There Be Enough Doctors?** Undated, Health Leader Media,
http://www.healthleadersmedia.com/content/MAG-92871/Will-There-Be-Enough-Doctors

...CEOs and board members of major corporations

Michel, Lawrence and Davis, Alyssa. **Top CEOs Make 300 Times More than Typical Workers,** June 21, 2015,
Economic Policy Institute, **http://www.epi.org/publication/top-ceos-make-300-times-more-than-workers-
pay-growth-surpasses-market-gains-and-the-rest-of-the-0-1-percent/.** THIS ARTICLE PROVIDES A LOT
OF TREND INFORMATION THAT IS IMPORTANT TO BOTH THE INVESTOR (EVEN IF YOU ARE
INVESTED ONLY THROUGH YOUR PENSION PLAN) AND THE USA CITIZEN. HAS A SENSE OF
ROYAL

Chapter 4 continued…

ENTITLEMENT DEVELOPED SIMILAR TO THAT IN ENGLAND BEFORE THE AMERICAN REVOLUTION? IS THIS SENSE OF ENTITLEMENT PART OF THE PROBLEMS THAT CAUSED EARLY AMERICANS TO REVOLT? IF THE CEO COMPENSATION TREND IS NOT REVERSED WILL AMERICA END UP WITH A PLUTOCRACY (I.E., ROYALTY)? CAN PLUTOCRACY AND DEMOCRACY CO-EXIST? WHAT IS IT THESE INDIVIDUALS DO IN A WORK DAY THAT MAKES THEM WORTH 300 TIMES THAT OF THE AVERAGE WORKING AMERICAN? ARE CORPORATE BOARDS OF DIRECTORS PROPERLY EXERCISING THEIR FIDUCIARY RESPONSIBILITIES?

Dill, Kathryn. **CEO Pay Has Risen More Than Twice As Much As The Stock Market**, Jun 27, 2013 **http://www.forbes.com/sites/kathryndill/2013/06/27/ceo-pay-has-risen-more-than-twice-as-much-as-the-stock-market/**.
"- More surprising than the WAGE chasm is how much it has widened over the past half century. In 1965 an AVERAGE CEO took home slightly more than 20 times what an average "production/nonsupervisory" employee earned." CITES EARLIER STUDY BY THE ECONOMIC POLICY INSTITUTE AND PROVIDES SEVERAL INTERESTING FACTS. THE POINTS AS RAISED ABOVE APPLY, ALSO, TO THE INFORMATION PRESENTED IN THIS ARTICLE.

…civil servants (primarily those in management and professional roles)

COMMENT:

It was very difficult to find articles or studies that provided a full view of the situation. However, it is clear that civil servants earn more (including benefits) than do private sector employees.

Several times in the private sector I have witnessed situations where individuals were promoted or hired into a senior management position; typically as a Division President (managing 500 to 3,000 employees). They subsequently established themselves as "empire builders." They both expanded and upgraded (?) staff. By upgrade, they meant – hire people with advanced degrees and at higher pay. The division profits, of course, diminished. The problem was the business did not need more and/or upgraded staff or just upgraded staff. What the business needed was the right number of people, properly qualified (but, not academically overqualified) and at the right wage to do the needed work. The CEOs of the respective companies eventually brought in someone new to run the respective divisions and the staffs were re-formatted and the profits improved. Competition forces this to happen in the private sector.

What were these division presidents after?

"Bragging rights." They wanted to tell their buddies and business acquaintances "I have 40 professionals on my staff, and 15 have master's degrees and 4 have Ph.D.'s. Additionally, the greater the number of high academically credentialed staff, the better the chances of a bigger pay raise for the presidents. However, the financial state of the businesses they were running didn't care about their "bragging rights" or the desired higher pay and the market forced a correction.

Competition does not force a correction in the public sector. Yes, there are reviews by "independent" wage and salary experts. I have never seen the results of one of these reviews for civil service personnel – but, I have seen several related to the private sector. I was not impressed (Do you think that any such expert would recommend a justified 50% cut in pay for a Division President or a CEO?). Because I was not impressed, I encourage the readers of this discussion guide to look to "common sense."

Now let us look at a "reality check." As a country, to remain competitive globally **the community's most capable young adults must choose careers in the private sector**. If we do not remain competitive, the private sector will diminish and take down the public sector with it. This means that job per job the private sector employees must earn significantly more than public sector employees. No, there are not direct competitive forces applied to the public sector; but, over the long term the same forces that apply to the private sector apply to the public sector. It is just a matter of time.

Zuckerman, Mortimer. **Public Sector Workers Are the New Privileged Elite Class,** Sept. 10, 2010, U.S. News & World Report, **http://www.usnews.com/opinion/mzuckerman/articles/2010/09/10/public-sector-workers-are-the-new-privileged-elite-class**.

Dennis Cauchon. **Wisconsin one of 41 states where public workers earn more,** 3/2/2011, USA Today, **http://usatoday30.usatoday.com/news/nation/2011-03-011A** publicworkers01_ST_N.htm.

Simon Rogers. **Public v private sector pay: who earns more?** March 27, 2012, The Guardian, **http://www.theguardian.com/news/datablog/2012/mar/27/public-private-sector-pay**.

Recap of Cato Institute study. **Historical Comparison of Public and Private Sector Compensation Levels,** undated, Intellectual Takeout, **http://www.intellectualtakeout.org/library/chart-graph/historical-comparison-public-and-private-sector-compensation-levels**. <u>EASY READ – ONE PAGE.</u>

FULL STUDY REFERENCED BELOW:

Edwards, Chris. **Public Sector Unions and the Rising Costs of Employee Compensation,** 2010, Cato Institute, **http://object.cato.org/sites/cato.org/files/serials/files/cato-journal/2010/1/cj30n1-5.pdf**. <u>IN DEPTH (114 pages)</u>

Ohanian, **Lee E. America's Public Sector Union Dilemma**, November 26, 2011, American Enterprise Institute, **https://www.aei.org/publication/americas-public-sector-union-dilemma/.** "There is much less competition in the public sector than the private sector, and that has made all the difference."

Drum, Kevin. **Chart of the Day: Federal Government Pay vs. Private Sector Pay**, Jan. 30, 2012, Mother Jones, **http://www.motherjones.com/kevin-drum/2012/01/chart-day-federal-government-pay-vs-private-sector-pay**, "The Congressional Budget Office (CBO) weighed in today on the fraught subject of whether federal employees are paid more than comparable workers in the private…"

CONGRESS OF THE UNITED STATES CONGRESSIONAL JANUARY 2012 BUDGET OFFICE. **Comparing the Compensation of Federal and Private-Sector Employees**, **http://www.cbo.gov/sites/default/files/01-30-FedPay_0.pdf**

Austin, PJ. **Different Worlds: Public vs. Private Sector Compensation**, December 2012, Wastewatcher, **http://cagw.org/media/wastewatcher/two-different-worlds-public-vs-private-sector-compensation.**

Smith, Lauren. **Correcting Myths About Federal Pay / Conservatives Compare Apples to Oranges**, October 25, 2010, Center for American Progress, **https://www.americanprogress.org/issues/open-government/news/2010/10/25/8480/correcting-myths-about-federal-pay/**. IS THE ISSUE THE SIGNIFICANT OVER GRADING OF JOB DUTIES? DO SPECIFIC EMPLOYEES TRULY NEED A BACHELORS, MASTERS OR Ph.D. DEGREE TO DO THE TASKS THEY HANDLE? DOES THE "OLDER AND MORE EXPERIENCED EMPLOYEE ASPECT BRING FOCUS TO THE RISK OF WORKING IN THE PRIVATE SECTOR? SHOULD THIS RISK BE COMPENSATED FOR WITH HIGHER PAY?

...Senior financial services managers and senior financial sales types

Delamaide, Darrell. **The failure behind Wall St. bonuses**, March 17, 2015, USA Today, **http://www.usatoday.com/story/money/business/2015/03/17/delamaide-wall-street-bank-bonuses-**

regulators/24912689/. *EXCELLENT ARTICLE*. SEE REMARK ON FISCAL MULTIPLIER AND SPENDING. HOW DOES THIS RELATE TO IDLE VERSUS ACTIVE MONEY?

Patel, Sital S. **Wall Street bonuses rose 15% in 2013 to post-financial-crisis high**, March 12, 2014, Market Watch, **http://blogs.marketwatch.com/thetell/2014/03/12/wall-street-bonuses-rose-15-in-2013-to-post-financial-crisis-high/**

Feng, **Felix Zhiyu. Why Paying Bonuses During a Financial Crisis Might Strengthen the Economy**, November 11, 2013, The CLS Blue Sky Blog, Columbia Law School, **http://clsbluesky.law.columbia.edu/2013/11/11/paying-bonuses-during-a-crises/**

CHAPTER 5 – Types of Economic Systems

Key Differentiating Aspects of Economic Systems

Laissez Faire Capitalism

…property rights, prevent theft, and prevent aggression

Wikipedia. **Laissez Faire Capitalism**, as of 07/07/2015, **https://en.wikipedia.org/wiki/Laissez-faire**

Unfettered capitalism:

…regulations against such practices being implemented in the 1940's

Yellowwitz, Irwin. **Child Labor – Facts & Summary** – History, undated, **http://www.history.com/topics/child-labor**

Semuels, Alana. **How Common Is Child Labor in the U.S.?** Dec. 15, 2014, The Atlantic, **http://www.theatlantic.com/business/archive/2014/12/how-common-is-chid-labor-in-the-us/383687/**

US Department of Labor, Wage and Hour Division (WHD). **Child Labor**, undated, **http://www.dol.gov/whd/childlabor.htm**
"The federal **child labor** provisions, authorized by the Fair Labor Standards Act (FLSA) of 1938, also known as the **child labor laws**, were enacted to ensure that…"

Benefits and Disadvantageous

Laissez Faire Capitalism:

Benefits and disadvantageous-

…were used by larger companies to put smaller companies out of business

Wikipedia. **Predatory pricing, https://en.wikipedia.org/wiki/Predatory_pricing**

Francisco, Bedoya. **Standard Oil: Cost Reductions and Predatory Pricing**, 4-1-2013, Trinity College, Trinity College Digital Repository, Senior Theses and Projects Student Works, **http://digitalrepository.trincoll.edu/cgi/viewcontent.cgi?article=1298&context=theses**

Folsom, Burton Jr. **Herbert Dow and Predatory Pricing**, May 1, 1998, **http://fee.org/freeman/detail/herbert-dow-and-predatory-pricing**. Foundation for Economic Education

Communism:

Disadvantageous -

...backfire on them within their own lifetime

Hoeppler, Christopher. **Russian Demographics: The Role of the Collapse of the Soviet Union,** McMaster University, URJHS Volume 10, http://www.kon.org/urc/v10/hoeppler.html

Wikipedia. **History of Russia (1992 to present),** as of 07/07/2015 https://en.wikipedia.org/wiki/History_of_Russia_(1992%E2%80%93present),

Cockerham, William C. **The Social Determinants of the Decline of Life Expectancy in Russia and Eastern Europe: A Lifestyle Explanation**, Published by: American Sociological Journal of Health and Social Behavior, Vol. 38, No. 2 (Jun., 1997), pp. 117-130, http://www.jstor.org/stable/2955420?seq=1#page_scan_tab_contents

Mydans, Seth. **20 Years After Soviet Fall, Some Look Back Longingly**, Aug. 18, 2011, NY Times, http://www.nytimes.com/2011/08/19/world/europe/19russia.html?_r=0.

CHAPTER 6: CURRENT ISSUES -Welfare Payments

(LAW) Federal Reserve Bank of Chicago. Last Updated: 06/23/15, **The Federal Reserve's Dual Mandate, What Is the Dual Mandate? https://www.chicagofed.org/publications/speeches/our-dual-mandate**. PREVIOUSLY CITED IN CHAPTER 2. VERY IMPORTANT TO THE ISSUE OF "WELFARE," AS WELL.

<u>Question:</u>

2.   **A reduction in welfare payments will:**

...living below the poverty line

Derek Thompson. **Get Rich, Live Longer: The Ultimate Consequence of Income Inequality**, Apr 18, 2014, The Atlantic, **http://www.theatlantic.com/business/archive/2014/04/more-money-more-life-the-depressing-reality-of-inequality-in-america/360895/**

Tavernise, Sabrina. **Life Spans Shrink for Least-Educated Whites in the U.S.**, September 20, 2012, NY Times, http://www.nytimes.com/2012/09/21/us/life-expectancy-for-less-educated-whites-in-us-is-shrinking.html.

S. Jay Olshansky, Ph.D., Douglas J. Passaro, M.D., Ronald C. Hershow, M.D., Jennifer Layden, M.P.H., Bruce A. Carnes, Ph.D., Jacob Brody, M.D., Leonard Hayflick, Ph.D., Robert N. Butler, M.D., David B. Allison, Ph.D., and David S. Ludwig, M.D., Ph.D. **A Potential Decline in Life Expectancy in the United States in the 21st Century**, March 17, 2005, New England Journal of Medicine, **http://www.nejm.org/doi/full/10.1056/NEJMsr043743**. <u>IN DEPTH</u>

CHAPTER 7: CURRENT ISSUES - Investment Shortfall, Idle Money, Repatriation, and Job Creation

Idle Money - Domestic

...USA businesses range from $1.7 trillion to $2.4 trillion

Johnston, David Cay. **Idle corporate cash piles up,** July 16, 2012, Reuters
http://blogs.reuters.com/david-cay-johnston/2012/07/16/idle-corporate-cash-piles-up/

Sánchez, Juan M.; Yurdagul, Emircan. **Why Are Corporations Holding So Much Cash**, January-2013, St. Louis Fed, **https://www.stlouisfed.org/Publications/Regional-Economist/January-2013/Why-Are-Corporations-Holding-So-Much-Cash**

Johnston, David Cay, **The great corporate cash-hoarding crisis,** March 2014.
http://america.aljazeera.com/opinions/2014/3/corporations-cashreservestaxavoidanceoffshore.html

Do USA Corporations have Money Needed to Invest More in America if They Want to Invest More in America?

...will in any way lead to increased investment in America

Richards, Kitty; Craig, John. **Offshore Corporate Profits, The Only Thing 'Trapped'** (*Offshore*) **Is Tax Revenue**, January 9, 2014, Center for American Progress
https://www.americanprogress.org/wp-content/uploads/2014/01/TrappedRevenues-brief1.pdf

Jeanne Sahadi, **The Myth of Corporate America's Offshore Cash,** July 10, 2013, CNN Money,
http://money.cnn.com/2013/07/10/news/economy/offshore-cash/

Will Corporations Invest in America and Create American Jobs if Another Repatriation Tax Holiday is Declared?

...in the USA? The answer is typically none of it

Rapoza, Kenneth. **Bringing Overseas Corporate Profits Back To US Not Necessarily A Job Booster,**
9/12/2011, Forbes, **http://www.forbes.com/sites/kenrapoza/2011/09/12/bringing-overseas-corporate-profits-back-to-us-not-necessarily-a-job-booster/**

Gale, William G. and Harris, Benjamin. **Don't Fall for Corporate Repatriation,** June 27, 2011, Brookings,
http://www.brookings.edu/research/opinions/2011/06/27-corporate-tax-holiday-gale-harris.

Peterson, Kristina. **Report: Repatriation Tax Holiday a 'Failed' Policy,** Oct. 10, 2011, Wall Street Journal,
http://www.wsj.com/articles/SB10001424052970203633104576623771022129888

CHAPTER 8: CURRENT ISSUES - Education and Welfare to Work

News 10. **Foreign workers fill hundreds of Sacramento-area IT jobs,** February 24, 2015
http://www.news10.net/story/news/investigations/2015/02/24/foreign-workers-fill-hundreds-of-sacramento-area-it-jobs/22603549/

Chapter 8 continued...

Preston, Julia. **Pink Slips at Disney. But First, Training Foreign Replacements,** June 13, 2015, NY Times, **http://www.nytimes.com/2015/06/04/us/last-task-after-layoff-at-disney-train-foreign-replacements.html?_r=0**

Miano, John. **The Bottom of the Pay Scale: Wages for H-1B Computer Programmers**, December 2005, Center for Immigration Studies, **http://cis.org/PayScale-H1BWages**. "computer occupations were for wages $13,000 less than Americans in the same occupation and state."

Matloff, Norman. **Data and implications for immigration policy / Are foreign students the 'best and brightest'?** February 28, 2013, Economic Policy Institute, **http://www.epi.org/publication/bp356-foreign-students-best-brightest-immigration-policy**.

CHAPTER 9: CURRENT ISSUES - Minimum Wage

What We Think We Know

Kyle, Jacoby. **The Winners and Losers of Raising the Minimum Wage**, June 9, 2014, St. Louis on the Air, **http://news.stlpublicradio.org/post/winners-and-losers-raising-minimum-wage**.

Sabia, Dr. Joseph. **Minimum Wages and the Business Cycle: Does a Wage Hike Hurt More in a Weak Economy?** January 28, 2014, Employment Policies Institute, **https://www.epionline.org/study/minimum-wages-and-the-business-cycle-does-a-wage-hike-hurt-more-in-a-weak-economy/**.

Mejeur, Jeanne . **Maximum Divide on Minimum Wage**, March 2014, State Legislatures Magazine, **http://www.ncsl.org/research/labor-and-employment/maximum-divide-on-minimum-wage.aspx**.

Discussion of Pros and Cons

PROS:

Doyle, Alison. **Pros and Cons of Raising the Minimum Wage**, as of July 15, 2015, About Careers, **http://jobsearch.about.com/od/minimumwage/fl/pros-and-cons-raise-minimum-wage.htm**.

... Americans the actual standard of living may not improve – at least not much.

Breslow. Jason M. and Wexler, Evan. **The State of America's Middle Class in Eight Charts,** July 9, 2013, PBS, **http://www.pbs.org/wgbh/pages/frontline/business-economy-financial-crisis/two-american-families/the-state-of-americas-middle-class-in-eight-charts/**

Thompson, Derek. The Incredible Shrinking Incomes of Young Americans, Dec. 3, 2014, The Atlantic, **http://www.theatlantic.com/business/archive/2014/12/millennials-arent-saving-money-because-theyre-not-making-money/383338/**

Mislinski, Jill. **Five Decades of Middle Class Wages:** June 2015 Update, July 7, 2015, Advisor Perspectives, **http://www.advisorperspectives.com/dshort/updates/Employment-Wages-and-Hours-since-1964.php**

Chapter 9 continued...

Short, Doug. **U.S. Household Incomes: A 46-Year Perspective,** September 17, 2014, Advisor Perspectives, http://www.advisorperspectives.com/dshort/updates/Household-Income-Distribution.php**DOES NOT TAKE INTO ACCOUNT THE SIGNIFICANT INCREASE IN FEMALE PARTICIPATION IN WORKFORCE, CHILD CARE COSTS, OR INCREASE IN EMPLOYEES' COST SHARE OF EMPLOYER-PROVIDED HEALTH CARE INSURANCE.**

Johnston, David Cay. **Compensation shrinks for all income groups – except the very highest,** October 23, 2014, Al Jazeera America, **http://america.aljazeera.com/opinions/2014/10/wages-compensationeconomystagnationsocialsecurityadministrationd.html**

Toossi, M. **A century of change: the U.S. labor force, 1950-2050,** May 2002, U.S. Bureau of Labor Statistics, **http://www.bls.gov/opub/mlr/2002/05/art2full.pdf**

"of **WOMEN, WHICH STOOD AT 34 PERCENT IN 1950** and **increased to 60 percent by 2000.** The number of women in the labor force rose from. 18 million in 1950 to 66…"

...as indicated by declining life expectancy.

Derek Thompson. **Get Rich, Live Longer: The Ultimate Consequence of Income Inequality,** Apr 18, 2014, The Atlantic, http://www.theatlantic.com/business/archive/2014/04/more-money-more-life-the-depressing-reality-of-inequality-in-america/360895/

For additional reading material, see listing for declining life expectancy under **CHAPTER 6: CURRENT ISSUES -Welfare Payments**

CHAPTER 11: CURRENT ISSUES - National Debt

Key Definitions of Economic Activity Measurement

National Debt-

Wikipedia. **National Debt of the United States,** definition, as of 07/10/15, **https://en.wikipedia.org/wiki/National_debt_of_the_United_States,**

Historically, Government has not Paid Down Debt

...averaged 17.4% of GDP and the shortfall has averaged 2.7% of GDP

Office of Management and Budget, **Table 1.1 Summary of Receipts, Outlays, Surpluses or Deficits,** Also see table 1.3, **https://www.whitehouse.gov/omb/budget/Historicals**

Tax Policy Center. **Summary of Receipts, Outlays, Surpluses or Deficits,** Source US Office of Management and Budget – table 1.3, Feb 2, 2015, **http://www.taxpolicycenter.org/taxfacts/displayafact.cfm?Docid=200.** THE SAME SOURCE AS ABOVE, BUT EASIER TO READ.

Intellectual Takeout, **1947-2012 Federal Government Tax Revenues vs. Spending,** Source – FRED (Federal Reserve Bank) October 4, 2012, **http://www.intellectualtakeout.org/library/chart-graph/1947-2012-federal-government-tax-revenues-vs-spending**

CHAPTER 12: CURRENT ISSUES - "Fix Social Security"

Desilver, Drew. **5 Facts About Social Security**, Oct. 16. 2013, Pew Research Center, http://www.pewresearch.org/fact-tank/2013/10/16/5-facts-about-social-security/

Fry, Richard and Kochhar, Rakesh. **America's wealth gap between middle-income and upper-income families is widest on record**, Dec. 17, 2014, http://www.pewresearch.org/fact-tank/2014/12/17/wealth-gap-upper-middle-income/.

Background

...No, it is not necessary to sacrifice for our children nor is it necessary to burden our children with debt to keep Social Security and Medicare intact.

Gardner, Marcie and Abraham, David – data researchers. **Income Inequality,** A project of the Institute for Policy Studies, after 2012, http://inequality.org/income-inequality/.

Stone, Chad;Trisi, Danilo; Sherman, Arloc and Debot, Brandon. **A Guide to Statistics on Historical Trends in Income Inequality**, REVISED, Feb. 20, 2015, Center on Budget and Policy Priorities, http://www.cbpp.org/research/poverty-and-inequality/a-guide-to-statistics-on-historical-trends-in-income-inequality.

Fry, Richard and Kochhar, Rakesh. **America's wealth gap between middle-income and upper-income families is widest on record**, Dec. 17, 2014, Pew Research Center, http://www.pewresearch.org/fact-tank/2014/12/17/wealth-gap-upper-middle-income/

Desilver, Drew. **5 Facts About Social Security**, Oct. 16. 2013, Pew Research Center, http://www.pewresearch.org/fact-tank/2013/10/16/5-facts-about-social-security/.

... refer to this phenomenon as "death creep."

Derek Thompson. **Get Rich, Live Longer: The Ultimate Consequence of Income Inequality**, Apr 18, 2014, The Atlantic, http://www.theatlantic.com/business/archive/2014/04/more-money-more-life-the-depressing-reality-of-inequality-in-america/360895/.

See other citations on declining life spans under Chapter 6, Welfare

...they did save for retirement – they put money into Social Security)

Social Security Administration. **Social Security Basic Facts, December 2013 Beneficiary Data, Social Security is the major source of income for most of the elderly,** April 2, 2014, http://www.ssa.gov/news/press/basicfact.html.

- Nine out of ten individuals age 65 and older receive Social Security benefits.
- Social Security benefits represent about 38% of the income of the elderly.
- Among elderly Social Security beneficiaries, **52% of married couples and 74% of unmarried persons receive 50% or more of their income** from Social Security.
- Among elderly Social Security beneficiaries, **22% of married couples and about 47% of unmarried persons rely on Social Security for 90%** or more of their income.

...many corporations are phasing out defined benefit pension plans

Employee Benefit Research Institute. **FAQs About Benefits – Retirement Issues. 1979-2011,** http://www.ebri.org/publications/benfaq/index.cfm?fa=retfaq14

Miller, Mark. **The vanishing defined-benefit pension and its discontents**, May 6, 2014, Reuters, http://www.reuters.com/article/2014/05/06/us-column-miller-pensions-idUSBREA450PP20140506

Fortified Cultural Fix

NOTE: Government engineering of family relationships is not a new idea.

…requiring siblings to help with their fair share financially.

Wikipedia. **Grandparent visitation**, as of 7/11/2015, https://en.wikipedia.org/wiki/Grandparent_visitation
Grandparent visitation is a legal right that grandparents in some jurisdictions may have to have court-ordered contact (or visitation) with their grandchildren. In the United States, all 50 states have a "grandparent visitation" statute that allows grandparents to ask a court to grant…

USA Today. **New Chinese law requires adult kids to visit parents**, December 12, 2012, USA Today, http://www.usatoday.com/story/news/world/2012/12/28/china-law-adult-children-visit-elderly-parents/1795721/

Pay-as-We Go

Siems, Thomas F. **Can Duct Tape Fix Social Security?** May 24, 2003, Investor's Business Daily / Cato Institute *(article was published in Investor's Business Daily),* **http://www.cato.org/publications/commentary/can-duct-tape-fix-social-security**

"First, Social Security's structure as a pay-as-you-go program — wherein taxes paid by today's workers provide benefits for today's retirees — saves nothing for the future. Surplus dollars are "invested" in special issue Treasury bonds (resulting in the so-called Trust Fund) to cover financial obligations in other parts of the government or to reduce the outstanding publicly held debt."

Raising the SS Retirement Age

…needing to continue in or return to the workforce.

The Editorial Board. **Beyond jobs numbers, labor shortage looms: Our view/** *It's time to plan for massive demographic shift. Discourage retirement; encourage immigration.* May 7, 2015, USA Today, **http://www.usatoday.com/story/opinion/2015/05/07/jobs-numbers-labor-shortage-baby-boomers-inflation-editorials-debates/70973518/**

John, David C. **Time to Raise Social Security's Retirement Age**, November 22, 2010, Heritage Foundation, http://www.heritage.org/research/reports/2010/11/time-to-raise-social-securitys-retirement-age

Schaefer, Patricia, **Impending Labor Shortage: Myth or Fiction**? Copyright 2006, Attard Communications, Inc. **http://www.businessknowhow.com/manage/labor-shortage.htm**

Advanced Technology Services. **What would Americans do if the retirement age were increased?** 10/25/2010, http://www.us.advancedtech.com/news-releases/10/25/2010/what-would-americans-do-if-the-retirement-age-were-increased

<u>Privatizing Social Security</u>

…this time with subprime automobile loans.

Silver-Greenberg, Jessica and Corkery, Michael. **In a Subprime Bubble for Used Cars, Borrowers Pay Sky-High Rates**, July 19, 2014, NY Times, **http://dealbook.nytimes.com/2014/07/19/in-a-subprime-bubble-for-used-cars-unfit-borrowers-pay-sky-high-rates/?_r=0**

McLaughlin, David and Schoenberg, Tom. **Auto Loan Securitization Probed by U.S., States**, Yates Says, Feb. 24, 2015, Bloomberg, **http://www.bloomberg.com/news/articles/2015-02-24/justice-department-probing-auto-loan-securitization-yates-**

Lawrence, John. **Wall Street's Latest Scam: Subprime Auto Loans**, Oct. 21, 2014, Sandiego Free Press, **http://sandiegofreepress.org/2014/10/wall-streets-latest-scam-subprime-auto-loans/**

Rudegeair, Peter. **Exclusive: U.S. regulators press banks for more on auto loan exposure to assess risks,** 10/12/2014, Reuters, **http://www.reuters.com/article/2014/10/12/us-autos-lending-regulators-idUSKCN0I10T320141012**

THE FOCUS SHOULD BE ON THE SECURITIZATION OF SUBPRIME AUTO LOANS. YES, WHAT THE LENDERS ARE DOING TO THE BORROWERS IN THESE CASES IS A QUESTION OF MORALITY; BUT THAT DOES NOT HAVE NEAR THE EFFECT ON THE ECONOMY OF THE SELLING OF TOXIC (SUBSTANDARD) SECURITIES TO PENSION FUNDS

THE AUTHOR

Charles Francus is a retired manufacturing executive and turnaround consultant. He previously held certifications in public accounting (CPA) and production and inventory management (CPIM).

Before stepping into the role of a turnaround expert, Charles' career included working in both staff and management positions at both Fortune 500 and middle market companies. Positions included Operations Analyst, Sales Manager, Controller, CFO, Vice President of Manufacturing and Engineering, Vice President of Operations, Division President, and Subsidiary Managing Director (CEO). Businesses he directed or helped direct ranged in headcount from 500 to 4,000.

During his 15 years as a turnaround consultant, he helped financially distressed businesses return to profitability. Charles observed that the foremost problem a distressed business's CEO and management team had is that they did not understand the business. This was true in spite of the fact that many of the team members had worked in the business for many years. He, therefore, initiated each engagement with a campaign to help the team learn their business. Subsequently, ideas and actions for true improvement begin to flow like water.

Charles, also, had the opportunity to review the operations of several profitable businesses. The level of understanding of the management teams, in all but one of these businesses, was not much different from that of turnaround clients. They were successful financially because they were in the right business at the right time. There was the same opportunity for operational improvement in these profitable businesses as in the financially distressed businesses – but, "understanding the business" was the first ingredient to getting there.

The moral of this story is that before people can improve on something they must first understand that something. In this discussion guide, the thing to be improved on is America's economic system. Hopefully, this guide will help American citizens understand the American economic system in a way that empowers them, as voters, **to make the changes necessary to improve the economic quality of life for all Americans**.

Dear reader,

You have completed the book. Congratulations.

There is an old adage that "to improve upon the sausage one must first know how the sausage is made." This is true whether the sausage is made of stuff you would rather not know about or of prime cuts. You now have a good idea of how the sausage is made.

You possess a reasonably sound understanding of the basics of America's economic system. While there is more to learn – you understand more than most of those who hold political office.

There are several things you can use your knowledge to accomplish:

- Assessing a political candidate's understanding of our economic system.

    Keep in mind that anything you want a candidate to do politically, (improve: healthcare, pay for military personnel, education, infrastructure, social security, etc.) can only be done if it fits within the framework of the economic system – all things done must be paid for. You can change the system because you own it. Sometimes it will be necessary for the system to be changed to enable the realization of the political goals you wish to see put in place. If your candidate does not understand that a change is necessary and what type of change is necessary – then you need to look for a different candidate to support.

- If you cannot identify a candidate who possesses an adequate level of knowledge – suggesting to the candidate you like, for other reasons, that he or she read this book.

- Running for office.

There is a caveat to what is said above. No system can provide all things a society may wish to have. Your knowledge of the basics of the system will help you decide what to balance against what in order to allow for the best overall outcome from government.

Have a good day,

Chuck

Made in the USA
San Bernardino, CA
11 July 2019